Guide to British Zoos & Aquariums

Tim Brown

To Sue

Thanks for all your help

Best wishes

Tim Brown

The IZES Guide to British Zoos & Aquariums

Tim Brown

The Independent Zoo Enthusiasts Society

First published in 2009

ISBN 978-0-9563831-1-2

Published by AAOS
PO Box 4
Todmorden
Lancashire OL14 6DA
United Kingdom
In association with the Independent Zoo Enthusiasts Society (IZES)
www.izes.co.uk

Tim Brown has asserted copyright law as the author. All rights reserved. Other than review material no part of this work may be reproduced without the written permission of the author

Design and Production by Alan Ashby
Cover photographs: Komodo Dragon/Shutterstock. Giraffes at Colchester Zoo, Brown Bear at ZSL Whipsnade Zoo and Budongo Trail at Edingburgh Zoo by Rob Vaughan.
Printed by Newton Print, Collett Way, Brunel Industrial Estate, Newton Abbot, Devon TQ12 4PH

A catalogue record for this book is available from the British Library

INTRODUCTION

BRITAIN IS arguably the most important of the zoo nations. Other countries may have more zoos, bigger zoos, maybe even some better zoos but no country has been more influential. We devised the first scientifically based zoo, the first aquarium, the safari park and the first insectarium. Much of today's conservational protocol in the zoo world has its roots in these islands and individuals such as Gerald Durrell or Sir Peter Scott.

The zoo history of Britain traces its beginnings back to the collection of Henry I at Woodstock in Oxfordshire which was moved to the Tower of London in 1235 by Henry III and existed there until 1832. By this time the Zoological Society of London had been formed (1826) with the zoo itself opening in 1828. There then followed a national explosion of zoological interest, with a variety of motivations, which saw at least eight zoos open around the country over the next ten years. Most of these ultimately failed but nonetheless established the country as an innovator within the zoo field. At this time neither Germany nor the USA had a single zoo. This was a rate of progress that couldn't be sustained of course and the next 120 years saw a much more sporadic and diverse development. It was at the end of this time (1957), that Geoffrey Schomberg wrote the first book about British zoos in general (*'British Zoos'*). There had been a number of books about specific zoos, mainly London, but none about the overall UK situation and Schomberg wrote broadly without any attempt to identify every collection. This was to change in 1970 when the same author wrote *'The Penguin Guide To British Zoos'* – reflecting the huge growth in the number of collections during the sixties. Aquariums per se were left untouched however, unless they existed within zoos themselves.

Although some catchpenny booklets also sought to detail the British zoo scene of the early seventies it was Anthony Smith who was to produce the only complete overview of UK zoos and aquariums with his *'Animals On View'* (1977) and a paperback update two years later. Throughout the seventies and eighties, books came and went with little satisfaction either in scope or depth of analysis. 1992 brought John Ironmonger's *'Good Zoo Guide'* which by its very name didn't seek to look in every nook and cranny for its inspiration but was nonetheless worthwhile.

It is now seventeen years therefore since the last overview of British zoos and obviously things have changed in that time, in fact British zoos have changed more quickly

INTRODUCTION

in that period than at any other time by some degree. A variety of factors brought about an age of remarkable dynamism but no factor was greater than the unjust and vindictive criticisms of zoos from the anti-zoo lobby, which first gained momentum in the mid-eighties. Rather than heralding the demise of UK zoos these criticisms brought forth a new era of higher standards and greater responsibility reflecting in renewed public approval and higher visitor numbers. Major aquariums also made their appearance in this country and took the genre to a new national level. At literary level therefore, a new perspective is probably overdue.

The IZES Guide to British Zoos and Aquariums seeks to detail all zoos, aquariums and wildlife attractions of the current time (October 2009), in that respect, it can only be compared to *'Animals On View'* in its scope. Yet in one respect it is different again in that it seeks to inform the serious enthusiast and zoo professional rather than the general public. And whilst the Independent Zoo Enthusiasts Society Guide recognises the current-day conservational role of zoos, this aspect has been deliberately underplayed in order to provide a critique of zoos as they appear on an actual visit. This is a book about zoos for zoo's sake.

ACKNOWLEDGEMENTS
Many thanks to Alan Ashby, Rob Vaughan, Brian Foster, Sean Rovai, John Tuson, Rick Foster, Russell Tofts, John Adams and Mike Grayson for updates, advice and opinion.

THE INDEPENDENT ZOO ENTHUSIASTS SOCIETY
Formed in 1995 by Tim Brown (author of this book) the Independent Zoo Enthusiasts Society exists to promote an interest in all aspects of good zoos around the world and to counter misinformation on the same subject. The Society publishes a quarterly newsletter *'Zoo Grapevine'* and has also published *'We Went To the Zoo Today...'* which looks at yesterday's British zoos through the medium of picture postcards.

Details of our subscription rates and publications can be found at www.izes.co.uk or by writing to the Independent Zoo Enthusiasts Society, P.O. Box 4, Todmorden, Lancs, OL14 6DA, United Kingdom.

ZOOS IN TODAY'S BRITAIN

THE UNITED KINGDOM probably has the highest standards of husbandry, welfare and educational output within its zoos of any nation. No other country can claim a larger conservational commitment. It could even be argued that a 'zoo for zoos sake' ethos has been lost in favour of policies geared to *in situ* projects. Yet there is an awareness that little can be done with natural habitats unless visitors come through the zoo turnstile at home for of course most British zoos have to stand alone unaided by taxational subsidy at either local or national level. Alongside Germany, USA and Holland, Britain is one of the leading zoo nations yet, by and large, has smaller collections and less visitors to its zoos than its peers. It is not short of captive animal collections as this book shows and these are maintained under a large variety of circumstances from charity-status zoological societies, to responsible privately-owned collections, a few municipally-supported establishments, right down to the make-me-a-wage catchpenny places and well-meaning sanctuaries which favour the individual animal rather than the species.

This book seeks to detail all of our current collections and forms two parts. The first and major portion reports on all the significant establishments whilst a further addendum lists smaller collections about which, it would appear, (and with apologies), there is comparatively little to say. Wildlife attractions in today's Britain can be said to fall within the following basic categories:-

GENERAL ZOOS
This is the traditional cross-section of species possibly exhibiting a selection of mammals, birds, reptiles, amphibians, fish and invertebrates but often stronger in one area of these than the others. The major zoos would carry representatives of all groups but quite a few collections, including some of significance, would leave out some orders and groupings altogether.

SPECIALIST ZOOS
There are actually only a very small number of zoos which specialize in a distinct group of animals or even one species. Primate collections, also pinnipeds and invertebrates come to mind. Zoogeographical aspects can also make for a specialist zoo and there are places which stick to African, Asian, European or British fauna for instance.

BIRD GARDENS
Following a path forged by Len Hill at Birdland in 1957 throughout the sixties and seventies bird-only collections proliferated around Britain. Many have since closed and it is quite a few years since any new bird garden opened. A few however remain, and those that have stood the test of time are largely of a good quality.

SAFARI PARKS
A rash of these drive-through wildlife parks opened in the late sixties and early seventies. They were invented in the UK by circus impresario Jimmy Chipperfield. Touted as the 'zoos of the future' by some critics this in fact never happened and the vogue for these things soon passed. Half of the UK's safari parks have now closed but such is the nature of the commercially-orientated beast after all.

AQUARIUMS
London Zoo opened a Fish House in 1853 but it would appear that the word 'aquarium' was first used in the context of an aquatic public exhibition seven years later in Vienna, Austria, (Aquarien-Salon of Ussner and Jager). Whatever the derivation of the word, the UK was first, with at least half a dozen other aquariums opening in the later part of the 19th century. By the late 1950s American oceanaria had taken the display of aquatic animals to a new level and the seventies saw the current trend for architecturally-inspired mega-aquariums take hold around the world. This is a trend that continues to this day and one which has almost bypassed the UK. Whilst there are perfectly good new aquariums in the UK at places like Hull and Plymouth these islands still do not possess a world class facility of the size and calibre to be seen in countries such as Japan and the USA. Indeed the main proliferation has been through the number of smaller, professionally-presented Sea Life Centres that have been built around the nation.

BUTTERFLY CENTRES
With its 1881 Insect House, London Zoo was the first place in the world to display living invertebrates. Almost one hundred years later and there was still scarcely another place like it in the land. There was, however, a butterfly farm in Sherborne, Dorset and perhaps it is here that the origins of the current swathe of butterfly attractions really began. So all-consuming is the desire for the *Lepidoptera* that even zoos now see butterfly houses as almost a 'must have'. Around the UK there is currently a host of greenhouses and other buildings given over to butterflies with the commercial beauty of an entrance fee that is perhaps half that of a zoo without the considerable overheads that the latter will incur.

FALCONRY CENTRES

At the risk of being deemed cynical I would venture that the same economics as are determined in butterfly centres (see above) account for the plethora of falconry and birds of prey centres which have grown around the nation in the last two decades. These places vary greatly in their commitment to conservation but almost all use the word with some abandon. The amount of aviculture differs enormously from place to place but serious breeding must involve aviaries and I would say that the number and nature of these is a good litmus as to the credibility of a particular establishment. Without exception a free-flying falconry exhibition is offered (sometimes little more) which in all fairness have rather added to our appreciation of the true nature of these birds.

APPOINTMENT-ONLY COLLECTIONS

There are a small number of appointment-only or schools-only collections around the country. These are often on the basis of photographic experiences. I have not included these collections as I do not believe them to be in the spirit of this guide and they may incur a needless journey for those without a prior arrangement.

AFRICA ALIVE!
Suffolk Wildlife Park, Kessingland, Lowestoft, Suffolk NR33 7TF
MAP REF: 1/D3
SIZE: 60 ACRES
OPENED: 1969
OWNERS: PRIVATE LIMITED COMPANY
SPECIES: 80

WITH THE re-naming of Suffolk Wildlife Park as *Africa Alive!* the metamorphosis became complete. In 1991 the rather run-down wildlife park was purchased by the owners of Banham Zoo and they have transformed it into a rather excellent medium-sized zoo which I actually now prefer to the parent collection.

Africa Alive! could almost be said to consist of three areas on the slope of a hill leading down to a rather marshy, flat area at the bottom of the slope. At the very top of the zoo is an area of particularly attractive small mammal enclosures fashioned largely from logs and also a range of aviaries for African birds. Aardvarks, Fosas, Bat-eared Foxes and Fennec Foxes kept diurnally (my preference) are just some of the species to be seen. Make a note too of some little 'specials' such as the African subspecies of Barn Owl *(Tyto alba affinis)* or Straw-coloured Fruit Bats. The labelling too is wonderfully informative including some zoo information of the origins of the animals.

The middle of the zoo contains 'Plains of Africa' a spacious savannah exhibit including the likes of Giraffe, White Rhino and Blesbok (the other subspecies, the Bontebok, has now disappeared from Europe). In the nature of these things it is as good as you will see in these islands. 'Big Cat Kingdom' for Lions is a wonderful wooded dell which reminds this writer of the old Lion enclosure at Whipsnade a little (and that is no bad thing).

The marshy area at the bottom of the hill has permitted not only some primate islands to be constructed – mostly for lemurs – but also paddocks for Kafue Flats Lechwe, Nile Lechwe, Nyala and Sitatunga. The zoogeographical direction pursued here has clearly worked well – the zoo has a defined profile built on quality foundations and is amongst the best smaller zoos in the whole of the country.

AMAZON WORLD ZOO PARK
Watery Lane, Newchurch, Isle Of Wight PO36 0LX
MAP REF: 2/C4
SIZE: 4 ACRES
OPENED: 1992
OWNERS: PRIVATE
SPECIES: 212

AMAZON WORLD, opened in 1992 is slightly unusual in as much as the zoo is mostly indoors. Nor is it entirely South American fauna, indeed it isn't entirely rainforest fauna either. Once through the impressive mock Mayan entrance a maze of buildings leads the visitor on a rambling journey through various ecosystems and themes. In addition to 'the Amazon' there is a desert region, a small nocturnal area, 'the canopy', 'the river' and so on, and so forth. Most of this is quite nicely done but not exceptionally so. However, the collection of animals is, in parts, rather unique with quite a number of species not to be seen anywhere else in Britain. Amongst birds these would include Crested Quetzal *(Pharomachrus antisianus)* and Plate-billed Mountain Toucan, both exquisitely beautiful birds to boot. Small mammals would include five species of armadillo, Hoffmann's Two-toed Sloth (Linne's are more common in this country), Kinkajous, Plains Viscachas and Southern Tamandua.

The outside area is a real hotchpotch of monkeys (up to the size of Black Howlers), lemurs, small cats, parrots, African Penguins and Giant Anteaters (which have recently bred here). It is all rather crammed in and the 'paddocks' along the rear wall are somewhat unsatisfactory for the range of larger species such as Brazilian Tapir, Capybara and Collared Peccary kept there. Despite that element the sheer diversity of species maintained at Amazon World is worthy of commendation in an age when uniformity of collections is becoming something of a concern.

AMAZONA ZOO

Hall Road, Cromer, Norfolk NR27 9JG
MAP REF: 3/D3
SIZE: 11 ACRES
OPENED: 2008
OWNERS: PRIVATE
SPECIES: 39

THE SMALL seaside town of Cromer has had its fair share of zoological spills and thrills over the years with both a zoo and a bird garden in the dim and distant past. Courtesy of Ken Sims, the owner of Thrigby Hall Wildlife Gardens, there is now a new zoo in town. Going under the name of Amazona not surprisingly the policy here is one of South American fauna.

At a cost of some £2 million Amazona has been established within mature woodlands and with the site leased (for the moment anyway) this has led to a rather curious non-permanent style of construction. Indeed some aviaries would appear to stand without any visible means of structural support whatsoever with the wire standing done in a circular method. There are big cats at Amazona and clearly this would not be adequate for these animals, as a result the cages are of a more standard kind for the Jaguars, Pumas and Ocelots. The most substantial building is the 'Amazona Hall' which is, as you might imagine, a tropical house with reptiles, birds and fish – nothing to challenge the seasoned zoo observer really with a Yellow Anaconda as the most noteworthy inhabitant. There is quite an element of the aquatic to Amazona and the area has a number of pools and lakes clearly flooded from a time when a small brickworks occupied the site. Wildfowl, Chilean Flamingos, Brazilian Tapirs and Capybaras are perfect for these conditions. Two small islands are given over to Brown Capuchins and Common Squirrel Monkeys.

The addition of a new small zoo to the nation's list is always welcome and coming from Ken Sims was always likely to be of quality. Given the semi-permanent nature of the site at the moment I will be interested to see how things progress in the future.

ANGLESEY SEA ZOO

Brynsiencyn, Anglesey LL61 6TQ, Wales
MAP REF: 4/A3
SIZE: 1.5 ACRES
OPENED: 1983
OWNERS: PRIVATE

ANGLESEY SEA ZOO overlooks the deceptively calm waters of the Menai Straits, only a meadow and a narrow road separates the site from the sea. Basically the zoo is an aquarium with a few added non-animal attractions on the outside. The origins of the establishment are unusual in as much as the founders were actually oyster farmers who became general seafood dealers. The main building itself was a lobster dealer's warehouse which was bought purely as a building and various enterprises were entered into before the idea of an aquarium which eventually materialized in 1983.

The Sea Zoo has decided to specialize in local marine fauna and in this respect they have both my admiration and support. Various brightly coloured tropical fish and a few Black-tipped Reef Sharks are easily touted as representing the world's oceans in small thematic aquariums. It takes rather more courage to specialize in our own fish which often appear as rather less glamorous. Obviously the Anglesey Sea Zoo must strike up its own local themes. So it is that we have 'Under The Pier' which has various flatfish and Ballan Wrasse in an exhibit which actually uses some of the old posts from the restoration of Bangor Pier, and 'Fish Farming' which is self-explanatory but also embraces the current fad for seahorse aquaculture.

My favourite exhibit has to be 'The Wreck' a dark, tangled, maze of old timbers with a real atmosphere into which are set various aquariums for the likes of Conger Eel and Pollock. Almost as good is 'Big Fish Forest', a large semi-circular window on a representation of the kelp forests which are to be found around some of the Anglesey coastline. Here the Cuckoo Wrasse belies the impression that all our local fish are silver or grey with its bright orange and turquoise hues.

I would also like to mention that the Anglesey Sea Zoo produces a quite excellent guide book with in-depth (sorry!) information on both the collection and local marine life in general. On the downside it is perhaps unfortunate that the external areas of the zoo are given over to such frivolous attractions as crazy golf but despite that this is a highly recommended small aquarium.

ARUNDEL WETLAND CENTRE (WWT)

Mill Road, Arundel, Sussex BN18 9PB
MAP REF: 5/D4
SIZE: 70 ACRES
OPENED: 1976
OWNERS: WILDFOWL AND WETLANDS TRUST
SPECIES: 82

OPENED IN 1976, Arundel is one of eight daughters of Slimbridge. In other words, when the Wildfowl Trust under Sir Peter Scott decided, metaphorically, to spread its wings, Arundel was one of the sites eventually chosen and as such was the seventh Wildfowl Trust centre. Each of the centres is quite different in appearance but perhaps Arundel is the most distinctive of them all with its great reed beds lying in the shadow of Arundel Castle. Not all of the Wildfowl and Wetland Trust's establishments have a captive collection, the two exceptions being Welney and Caelaverock but I would venture that aviculture is as high up on the agenda at Arundel as any of the centres. Particularly interesting in this respect is the Blue Duck kept in an enclosure which seeks to replicate the mountain streams of its native New Zealand. Clearly something was correct in this replication, because a world first captive breeding outside of the species' native islands occurred here in 1988. As zoo animals these are perhaps as rare as any because only this WWT centre maintains the species in the Northern Hemisphere. One other aviary visits the volcanic outcrops of Lake Myvatn, Iceland, in its orientation and is therefore looks a little odd with its dark grey rockwork but then the world doesn't turn according to Gardeners' World! Species such as Common Scoter and Common Eider can be seen here. Other features of Arundel include a pond life exhibit and the usual high standard of visitor centre associated with the WWT.

AUCHINGARRICH WILDLIFE CENTRE

Comrie, Perthshire, PH6 2JS, Scotland
MAP REF: 6/C2
SIZE: 170 ACRES
OPENED: 1991
OWNERS: PRIVATE LTD COMPANY

IF ZOOLOGICAL collections were judged by their position and surroundings then this would be one of the best, staring, as it does, at the Scottish Highlands. In the event the zoo itself is a mixture of good, bad and downright bizarre. The good would be large, naturalistic enclosures for Corsac Foxes and Asiatic Small-clawed Otters. The bad would be the ranges of dark, dingy and dusty aviaries and cages around the old barn, some of which include species as interesting as Potoroos and Common Genets. The downright bizarre would be the system of covered walkways that stretch around the centre of the park presumably as an all-weather feature but in reality serving as nothing more than an eye-sore in such a glorious setting. A fair collection of waterfowl is diluted by the liberal application of domestic breeds which is a shame because Auchingarrich's original purpose was to specialise in exotic ducks and geese.

All of our native deer species are exhibited and the Highland Falconry Bird of Prey Centre is also to be found here although it is operated by a separate enterprise. Reindeer, Raccoons, Scottish Wildcats and Crested Porcupines are amongst the highlights of the remainder of the collection. As it stands I feel that a unique opportunity has been lost by pampering to the demands of the majority of visitors and not being pro-active enough to redress the balance by leading them in the right direction by means of presentation. Auchingarrich feels like a farm with some wild animals and could, quite easily, be much more. Excellent home-cooked food in the coffee shop by the way. Very recent news is of new ownership so it will be interesting to see if the bad and downright bizarre remain.

AXE VALLEY BIRD & ANIMAL PARK

Summerleaze Farm, Kilmington, Axminster, Devon EX13 7RA
MAP REF: 7/C4
SIZE: 1.5 ACRES
OPENED: 2008
OWNERS: PRIVATE

Around one-and-a-half acres of a Devon farm have been turned into a bewildering jumble of wooden framed cages and small enclosures. Axe Valley Bird and Animal Park has a surprisingly large number of animals such as Coatis, Meerkats, a Raccoon, Green Peafowl, Sacred Ibis, Ypecaha Wood Rail, a variety of pheasants and waterfowl, even comparative rarities such as Black and White Ruffed Lemur and Blue-winged Kookaburra. Best exhibit (without much competition) is an open-air oval one for Canadian Tree Porcupines although even here I would like to think that more substantial shelter was provided in winter. And whilst the owners are perfectly well-intentioned, it is surprising to see that the 'sixties zoo boom' type of collection can still start up in the modern age – possibly the owners are too young to remember them! Certainly there are a lot of animals here defined by that curse of the less professional collection – domestic animals mixed with exotic taxa – something a serious establishment would never do. It might have been advisable here to move a little slower and do fewer exhibits well, rather than so many animals displayed so uninspiringly! 'Start again' would be my advice – after all they do have the stock! A further note to the owners would remind them that birds *are* animals of course.

BANHAM ZOO

The Grove, Banham, Norfolk NR16 2HE
MAP REF: 8/D3
SIZE: 42 ACRES
OPENED: 1968
OWNERS: PRIVATE LTD COMPANY
SPECIES: 158

A VISIT TO the tiny village of Banham in 1966 would have found Grove Farm selling its produce to a newly car-enabled public. There was even the chance to visit the Rentafridge Electrical Showroom or buy some furniture; an early out-of-town retail outlet in fact but missing anything to seriously keep the children amused. In those days it was easier to buy a bear than a carousel, so a small zoo was installed in 1968. This was fairly common policy in the British Isles of the time and zoos, big and small, sprang up all over the nation. Most have long since fallen by the wayside and the vast majority are not missed. The survivors have all gone on to much better things and such an example is Banham Zoo.

From the outset Banham specialized in primates, today this aspect is still strong but the collection is housed in spacious cages for Siamangs, Mueller's Gibbons, Black and White Colobus, Black-headed Spider Monkeys and Black Howlers plus a variety of callitrichids. Forty years ago you might see an odd lemur or two around the British zoo scene but these days Banham epitomizes the change by exhibiting varieties such as Sclater's, Red-bellied and Crowned types as well as common-in-zoos (but very rare in the wild) Black and White Ruffed Lemurs and still-quite-common-but-popular Ring-tailed Lemurs.

Another strength is felines with a large Siberian Tiger enclosure and similarly open-topped affair for Sri Lankan Leopards *(Panthera pardus kotiya)*. In the case of the latter it is unusual to see these noted climbers in uncovered accommodation but it has worked for 6 or 7 years at Banham now without a problem so we can all sleep easily. Although the taxonomy of this particular subspecies is debatable, it is beyond debate that this island form is very rare in the wild as well as in captivity. Cheetahs have a large paddock and small cats consist of Ocelot, Fishing Cat and Geoffroy's Cat. In 2009 a new Snow Leopard habitat was opened which is decorated in a montane manner with a rock face and meandering stream although, regrettably, much of the 35 feet of netted height remains unused.

The remainder of the mammal collection shows a reasonable cross section without any further areas of speciality. For instance: Grevy's Zebras, Maned Wolves, South African Fur Seals and Bactrian Camels. The bird collection has steadily enlarged over the years to over 70 species including 25 of bird of prey or owl. Rather less impressive is something of a shed for reptiles and invertebrates, every time I visit Banham I expect it to have been pulled down but it's still hanging on twenty years after my first visit.

I have seen Banham Zoo described as 'handily placed' which rather exaggerates a rural position in the middle of Norfolk, although Norwich is little more than half an hour by car. At one time Banham even had to compete with Kilverstone Wildlife Park around a dozen miles away which really was saturation in an area largely populated by villages. Now alone, this zoo seems to be doing rather well for itself and improving all the time (which zoos should do of course).

BATTERSEA PARK CHILDREN'S ZOO

Battersea, London SW11 4NJ

MAP REF: 9/D4
SIZE: 2 ACRES
OPENED: 1951
OWNERS: PRIVATE LTD COMPANY

UNTIL 2003 this children's zoo in a famous park alongside the south bank of the Thames was maintained by the local Wandsworth Borough Council and actually had quite a decent reputation. Now it is run by Roger Heap who also owns the Chestnut Centre and New Forest Owl and Otter Centre. In truth he has not done a great deal other than to spruce the place up a little. The expected Asiatic Short-clawed Otters, Meerkats, callitrichids and lemurs are here together with a couple of nice aviaries but any enthusiast will be frustrated with the amount of space in such a tiny area given over to domestic animals. Of course, the policy in places such as this is not dictated by hardened zoo veterans and without a doubt the family orientated visitors who make up the majority find it meets their needs. Enthusiasts may not find the enormous effort of negotiating the capital's tiresome transport systems to be worth the effort quite frankly.

BEALE PARK WILDLIFE PARK & GARDENS

Lower Basildon, Reading, Berkshire RG8 9NH

MAP REF: 10/C4
SIZE: 76 ACRES
OPENED: 1956
OWNERS: CHARITABLE TRUST
SPECIES: 120

A LARGE PARK of some 76 acres running alongside the Thames around 5 miles west of Reading is home to the Beale Park Wildlife Park & Gardens. It would be fair to say that in over 50 years of existence it has kept a low profile although in its time and at different times the collection was noted for pheasants and laughing thrushes. Clearly then, birds have always been a priority and remain so today although the speciality is probably now

17

with owls. The Owlery, where the collection is held, is a long row of wooden aviaries with a couple of adjoining 'courtyards' for more aviaries, most of which are defined by their height. In some cases, for species such as Great Grey, Ural and Spectacled Owls the aviaries are 15 feet or more high. Other aviaries hold Ashy-faced Owls, Brown Wood Owls even Striated Caracaras and Black Turkey Vultures. In all there are around 15 sizeable cages.

Many of the small aviaries that held the taxonomic collections of days gone by are now gone and four larger zoogeographic aviaries have taken their place in the shape of Australasia, Africa, South America and the Himalayas. The last of these is easily the most interesting with a pair of rare Rufous-vented Laughing Thrushes mixing in with White-winged Starlings, Red Turtle Doves, Satyr Tragopans and Collared Hill Partridges to make for an eclectic exhibition. By contract the other aviaries seem markedly down on species to be perfectly honest, even if the Australasian aviary compensates by being superbly planted with cycads. Nearby a couple of aviaries house Lesser Vasa Parrots (the Greater species is also kept here) and Madagascan Lovebirds respectively, giving a signpost to a small Madagascan area of the park and a further clue to the development of Beale Park by way of an increased mammal collection in the shape of Ring-tailed Lemurs in this area. Over the last few years it has clearly become policy to widen the collection of small mammals here and these are in two major areas. Firstly a series of some five cages for South American small primates such as Squirrel Monkeys, Goeldi's Monkey and Cotton-top Tamarins and then a series of large, somewhat functional (to be kind), metal-sided enclosures for Meerkats, Black-tailed Prairie Dogs, Raccoons and Yellow Mongoose. At an aesthetic level these don't really fit in here it must be said. Elsewhere are Capybaras, meadows with domestic animals and the likes of Parma Wallabies and Rheas plus quite a lot of waterfowl if you look hard.

All in all some 120 species of bird are kept at Beale Park which places it amongst the larger avian collections in this land but there is a sense that the park doesn't quite know what it is. Are we a zoo or a park? Are we commercial or a cultural amenity? In places Beale Park is ornamental to a quite extraordinary level in other places untidy to farmyard level. I can't help but feel that if someone wanted a really top class zoo here they would have a perfect spot for it.

BEAVER WATERWORLD ZOOLOGICAL GARDENS

Waylands Farm Approach Road, Tatsfield, Nr. Westerham, Kent TN16 2JT
MAP REF: 11/D4
SIZE: 1.5 ACRES
OPENED: 1980
OWNERS: REGISTERED CHARITY

THE AIMS of Beaver Waterworld in Kent are totally laudable in that this small centre originated from, and is dedicated to, providing rescue facilities for unwanted reptiles and other animals. It was started by Stella Quayle in 1980 and occupies a number of buildings at the back of a small, unglamorous, industrial estate off a country lane in West Kent (almost Surrey in fact). A bewildering array of Green Iguanas, Bearded Dragons, Red-eared Terrapins, Burmese Pythons and the like are housed in a maze of vivariums. As might be expected from the name a breeding colony of Canadian Beavers can also be found here housed in a rather uninspiring concrete paddock and pond. Some other small animals such as Common Marmosets can be seen and there is a row of aviaries which more or less amount to the zoological garden aspect of the name.

In some ways it is difficult to write about Beaver Waterworld because they clearly have a role to perform, not only in direct rescue work, but also in informing the general public about the keeping of exotic pets. The difficulty is that the place itself is an untidy mess to which the public should not be given any access in my opinion. A leaflet for the centre stresses that educational facilities are available for school parties and youth groups, it is hoped that these same bodies of youngsters waiting to be inspired by the wonders of the natural world do not take any notice of the woeful labelling or ramshackle housing. In the seventies a plethora of tiny zoos hoping to make a quick buck broke out like a rash across the nation; at Beaver Waterworld the motives are entirely different but appearances are much the same.

BELFAST ZOO
Hazlewood, Antrim Road, Belfast BT36 7PN, Northern Ireland
MAP REF: 12/B2
SIZE: 60 ACRES
OPENED: 1933
OWNERS: LOCAL AUTHORITY
SPECIES: 156

BELFAST ZOO represents one of the bolder moves within British zoo history. Founded in 1933 as the Bellevue Zoological Gardens, the zoo was literally an attraction at the end of a tramline built as part of an existing pleasure garden, courtesy of Belfast Corporation. Indeed for many years the zoo was under the control of the Corporation Transport Committee of all things! Inertia set in and, despite immense local popularity, by the late sixties the zoo was tired and dated. As the modern day axiom goes, it was time to 'put up or shut up'. At this juncture the zoo was fortunate that the local council took the former option. Municipal recreation became vitally important as the political and social turmoil of Northern Ireland threatened to create an economic vacuum. The ordinary people of Belfast deserved some good news and in the shape of a brand new zoo they got it. Belfast Zoo lies on the slope of a towering hill (Cave Hill) of montane proportions and it was literally decided to build the new zoo on the land above the old zoo. Manager John Stronge saw to it that the latest ideas on zoo design were put into practice and the result was a zoo of modern homogeneity. Local authority support gave it the positive and professional feel of a continental zoo in northern Europe. The new Belfast zoo was started in 1974 – it was a period when the usual commonplace worldwide model of zoos as municipal amenities briefly flourished in this country and councils in Blackpool, Morecambe, Newquay plus a few other places thought that a zoo might be a good idea. Belfast built a better zoo than any of those places however, and treated its zoo with respect as well. Unlike most of its municipal bedmates of the time, Belfast Zoo has gone from strength to strength – the ragged zoo of the fifties and sixties has become one of the country's finest.

As indicated the zoo here occupies a steep hill and use has been made of the incline to create some stunning enclosures. I particularly like the old Polar Bear exhibit now converted for Spectacled Bears. This was also one of the first zoos I saw keeping monkeys in meadows. The zoo has tried to keep rarer and endangered taxa wherever possible, nor have they been afraid to break the mould and bring in species new to the UK or even Europe as a whole. Today's zoo manager Mark Challis has instigated much of this vibrant collection planning and continues to encourage it. Rare primate species such as Crowned Sifaka and Francois' Langur were brought first to the UK by this zoo.

Of course any zoo needs its stars, its 'ABC' animals, and Belfast has its share of charismatic mega vertebrates including Asian Elephants (Belfast was only the second UK zoo to breed an elephant back in 1997), Giraffes, Asian Lions and Tigers. Gorillas and

Chimpanzees are also kept here but I think that it is often the unusual smaller species which makes this a 'zoo man's zoo'. In some ways I'm reminded of Frankfurt under its heyday with Grzimek when something really 'choice' awaited the connoisseur at every visit. And it's a lot more difficult to do these days as well in an age when animal dealers have largely vanished or are not particularly acceptable to many.

I didn't think, in my childhood, that the day would come when the Sun Bear was a zoo rarity but there is only one other pair in the United Kingdom apart from Belfast's and the species is under threat in the wild. Amongst the cats there are Asian Golden Cats and Black-footed Cats with the Fosa rather cat-like, although it is one of the curious Madagascan carnivores now placed in the family Eupleridae. Lemurs and callitrichids in particular are strong here – make a note of the Pygmy Marmosets here for they are the unusual White-bellied subspecies *(Callithrix pygmaea niveiventris)*. Ungulates include Malayan Tapirs, Mhorr Gazelles, Sitatunga and Nile Lechwe in large, grassy, paddocks running down the hillside.

It seems from this review that mammals dominate at Belfast and this is true but the birds are quite nicely done too with specialities being made of groups such as cockatoos, touracos and tragopans. In the walk-through aviary it is an enormous pleasure for the enthusiast to see Southern Bald Ibis with its distinctive scarlet skullcap – the Waldrapp may be far more endangered, even critically so, but they are quite ubiquitous in captivity now so it is a pleasure to compare their southern hemisphere relation.

Northern Ireland has found a compromise to its problems that seems to be working and as a result tourism is on the agenda once more. The Belfast Zoo is proof that ordinary life went on through 'the troubles', sometimes with a degree of success, I know of a few non-zoo people who have recently visited this place and been pleasantly surprised – they should be, because the zoo is a testament to resilience and determination as well as quality.

BENTLEY WILDFOWL COLLECTION

Halland, Nr Lewes, East Sussex BN8 5AF

MAP REF: 13/D4
SIZE: 25 ACRES
OPENED: 1966
OWNERS: LOCAL AUTHORITY
SPECIES: 110

THE WILDFOWL COLLECTION at Bentley was created by Gerald Askew in 1962, following inspiration from Slimbridge. It opened to the public in 1966. Sadly Askew was to die in 1970 and in 1978 his widow gave the nucleus of the estate to East Sussex County Council. When we refer to the dearth of municipal collections in the UK, this one is usually forgotten about. An interesting motor museum is on the same site. With over a hundred species of waterfowl, the collection is well organised and particularly strong on geese and swans. Most of the world's taxa of swans can be observed here and the collection has Chilean and Greater Flamingos too. As might be expected, the wildfowl are kept on a series of meadows to the east of a substantial house. There is no zoogeographical policy and species are mixed on the basis of husbandry and compatibility. Not surprisingly therefore, many of the geese inhabit individual pens. With the Wildfowl and Wetlands Trust moving away from a taxonomic approach, substantial collections such as this one are to be valued as a different but quite valid approach to biodiversity.

BIRDLAND

Rissington Road, Bourton-On-The-Water, Gloucestershire GL54 2BN
MAP REF: 14/C4
SIZE: 10 ACRES
OPENED: 1957
OWNERS: PRIVATE LTD COMPANY
SPECIES: 133

NOW AT ITS second location, Len Hill's original Birdland in the heart of the quaint village of Bourton-On-The-Water was unique. Started in 1957 it closed in 1986 after Hill's death in 1981 and was moved by his son Richard to the outskirts of the village and a former trout farm in 1987. Following a number of financial twists and turns Eddie Trigg bought Birdland in 1993. With all due respect to the current owners, the original magic of Birdland is almost impossible to recreate but the site has grown and matured in over twenty years to overcome this writer's initial trauma at the change.

    Situated amongst tall trees and with the River Windrush dancing through the site, the 'new' Birdland has acquired an identity of its own and one or two of the newer aviaries equal those created by Len Hill himself in their attractiveness. Sadly the days of Lear's Macaws, Cock-o'-the-Rocks and Quetzals are gone and the collection is much more mainstream. However, a group of King Penguins remains; rather soberingly they are now the only ones in England. A small Desert House, a Tropical House (now themed under 'the egg'!) and a Toucan House represent the indoor accommodation, with Double-wattled Cassowaries as the largest birds in the gardens. Three taxa of flamingo are on display (Greater, Rosy and Chilean) using the river to provide more volatile waters than are normally the case for these birds.

    Some 135 species of bird are currently to be seen which compares favourably with the number in the heyday of the 'old' Birdland. Even Walsrode, Berlin or Jurong would struggle to match the rarities of the collection's heyday but some unusual species do remain in the shape of Bare-faced Curassow, Grey Tree Pie, Red-crested Touraco and San Blas Jay.

    It is difficult to forgive Richard Hill his decision to move Birdland and build houses on the famous gardens. In doing this he murdered one of this country's most noteworthy institutions. The Birdland of today is still amongst the country's best bird gardens but it is not unfair to compare it with such a glorious past when the comparison could so easily have been avoided. A footnote to the above concerns the two Jason Islands in the Falklands, which Len Hill bought for £5,500 in 1970. Semi-seriously, Hill even issued stamps and banknotes for his islands, both depicted penguins. These islands were also sold by Hill's descendants being purchased by Michael and Judy Steinhardt who in turn donated them to the Wildlife Conservation Society (Bronx Zoo).

BIRDWORLD

Holt Pound, Farnham, Surrey GU10 4LD
MAP REF: 15/C4
SIZE: 26 ACRES
OPENED: 1968
OWNERS: PRIVATE LTD COMPANY
SPECIES: 190

DOUBTLESS INSPIRED by Birdland in the Cotswolds, bird gardens spread like a rash around the UK in the sixties and early seventies. If we accept that wildfowl collections are a slightly different thing and that Birdland itself isn't the original one, then Birdworld is the oldest surviving bird garden having opened in June 1968 and seen most of its genre fall by the wayside. Birdworld expanded rapidly throughout the seventies and in 1977 Underwater World was added, a 132' long aquarium which still exists to this day. A further innovation was Seashore Walk in 1979, a walk-through aviary for seabirds and waders which featured the novelty of a wave-making machine for the first time in a UK zoo. Additional land around the bird garden was always acquired if possible. Having been instigated by the Harvey Family, Birdworld was sold to the company which owns the adjacent garden centre in 1996 and they were able to make additions and upgrade the bird garden.

The Crescent Aviaries were one of the additions made and this range does feature some interesting species, including Nocturnal Currasow for which a first UK breeding has been achieved. Hornbills are quite well presented too, with Blyth's, Trumpeter and Rhinoceros species amongst others, Birdworld was the first to breed Casqued Hornbills (1972) and Northern Ground Hornbills (1989). Also created was a large free-flight aviary for macaws, cockatoos and larger parrots. On the other hand the 1984 Penguin Pool and a row of rather dull lorikeet aviaries are looking their age.

The gardens occupy a pleasant semi-wooded site a couple of miles outside of Farnham and are incredibly well-signposted on the myriad of major roads in this neck of the woods. A stoutly built brick and timber Temperate House bodes well but seems to have rather retracted its capacity, it is comprised of individual aviaries and a small walk-through area. An impression is formed that it was once a bigger affair. Zoo 'spotters' should take care to look out for the Vinous-throated Parrotbills and Rufous-crowned Roller, both unusual in aviculture.

Birdworld claims to be the largest avian collection in the country – this is not now true due to the collection at Blackbrook Zoo, but it is certainly the biggest bird garden as such. The aquarium is a worthy diversion too even if it is mainly hobbyist fish on display. Although we in the UK more or less invented the bird garden, places such as Walsrode in Germany or Jurong or Loro Parque took the concept to another level. Birdworld near Farnham is probably the nearest we ever got to that size of bird zoo but sadly still doesn't occupy the same league.

BIRMINGHAM NATURE CENTRE

Pershore Road, Birmingham, West Midlands B5 7RL
MAP REF: 16/C3
SIZE: 6.5 ACRES
OPENED: 1964
OWNERS: LOCAL AUTHORITY
SPECIES: 154

ORIGINALLY KNOWN as Birmingham Zoo this small zoo was opened, with some haste, when the parent zoo Dudley heard of plans by the Chipperfield organisation to open in England's second city. Hurried or not, the new zoo had a uniformity which was well received by those 'in the know' at the time. Despite this by 1973 it had closed and was reopened in 1975 as Birmingham Nature Centre under control of the City Council. The idea was to specialize in European animals and although this policy now seems to have been largely abandoned with an entrance fee of only £3 for adults the Nature Centre is not surprisingly very popular with locals. European Lynx, Black and White Ruffed Lemurs, Mouflon, Canadian Beaver and White-naped Crane give some idea of the diversity here and around 130 species are kept even if the ad hoc distribution of domestic breeds around the place rather dulls the definition of a conservation centre. There is a small Reptile House and even a house for rodents called the Mouse House which could be much better than it is due to the preponderance of pet-type breeds. All in all it is churlish to complain however, and I only wish that more local authorities could come up with nice little zoos such as this one.

BLACK ISLE WILDLIFE & COUNTRY PARK
The Croft, Drumsmittal, North Kessock, Ross Shire IV1 3XF, Scotland
MAP REF: 17/B1
SIZE: 20 ACRES
OPENED: 1993
OWNERS: PRIVATE

BRITAIN'S MOST northerly zoo lying between Inverness and Dingwall in the north of Scotland. The feeling is of a farm around and in between which a zoo is growing, but unfortunately in a rather haphazard manner. The only truly satisfactory area for the enthusiast is the initial area of aviaries containing a reasonable selection of owls but with no real surprises (well maybe Ural Owls aren't seen too often). In amongst paddocks containing sheep, goats and rabbits are Emus, Rheas and Bennett's Wallabies with the more surprising addition of a Damara Zebra. A further selection of mammals such as Black and White Ruffed lemurs, Raccoons, Pine Martens and Meerkats all kept in fairly uninspiring cages left this writer with the impression that Black Isle Wildlife Park would have done better to deal with a smaller collection more adequately and professionally housed than is the current case.

BLACKBROOK ZOOLOGICAL PARK
Winkhill, Nr Leek, Staffordshire ST13 7QR
MAP REF: 18/C3
SIZE: 38 ACRES
OPENED: 1991
OWNERS: PRIVATE
SPECIES: 290

QUITE A NUMBER of the general public have a vague conception that all zoos are the same. A tour of the collections in this book would prove conclusively that this is not the case and no place can be compared with Blackbrook which is a very large collection situated on the Staffordshire moors some miles away from any kind of town or village. The buildings of the zoo are squat, stone edifices of some permanence whilst various paddocks and grass enclosures spread out across a site of gentle inclines whatever the altitude of the whole. An abandoned railway line runs alongside the zoo lending a strange air of the forgotten up in these hills. The emphasis here is on birds, particularly waterfowl, and Blackbrook now houses the largest collection of birds in the country. All seven species of swan can be seen here, there is a decent sea duck collection (four species of merganser for instance) and the country's only Kelp Geese which is surprising considering that this species is found in the Falklands Islands. Cranes and storks are also well represented with rarities such as Black-necked Crane, Wattled Crane, the Australian subspecies of Sarus Crane, Maguari Stork and Lesser Adjutant Stork.

Blackbrook continues to march on with its avian collection and 'Pelican World' shows the country's largest selection of pelicans behind enclosures bounded by large rocks. A penguin exhibit (for Humboldt Penguins) is brand new as well including a simulation of a cave with underwater viewing. There are owl aviaries and pheasants. Indeed the dishonest visitor could get quite a show out of the aviaries surrounding the car park alone. One unusual house known as 'Water, Wings and Webs' combines invertebrates, reptiles, indoor aviaries, an open-topped marine pool for rays and small sharks as well as a glass-fronted view into a waterbird aviary containing Purple Sandpipers amongst many others. Squacco Herons, Boat-billed Herons (a UK first captive breeding here), Asian Openbill Storks (Britain's only ones) are also in the gardens, the list could go on and on. This is a connoisseur's collection with plans to develop the largest river aviary in Britain in the near future.

Although birds make up 90% of the collection at Blackbrook there is a small move to the mammalia with more to come. At the moment a Lemur House includes White-fronted, Mongoose and Mayotte Brown Lemurs and elsewhere Red Kangaroos can be seen with Red River Hogs promised as I write.

At one time this was the sister collection to a tiny bird garden in Cheshire by the name of Hillside which is now an off-show facility. Those who increasingly feel that they are looking at the same species in zoos around the country should delight in the idiosyncrasy and diversity at Blackbrook Zoological Park.

BLACKPOOL SEA LIFE
Promenade, Blackpool, Lancs FY1 5AA
MAP REF: 19/C3
OPENED: 1990
OWNERS: MERLIN ENTERTAINMENTS

SHOE-HORNED in amongst the brash 'glamour' of Blackpool's Golden Mile is one of Sea Life's most prominent aquariums which claims to have Europe's most comprehensive collection of tropical sharks housed here in their own dedicated area and also in the 'Lost City of Atlantis'; so no 'sanctuary' here then (Sea Life seems to have a thing in general about 'sanctuaries'). Perhaps the owners realise that even sharks are not safe from the public in Blackpool! Further reinforcing the 'thrills and spills' profile of Blackpool's Sea Life Centre is 2009's new attraction 'Scary Monsters' – a rather negative slant on a rather interesting selection of Japanese Spider Crabs, frogfish, even Deep Sea Isopods. Some 13 Sea Life and related aquariums are to be found around the UK, time and time again these places return to the same tried and tested exhibits. So, and not for the first or last time, say hello to 'Kingdom of the Seahorse', 'Nemo', small walk-through tunnels, a ray exhibit, Amazon area etc. I would also add that Sea Life centres tend to have something new for each summer season and these often rotate around the various centres. It may well be that 'Scary Monsters' is at Scarborough or Birmingham in 2010. This book covers all of the UK Sea Life Centres but without a great deal of detail, a circumstance brought about by unadulterated repetition of exhibits I'm afraid.

BLACKPOOL TOWER AQUARIUM
Promenade, Blackpool, Lancs FY1 4RZ
MAP REF: 20/C3
OPENED: 1875
OWNERS: PRIVATE LTD COMPANY

BLACKPOOL TOWER is an icon of English tourism, standing tall as a signpost to a good time for generations of holiday makers. Most people do not associate the Tower with zoology but there have been substantial exhibitions of animals on this site even before the Tower opened in 1894 and for over seventy years a substantial indoor menagerie was maintained here. What's more, by and large, animals did well in the menagerie even if conditions would be unacceptable today.

The eagle-eyed amongst you may have noticed that the aquarium would have appeared to have opened almost twenty years before the Tower proper. This is indeed correct because an aquarium owned by Dr. Cocker was here first. Cocker merely incorporated the aquarium into the Tower. Although smaller today it is still quite substantial. The centrepiece of the aquarium is a large tank some 30 feet long by 24 feet wide, with a depth of 12 feet constructed at a cost of £2 million little more than a decade ago. Built to house now-departed Green and Loggerhead Turtles, it now houses a large coral reef exhibit. A variety of tanks around the edge of the hall house tropical and coldwater species of both marine and freshwater types. There are no particularly unusual species but nonetheless this room is a tranquil haven from the cheap hurley burley of Blackpool itself. As is often the tradition in public aquariums the collection is housed in the style of a cave toned now in aquamarine throughout. Despite the presence of a Sea Life Centre only yards away the various and ever-changing ownership of Blackpool Tower has kept the aquarium going and long may it do so!

BLACKPOOL ZOO
East Park Drive, Blackpool, Lancs FY3 9RS
MAP REF: 21/C3
SIZE: 36 ACRES
OPENED: 1972
OWNER: PRIVATE LIMITED COMPANY
SPECIES: 193

I WELL REMEMBER a number of covetous remarks from zoo professionals about the new municipally-owned Blackpool Zoo when it opened in 1972. What was more the new zoo was little more than a third of what was envisaged. Twenty years later and the zoo had almost become a political football with anti-zoo factions pressurising a facility funded by ratepayers' money. In the process the zoo rather lost momentum – an additional two phases of enlargement didn't happen and the sixties-styled modernist architecture employed quickly became dated. Dreams had burst almost as quickly as the zoo's unique, inflatable Tropical Bird House. Despite the best efforts of a number of noted managers, it was probably desirable that Blackpool Zoo was sold to private enterprise in the shape of Grant Leisure in 2003; they in turn sold to the Spanish chain Parques Reunidos in 2007. The Spanish company are no strangers to the zoo community, owning a number of facilities in Spain as well as the Lakes Aquarium and Bournemouth Oceanarium in the UK.

Under Parques Reunidos change has been conspicuous as a result of investment. Blackpool Zoo occupies the site of an old aerodrome including a number of sizeable, old, brick-built hangars and a flight control building which became the zoo's offices as well as a rather unusual backdrop to the elephant paddock. Most of the hangars were perfectly usable but until recently functioned as little more than storage (if at all). Today several of the hangars have been painted, upgraded and pressed into service. And whilst the enthusiast could have imagined almost a set of tropical houses, then a pristine, modern entrance area and a children's playbarn are probably more commercially pragmatic.

The challenge at Blackpool has been to deal with all that seventies concrete architecture. The new owners should have experience in that area as they also now own possibly the classic example in the shape of Madrid Zoo. A penguin pool of almost naïve simplicity never really worked and has been landscaped into an otter enclosure. Two flat and rather boring fields for Amur Tigers and African Lions have been brought to life – the simplistic indoor housing extended for the public to include interpretation and a Meerkat exhibit. A goat mountain that once displayed Chamois (amongst others) has been turned over to Lowland Gorillas by connecting it to the Ape House. There are other examples too, but I can't give Parques Reunidos all the credit here, many of these changes started in the old council days particularly under Iain Valentine.

The new owners are, however, responsible for the biggest raft of changes and the best of these is 'Amazonia'. This saw the concrete base of the old inflatable bird house spanned by some very substantial girders and meshed over. Nothing had stood the test of Blackpool's coastal gusts before – this covering will, I assure you. Inside is an excellent walk-through exhibit combining South American primates (Red Titi, Squirrel Monkeys, White-faced Saki, Goeldi's Monkey) with birds from the same continent such as Black Curassow, Blue-throated Conures and various whistling ducks amongst others. Tree nesting waders have proved incompatible with the monkeys, which is a great pity, nonetheless 'Amazonia' is nicely planted around a significant water feature. I would rate it as the best exhibit in the zoo.

'Amazonia' connects to the Elephant and Reptile House where it is still not too difficult to imagine an industrial past in a converted hangar. At one time Giraffes, as well as White Rhino, could be seen in this house utilizing the two (at the time) outdoor paddocks on a rotary basis. Now it is all for three female Asiatic Elephants and the two paddocks have merged into one. Despite the fact that this house was obviously fairly cramped at one time, the public area always was rather spacious. Over the years this area has seen various vivaria emerge, initially for reptiles and increasingly including invertebrates. At one time an attempt was made to maintain Army Ants, which was a fascinating, although ultimately futile, concept. With the exception of a lone Utilan Spiny-tailed Iguana, the collection in this part is rather perfunctory in all aspects.

Blackpool Zoo has become rather strong on primates over the years. The original Animal Nursery eventually became a monkey house now with the name of 'Small Primates'. A large group of King Colobus are the most noteworthy inhabitants here (small primates?), but also Pileated Gibbons (small primates?), Ring-tailed Lemurs, De Brazza's Monkey, Red Titis, Geoffroy's Marmoset, Pygmy Marmoset and Grey Mouse Lemurs. Elsewhere hot wired meadows are utilized for Black Howlers and Black-headed Spider Monkeys. The small lake around the Gibbon Islands is home to Capybaras these days. Another Blackpool 'original' is the Ape House and again changes have been enormous. For the plain, grass, outdoor enclosures this was very much needed, but the transformation of the indoors into 'peep hole' viewing has not worked for this writer. It is a dark and uninspiring environment for the public with uncomfortable and difficult viewing of the Lowland Gorillas and Bornean Orang Utans which live here.

One element of the original Blackpool which I always liked was the spacious Sea Lion Pool, even 37 years on it still seems large, possibly a little plain today but tell that to the mercurial Californian Sea Lions who make good use of it. Nearby is a brand new Penguin Pool which has done its best to recreate 'marineland' architecture of the seventies I would say and mostly in the name of providing underwater viewing. I don't like it at all, it appears as a great, light brown, gunnite wart, stuck on the lawn and quite out of keeping with the grounds around it – if not also the seventies brutalism of nearby animal houses. The Magellanic Penguins it houses are now quite unusual in UK zoos and, at the time of writing, are the only ones in this country.

Another new exhibit is the Giraffes which returned to the collection in 2008, viewing inside is on two levels in exactly the same type of green agricultural building as everyone else in the UK has built for this species in the last fifteen years! I suppose this is with good reason as far as husbandry is concerned but is still rather uninspiring (and not just here obviously). Other ungulates around this zoo include Hartmann's Mountain Zebra, Eastern Bongo, a profligate group of Turkmenian Markhors, Vicuna and Reindeer. The Camel House (Bactrian Camels) remains unchanged but still looks sturdy and professional. Birds are not really a strength at Blackpool but the waterfowl lake is quite nice with a flock of Rosy Flamingos, and psittacines are represented strongly too. With regard to the latter, the Keas have an unusual but imaginative glass-fronted habitat which recreates a New Zealand sub-alpine scene.

Apart from the first few halcyon years of municipal ownership, Blackpool Zoo is probably in the best hands that it has ever been. It should be the case in all zoos that they now look better than ever, but this isn't always true. It is here. I can't quite get to grips with an overly-dramatic, garish and probably costly 'Dinosaur Safari' but, that apart, the dynamism of the new ownership is palpable. Potential for a zoo in Britain's premier seaside resort was enormous, is enormous, but was woefully unfulfilled in the past. I can see that changing before my very eyes.

BLAIR DRUMMOND SAFARI & ADVENTURE PARK

Nr, Stirling, FK9 4UR, Scotland
MAP REF: 22/C2
SIZE: 120 ACRES
OPENED: 1970
OWNERS: PRIVATE LTD COMPANY
SPECIES: 58

EVERY ONE OF Britain's remaining safari parks is partially the creation of Jimmy Chipperfield, and he seemed to operate under differing circumstances in each and every one. In 1970 he formed a partnership with Sir John Muir to open a park at the Muir estate some 30 miles equidistant from Glasgow, Edinburgh and Perth. Today the park is privately owned and after many changes of name is now Blair Drummond Safari & Adventure Park.

In terms of area Blair Drummond is the smallest of the British safari parks and at 120 acres is only slightly larger than Chester Zoo and much smaller than Whipsnade, all crammed in on a flat site under the turrets of the Victorian mansion house which looks down on it all from the hillside. Possibly because of the restrictions on space many of the enclosures are not drive through but drive-past and the public are encouraged to get out of their cars at these paddocks, all of which is much more conducive to leisurely contemplation I must admit and the result is almost half zoo, half safari park. Not that the African Elephant, Giraffe, Brown Bear and Amur Tiger exhibits (which are all walk-round) are anything less than spacious you understand. Some of these exhibits have timber walkways-in-the-sky alongside permitting an almost birds-eye view of the animals, I particularly like the Brown Bear enclosure with its ponds and trees.

BLAIR DRUMMOND SAFARI & ADVENTURE PARK

Other animal exhibits exist in the concreted, 'adventure' portion of the park. As with all the safari parks a fairly brash theme-park style has been adopted here with amusements, dodgems, and high calorie food sending the spirits low and the cholesterol count high. In the seventies an unheated Dolphinarium was the centrepiece of this part of the park with the unfortunate cetaceans having to be transported to the Mediterranean every winter. Imagine the outcry today! Instead the sizable indoor pool is used for Californian Sea Lions which is just as well because the glass-surrounded outside pool is diminutive. Continuing the aquatic theme a recently renovated Penguin Pool (Humboldt's) is next to the Asiatic Short-clawed Otter exhibit and Meerkats (never!) are not too far away. A recently added lemur walk-through is as large as I've seen

As is often the case with these country estates a large lake exists although the keeping of pinnipeds in it Longleat-style was abandoned long ago due to frequent escapes, but at least the island is rather more substantial for apes (in this case Chimpanzees) than its counterpart at Longleat.

The true, drive-around traditional safari takes a somewhat convoluted route over three comparatively small areas (hence the convolutions presumably). First of these is something of a mixed bag geographically, so expect anything from Bactrian Camels to American Bison to Ankole Cattle and Kafue Flats Lechwe mixed up with Ostrich and Pere David's Deer. Less of a mix are three White Rhinos obtained from the rather sensible auction that the parks authorities have for surplus stock in South Africa these days.

That leaves a rather spectacular group of lions which on the day of my visit contained no less than five fully maned males. Whether or not the dynamics of the group here are affected by a rather equal ratio of males to females I wouldn't know but they do make for a spectacular show.

The future role of serious zoos has evolved and been defined over the last quarter of a century. It seems that safari parks exist only on the periphery of serious intention – that they exist almost to a man, as money-making enterprises is partly the problem, but too often the infrastructure goes uncomfortably close to theme park culture. Once touted as the 'zoos of the future' they are in danger of reaching an evolutionary dead end despite the fact that they have deflected much welfare criticism by virtue of painting a convincing illusion of freedom. I look around at Blair Drummond and the only truly endangered species I can see are surplus populations of Amur Tigers and Pere David's Deer from zoo breeding programmes. The scottish safari park is not on its own and given the sheer space and room these places have at their disposal, a serious bout of self analysis is long overdue.

BLUE PLANET AQUARIUM
Ellesmere Port, Cheshire CH65 9LF
MAP REF: 23/C3
OPENED: 1997
OWNERS: DEEP SEA LEISURE PLC
SPECIES: 405

SOME FIVE MILES away from Chester Zoo and on the edge of the Merseyside town of Ellesmere Port is the glistening steel shed that houses the Blue Planet Aquarium. It is actually one of our best aquariums and unusual in as much as it is comparatively inland. Granted, the Irish Sea is not that far away but there are no waterfront or quayside associations here. Not surprisingly Chester Zoo was vehemently opposed to Blue Planet when it was first proposed, particularly as the aquarium's location meant that it qualified for E.E.C. financial assistance. All that is water under the bridge now! (with apologies). Quite honestly it would appear that the aquarium draws visitors who do the usual hour or two in such a place then emerge into the daylight with the exclamation 'what now?'. I know of only a handful of aquariums in the world that can sustain a day visit and we don't have one in the UK. In the case of the Blue Planet a logical answer to filling out the rest of the day is a certain quality zoological garden just up the road, of that I'm sure. So in actuality the zoo has benefited from the aquarium development.

So what is it that makes me fonder of Blue Planet than your average Sea Life? Well I do like the fact that freshwater exhibits do not live in the shadow of marine aquaria as some kind of afterthought as in the coastal aquariums. The temperate zone gives over quite a lot of space even to the likes of Dace or Minnow. The Amazon has one of the few Arapaimas in the country, also Freshwater Pipefish as an oddity and there is a positively teeming Lake Malawi exhibit. A mangrove tank holds the usual Archerfish and Argus Scats but also the rarely seen and impressive Tiger Fish (which is actually not a mangrove species being from the waterways of tropical Africa dependent on the taxon). Both Coral Bay and the extensive Aquatheatre (a walk through tank) are packed with interesting fish, in fact the latter tank holds no less than ten species of shark. The usual problem of inadequate labelling abounds here but I know of no aquarium that has a really satisfactory solution to this apart from some zoo aquariums with smaller tanks and a commitment to full information about the collection.

At over 400 species Blue Planet has the largest aquatic collection in the country and has to be rated by that criteria alone. Together with high exhibition values I would rate it as Britain's best aquarium. It is owned by the same company as Deep Sea World in Scotland.

BORTH ANIMALARIUM

Ynys Fergi, Borth, Cardigan SY24 5NA, Wales
MAP REF: 24/B3
SIZE: 12 ACRES
OPENED: 2000
OWNERS: PRIVATE
SPECIES: 53

BORTH ANIMALARIUM is a long way from any other kind of collection and quite honestly I am not sure it would be worth the significant effort of virtually every zoo enthusiast to get there. This small zoo has a rather ramshackle appearance derived from a wild assortment of largely timber framed buildings. To describe it as homemade would be quite charitable. There is a zoo rarity in the form of a genuine African Leopard and as this taxon has been largely overtaken by the rarer Asiatic subspecies in captivity then the long and winding road does at least have some sort of reward at its end. Ocelots and Geoffroy's Cats can also be found here. Vervet Monkeys are another species knocked off their zoo plinth by virtue of conservationally important taxa and they too can be found as well as Brown Capuchins. A small reptile house will not add glory to any zoo chapter and Meerkats live in a concrete bowl. Clearly Borth has taken a number of animals which were unwanted at other collections and apart from that laudable reason I cannot really see that this small zoo performs any worthwhile function at all.

BOURNEMOUTH OCEANARIUM

Pier Approach, West Beach, Bournemouth, Dorset BH2 5AA
MAP REF: 25/C4
OPENED: 1998
OWNERS: PRIVATE LIMITED COMPANY
SPECIES: 258

A SPARKLING white building on the very edge of the beach at Bournemouth is the home of the Oceanarium. From a global perspective the name 'Oceanarium' is rather grandiose and in most of the world would probably entail dolphins, penguins, seals and many more fish than are on view here – in truth a name such as 'the Bournemouth Aquarium' is much more accurate. That said, this medium-sized aquarium has a number of interesting aspects and rather breaks the mould of formularized aquariums that are now the tendency in the UK. A number of rooms are thematically arranged such as the Mediterranean, Africa, Ganges River, and the Abyss for nocturnal fish such as the Short Bigeye and Pinecone Fish. The zoogeographic policy occasionally falls apart but as previously stated makes for something of a change. A small walk-through tank bases itself upon the Great Barrier Reef and amongst the Blacktip Reef Sharks and Bannerfish are a pair of large Green Turtles (sea turtles are now uncommon in British aquariums). As usual, labelling is woefully inadequate in here. The last exhibit in the aquarium has a nice touch in that a rather standard ray tank as popularized by the Sea Life group of aquariums has been converted to a Key West theme and as such holds a number of interesting species including the strange Jackknife Fish which is quite difficult to keep. The breeding of many marine animals is still in its infancy but the Oceanarium here has succeeded with a couple of ray species for the first time in the UK (Southern Stingray and Cownose Ray). In 2007 ownership of the Oceanarium changed to the Spanish group Parque Reunidos who also own Blackpool Zoo and the Lakes Aquarium, it will be interesting to see if they do anything different with this aquarium in the light of space constraints that restrict major changes in many such establishments.

BREAN DOWN TROPICAL BIRD GARDEN

Coast Road, Brean Down, Burnham-on-Sea, Somerset TA8 2RS

MAP REF: 26/C4
SIZE: 0.4 ACRES
OPENED: 1972
OWNERS: PRIVATE

BREAN DOWN is a National Trust headland to the south of Weston-Super-Mare. That said, it requires something more than a short journey to reach it from the famous seaside resort. After you've wound your way around various small roads and lanes and through acres of caravan parks you will see the peninsula looming up in front of you. Before you can climb up on to it you will observe a plain sixties-style house that seems to be a café at first, however, this is also the entrance to the small walled bird garden behind. Assembled mainly around the walls are a collection of no less than 47 aviaries surrounding a formal lawn. These aviaries contain mostly parrots and as such are the traditionally formal psittacine aviaries denuded of naturalistic effects that do not last long under the attention of such birds in smaller aviaries. Most of the species are the commonly seen amazons, Grey Parrots, commoner cockatoos but also some rarer species exist in the form of Red-fronted Macaws, a few *Pionus* Parrots and King Parrots. In truth the serious aviculturist might find the collection somewhat unexciting and certainly the lack of beautifully-planted aviaries is also a further detraction – some softbills might not go amiss here! That said, the place is probably quite an amenity for all those surrounding caravan dwellers who can also buy a decent breakfast here!

BRIGHTON SEA LIFE

Marine Parade, Brighton, Sussex BN2 1TB
MAP REF: 27/D4
OPENED: 1872
OWNERS: MERLIN ENTERTAINMENTS
SPECIES: 160

W̲h̲i̲l̲s̲t̲ I̲ h̲a̲v̲e̲ a tendency to be a little dismissive of Sea Life's identikit approach to their various aquariums, there is no doubt that their acquisition of the Brighton Aquarium in 1991 cannot come within that category. This aquarium is in fact the oldest in the world (if we accept that the one at Liverpool's World Museum is not quite the same one as the original). Brighton opened in 1872 and the main hall with its neo-trecento style arches remains much intact. It has the sturdy clumsiness of a great deal of Victorian architecture and whilst frequently defined as 'Moorish', has more of the feel of a church or chapel with each aquarium inserted between the stone arches. In total this room is 224 feet in length. The architect, Eugenius Birch, was the same one who designed the nearby pier. Such was the importance of the Brighton Aquarium that Prince Arthur (Queen Victoria's third son) undertook the official opening.

Today some 57 separate tanks house over 150 species, these include a large walk-through Tropical Reef with many of the standard species to be seen in this type of thing, but including some Green Turtles that have now been in the country for over fifty years, having originally been brought in for a soap advertisement and subsequently housed at London Zoo, then Blackpool Tower Aquarium. 'Tropical Reef' occupies the area once given over to dolphins in the heyday of these exhibits in the UK, around thirty years ago. Other exhibits include 'Kingdom of the Seahorse' and ones for local species – some aquaria are more variable and in recent times have included temporary ones for octopuses, also crabs. Sea Life Centres have a tendency to do this, in order that the various aquariums can offer 'new' attractions each season. This can make things awkward for the reviewer.

Throughout its history Brighton Aquarium's clock tower has been a famous landmark and today the visitor can still descend the steps behind it to visit a decent facility, but for the enthusiast the descent is one into history and it is for this reason more than any other that a visit here is essential for the serious zoo observer.

BRISTOL ZOO

Clifton, Bristol BS8 3HA
MAP REF: 28/C4
SIZE: 12 ACRES
OPENED: 1836
OWNERS: NON PROFIT ZOOLOGICAL SOCIETY
SPECIES: 419

ONE OF THE oldest zoos in world, Bristol originally took its cue from the Zoological Society of London and aimed itself at the well-heeled middle and upper classes of the region, opening its doors on Monday, 11 July 1836. It was in connection with Bristol that the word 'zoo' was actually first-recorded, in Lord MacCauley's diaries, "we treated the Clifton Zoo much too contemptuously. I lounged hither, and found more than sixpenny worth of amusement". This is between 1847 and 1849. Bristol wasn't the only city to try to emulate the capital at the time and similar schemes in places such as Manchester, Cheltenham and Leeds quickly floundered due to an essential lack of monied patrons. And indeed Bristol was lucky to hang on – it had a roller coaster, turbulent, first century where all manner of unsuitable activities such as fireworks, bands and sporting contests were added to the compact gardens by way of money-making potential. It was one Dr Richard Clarke who was to put Bristol Zoo firmly back on the zoological tracks in the late 1920s. However, they say that time is a thief and by the end of the seventies Bristol's now hugely popular zoo looked very dated indeed.

The last thirty years has seen Bristol Zoo undergo almost total transformation. Aided and abetted by its small, almost tiny, size almost every building has undergone transformation or replacement. Indeed, so vigorous is the change that quite a lot of the improvements have since been replaced! When you are small, neat and successful this is easier to do of course. In the process of all this new development Bristol also decided that many large mammals were too big for the gardens. Gone now are Giraffes, elephants, rhinos (the first Black Rhino born in the UK was here), Tigers (Bristol was once famous for its white Tigers), Polar Bears indeed any bears, Chimpanzees (another UK or even European 'first') and more. Granted, there isn't really room for most of these now but I still think they went a little too far and it might just be that the general public agrees with me because, against a nationwide trend, attendances have slightly fallen at Bristol Zoo in the last few years. Bristol even has to suffer the indignity of the trivial and bizarre Noah's Ark Zoo Farm, seven miles to the south, marketing itself as 'the home of the BIG animals' in a totally unwarranted attack on a serious establishment. Fortunately plans are in hand to reintroduce large mammals to Bristol under scientific protocols, but more of that later. As it is the response is rather unsatisfactory, consisting of the conversion of the excellent Wallace Aviary into a popularist lorikeet-feeding aviary.

Apart from the last-named development Bristol's reinvention has been rather superb.

It is difficult to select the best of these but I rather like 'Twilight World' which occupies the old Ape House. Bristol had the world's first nocturnal house in 1953 and the idea is usually credited to Dr Richard Clarke – I don't know when the idea entered his head but there is clear evidence that Wroclaw Zoo (now in Poland, then in Germany) had plans for such a development in 1941. Whatever the truth, Bristol's was actually the first to exist and the tradition is excellently maintained today (in a different spot). Three different night-time environments (Desert, Subterranean, Tropical Rainforest) are imaginatively presented with Aye-ayes as the most notable inhabitants. A final fourth environment is more surprising in that it is a typical house (human) overtaken by Brown Rats and House Mice plus a few invertebrates. I quite like its light-hearted approach. At the very end of the 'Twilight Zone World' is a walk-through outdoor flight cage for Livingstone's Fruit Bats – for my money the most impressive species of their type and critically endangered to boot. Here, in broad daylight, you can see their jet-black fur flecked with gold rather like a pollen dusting. Follow the path around and you will come to exhibits for Red Pandas and Keas, which also use the retaining wall of the old Ape House as their backdrop.

Not too far away (nothing is at Bristol) an ancient bear pit has been converted into a small aquarium and manages to squeeze in a variety of freshwater and marine exhibits. It doesn't seem at all tiny but it is. Very imaginative, very good. The Reptile House is next door and was amongst the first conversions in the early 1980s. Surprisingly the visitor heads up a slope passing various vivaria (look out for some wonderful Meller's Chameleons) and a breeding room in which Splendid Leaf Frogs are to be seen (very scarce in captivity) before winding down again via pools for turtles and West African Dwarf Crocodiles. 'Bug World' occupies the upper level of the neo-modernist restaurant. In a manner not unlike 'Twilight World' this invertebrate house meanders through various biomes such as rainforest, desert and marine before, yet again, replicating human dwellings. I'm sure the mock toilet with its Black Widow Spider stays in the mind of many a visitor!

'Monkey Jungle' is the name for the new Monkey House with a stout, solid, approach to its construction which would not disappoint a German zoo director! Four indoor enclosures link to imaginative outdoor ones for Lion-tailed Macaques, De Brazza's Monkeys, Black Howlers and various lemurs (complete with an outdoor walk-through). In fact the De Brazza's Monkeys can even access the adjacent gorilla enclosure. The Lowland Gorillas in fact have an island and half of the indoor usage of the extended old Elephant House, the other half is given over to Okapis. This is an appropriate coupling as Bristol was the first British zoo to breed both species. Pygmy Hippos are to be found in a suitably 'earthy' tropical house next door.

It is difficult to believe that 'Seal and Penguin Coasts' is now ten years old, it seems like only yesterday that it opened and, thankfully, it still looks like new as well. This is a combination of walk-through seabird aviary and separate seal exhibit (South American Fur Seals) both with underwater viewing. The birds consist of a large group of African Penguins, Inca Terns, Common Eider and a solitary Little Penguin, which is the only one to be kept alive in this country for decades. 'Zona Brazil' takes us around South America with Black Lion Tamarins as the highlight. The exhibit is mostly outdoors with one small walk-through greenhouse and, to my mind, very unlike 'new' Bristol in that it has something of a homemade feel about it. Various aviaries are dotted haphazardly around the grounds making the bird collection seem smaller than it is (around 70 species) although I do like the fact that the Flamingo Pool near the entrance is netted giving the Chilean Flamingos a chance to flap about a bit.

So what of the previously mentioned large mammal return? Well, as is commonly known Bristol Zoo owns a country estate of around 100 acres, about 8 miles away alongside the M5, known as Hollywood Towers. Plans are in hand to construct a major zoological park on this site that has been owned by the Society for well over 40 years. The recent economic downturn has cast doubt over a timescale but I am sure it will happen. The Bristol, Clifton and West of England Zoological Society should be the home of BIG animals in these parts!

BRITISH WILDLIFE CENTRE

Gate House Farm, Eastbourne Road, Newchapel, Lingfield, Surrey RH7 6LF
MAP REF: 29/D4
SIZE: 50 ACRES
OPENED: 2000
OWNERS: PRIVATE
SPECIES: 43

DAVID MILLS had the dream that many of us have had or still have. He wanted to open a zoo. He also wanted to specialize and the British Wildlife Centre is the result – you will find it right on the A22 heading towards East Grinstead. With its impressive entrance signage you can't really miss it. Due to the restrictions of local council protocol the centre is only open at weekends and public holidays through March to October, also school holidays.

Now, BBC Wildlife Magazine would not thank me for saying it but Britain is not exactly Madagascar or New Guinea, whilst we have quite a wonderful and varied fauna we are not over-endowed with charismatic mammals or gigantic snakes, our birdlife has a tendency toward the brown spectrum rather than gaudy scarlets or spectacular ultramarines. There is still much of interest however, yet a further problem remains in that much of what we have is shy, secretive and occasionally difficult to keep in captivity. The zoo here has addressed those problems and the result is a quite delightful meadow full of interesting animals or maybe that should be animals made interesting (at public level at least).

Initial impressions are positive indeed with a very large old barn converted into an impressive visitor centre complete with a museum, café and gift shop, even better are two adjoining animal houses with the theme of 'The Barn' and 'The Hedgerow'. The former is authentic and nicely done; however 'The Hedgerow' is a little gem of an exhibit quite unlike anything I have ever encountered. Naturalistic vivaria show us Common Moles (in a cutaway burrow – come on now, have you ever seen a mole enclosure before?) Wood Mice, Bank Voles, Hedgehogs and Yellow-necked Mice working up in size to the likes of Stoats and Weasels scuttling around in wirework runs above your head. Lots of informative labelling – who needs Clouded Leopards?

Out and about in the 20 acre meadow that comprises the majority of the centre are enclosures for Pine Martens, Common Foxes, four species of deer (including the fairly-tricky-in-captivity Roe Deer) and the now endangered (in Britain at least) Water Vole. Two large ponds for European Otters are beautifully presented in a naturalistic style and the Scottish Wild Cat's cages made me smile, in as much as they utilise the framework of a roof set against a small hillock – exactly the same thing was once done at South Lakes Wildlife Park – convergent evolution at architectural level therefore! Of course walk-through enclosures are all the rage currently, in an interesting slant on the concept the British Wildlife Centre is about to enclose Red Squirrels in such a fashion

Some outdoor vivaria for reptiles have been made from converted pig sties and the artificial Badger sett is another very professional exhibit adjacent to a wildlife theatre containing a rolling programme of pertinent footage. There are also some aviaries for birds of prey and owls although the bird collection could be larger given that these isles are home to more than three hundred species.

The British Wildlife Centre now includes a wetland reserve and the collection is increasing to become as comprehensive as possible. If there was ever a doubt that our country's fauna could sustain an interesting living collection then this fascinating small zoo instantly disabuses any such notion.

THE BUG WORLD EXPERIENCE

The Grand Hall, The Colonnades, Albert Dock, Liverpool, Merseyside L3 4AA

MAP REF: 30/C3
OPENED: 2009
OWNERS: PRIVATE LIMITED COMPANY
SPECIES: 37

NEARLY 130 YEARS had to elapse after London Zoo created the world's first living invertebrate display before the nation was to encounter its first stand-alone insect zoo outside of the butterfly syndrome. Much emphasis has been placed on high quality presentation and professionalism at The Bug World Experience. Even though the species count is quite small it is quality rather than quantity on display here.

Unusually for Britain (but seen occasionally in the US) the visitor is introduced to the collection by a short film courtesy of television star Craig Charles before finding the living animals displayed in various biotopes. These are tropical rainforest, savannah, desert, water, woodland, garden and 'Your World' (domestic environments). Nor are these areas populated by the oft-found over-reliance on bird-eating spiders and stick insects. There are Seychelles Millipedes, Sacred Scarab Beetles, Scolopendra Centipedes, White-clawed Crayfish even Medicinal Leeches in a naturalistic environment rather than an apothecary jar. We have seen Partula snails presented before but here at Bug World we can see the other participants in the ecological disaster on Moorea in the shape of the Rosy Wolf Snail and the Giant African Snail. Included are further zoo rarities such as the Deathstalker Scorpion, a highly venomous Middle East species, or the South American Fishing Spider *(Ancylometes bogotensis)*. Panamanian Paper Wasps *(Polistes canadensis)* were also a personal 'first' and if you have forgotten that we now have scorpions in the UK then try Kent's Yellow-tailed Scorpion on show in the garden area here. Finally in the shop edible invertebrates can be purchased reminding us that they are common food fare around much of the world (and they sell well too!)

It would have been quite easy for The Bug World Experience to offer the distorted view of invertebrates that the usual 'ooh' and 'aah' creepy crawly corners give us in many butterfly centres. A more holistic approach is on offer here and is so well done as to be a very welcome newcomer to the British zoo scene.

CALDERGLEN CHILDREN'S ZOO

Strathaven Rd, East Kilbride G75 0QZ, Scotland
MAP REF: 31/B2
SIZE: 3 ACRES
OPENED: 1980
OWNERS: LOCAL AUTHORITY

THE ONLY ZOO I can think of that opened to commemorate the United Nations 'Year of the Child' in 1980! Many a park around the nation has seen a pets corner or an aviary or two – my local park has a small vivarium for instance, but most of these must fall outside the scope of this book by virtue of size. One or two however have grown into zoos by any definition of the word. Such a place is Calderglen Children's Zoo which now comprises of three distinct parts. First up is the 'Conservatory' which is, in effect, a small tropical house with a tank for Malawi cichlids, a few reptiles and a group of Common Marmosets housed above an Amazonian pool with fish to match. Then there is 'Hidden Worlds' which takes you into a cave-styled room with various small glass-fronted exhibits set into the walls but, unusually, representing native wildlife such as the various stages of river life from source to sea as well as a Honey Bee colony. Finally there is a small outdoor zoo for the likes of Parma Wallabies, Coatis, Meerkats, Black Turkey Vultures and Temminck's Tragopans. Needless to say there are domesticated animals as well. Amazingly Calderglen Children's Zoo can boast of over half a million visitors per year, many of these visit the zoo as only one part of the diverse attractions of Calderglen County Park.

CAMPERDOWN WILDLIFE CENTRE

Camperdown Park, Dundee DD2 4TF, Scotland

MAP REF: 32/C2
SIZE: 10 ACRES
OPENED: 1968
OWNERS: LOCAL AUTHORITY
SPECIES: 48

OPENED IN 1968 as a children's zoo within the greater area of Camperdown Park, the collection evolved to become a specialist collection of European fauna. Recent times have seen a minor move towards some taxa outside of a European remit. Britain is of course unique amongst the major zoo nations in that there are very few municipally supported collections and only one at governmental level in the Isle of Man. Camperdown is one of the tiny band partly supported by the ratepayer, a fact that reflects itself in a very low admission fee. And whilst the local populace can bask in the glow of a subsidized collection, there do seem to be contradictory forces at work with some exhibits running down, others brand new and others beyond repair.

Camperdown Wildlife Centre is comprised of an old walled garden area, a semi-wooded area to one side of this and an open grassed area on another side of the wall. The entrance gate is as solid as you might expect from a municipality. In many ways the old walled garden and its contents epitomizes the hotchpotch of situations here. A new Brown Bear enclosure dominates around half of the garden replacing a cage thought modern when it replaced a tiny bear pit in 1979. Both cage (used now for owls) and pit (now unused) are still in existence. That the two bears have a magnificent grassed enclosure now is beyond dispute. Towards one corner is a substantial visitor viewing tower cleverly built as to reinforce age-old zoo notions of bears and castles. I can only assume that this will be utilised educationally at some point because there wasn't one printed word in there. Easily solved however, (although labelling is generally poor at the zoo). To the centre of the walled garden is a very bare otter enclosure and of course the style and colour of the fencing is entirely different from that of the bears. On one side of all this are ramshackle overgrown old paddocks and on the other side a nocturnal house and a rodent house, both containing lots of unused vivaria, some with empty pots of paint and rubbish in them. Black and White Ruffed Lemurs and Seba's Short-tailed Bats are just two species illustrating the move away from European fauna living in this particular area of the zoo. On the other side of the wall an old, rather strange, Snowy Owl aviary now houses Guinea Pigs and Domestic Rabbits alongside a brand new Golden Eagle aviary. This is a place of jaw-dropping contrasts, which seems to be unsure which way to go.

Around Camperdown are Wolves, European Lynx, Scottish Wildcats, Pine Martens, deer and Ring-tailed Lemurs amongst others. It could (and should) be a nice little zoo but sensible touches, consistency and an amount of awareness seem to be missing.

CASTLE ESPIE WILDFOWL & WETLANDS TRUST

Ballydrain Road, Comber, Co Down BT23 6EA, Northern Ireland
MAP REF: 33/B2
SIZE: 60 ACRES
OPENED: 1989
OWNERS: REGISTERED CHARITY

THE ORIGINS of the Wildfowl and Wetlands Trust's Irish centre at Castle Espie go back to 1978 when a private concern known as the Castle Espie Conservation Centre was opened by one Paddy Mackie. In 1989 as a memorial to his brother who had been killed in an accident, Paddy Mackie gave the centre to the Wildfowl and Wetland Trust. The centre is situated on Strangford Lough, a body of water with enormous natural significance and which attracts huge numbers of waterfowl and waders – particularly famous is the over-wintering flock of Light-bellied Brent Geese *(Branta bernicla hrota)* which can number in excess of 20,000. An accurate assessment of the captive collection is, at the time of writing, rather difficult due to extensive redevelopments. Already a new visitor centre has opened and other work is underway, scheduled to be completed in 2010. In the past Castle Espie has tended to hold about 50 species of wildfowl which is around half the number at Slimbridge or Martin Mere, but this did include some interesting sea ducks such as Common Scoter and Red-breasted Merganser, uncommon at other WWT centres.

CHESSINGTON WORLD OF ADVENTURES & ZOO

Chessington, Surrey KT9 2NE
MAP REF: 34/D4
SIZE: 17 ACRES
OPENED: 1931
OWNERS: MERLIN ENTERTAINMENTS
SPECIES: 181

CHESSINGTON WORLD OF ADVENTURES opened as Chessington Zoo in 1931 and drew its success from the inexorable growth of London south of the Thames. Indeed the leafy and semi-rural parts of Surrey begin almost at Chessington's gates and until that point Surrey runs seamlessly into London proper. Like half a dozen other zoos Chessington zoo became a theme park when purchased by Madame Tussauds in 1978. It is now owned by Merlin Entertainments who also own Warwick Castle, Madame Tussauds, the London Aquarium and the burgeoning Sea Life chain as well as others. That Chessington like, for instance, Flamingo Land and Drayton Manor found greater success with the cheap thrill of the fairground is depressing if not surprising and a familiar scenario emerged whereby the retained zoo became a sideshow in its own right. By the early nineties there was a pressure to 'put up or shut up' with the zoo proper and wisely the former course was taken – with a little downsizing as an acceptable side-effect, after all Chessington always was a place with a commercial outlook and a fairly sizeable portion of the park was always allocated to non-zoological attractions.

The first notable product of the 'new age' actually dated from the late 1980's and was a tremendous bird garden known as 'The World of Birds'. Chessington always did well with birds and created a meandering maze of aviaries fashioned from telegraph poles amongst swathes of vegetation. I thought at the time that it was the best such facility in the land. The quite awful Ape House from 1967 was replaced by a Gorilla exhibit in the manner of an Aspinall-styled cage complete with deep straw litter. A new range of small cat enclosures pleasantly fronted in logs and with glass viewing windows complimented two upgraded grassy enclosures for Asiatic Lions and Sumatran Tigers. The Sea Lion Pool was modernised and eventually the Reptile House found a home in a converted Polar Bear pit under the melodramatic name of 'Creepy Caves'. It was difficult to escape the thought that the zoo still wasn't the main item on the menu at Chessington but still the portions that remained were appetising enough.

Just a few years ago it appeared that Chessington World of Adventures was really going to embrace the zoo philosophy once more. Possibly inspired by the success of Disney's Animal Kingdom in Florida planning permission was obtained for a hotel which in turn would overlook an African savannah full of animals. As I write the hotel has been completed for some time without any sight or promise of a Serengeti in Surrey. To add insult to injury this particular development also resulted in the demolition of 'Monkey Walk' (which had only recently been renovated) and the introduction of some of the said simians to the bird garden. Neither birds nor monkeys have profited from further retraction of the collection.

For some years now Chessington has held an interesting collection of reptiles and the collection has moved around the grounds too with at least four different locations over the years. 'Creepy Caves' as the most recent should be the best of these houses. And it is, but the initial impetus that saw species as interesting as Crocodile Monitor and Timor Python on display seems to have been lost and already this underground display looks tired and unloved, decidedly worn around the edges.

At least the acquisition of Chessington by Merlin Entertainments has resulted in a new zoological attraction – not surprisingly this is a Sea Life Centre and not surprisingly it is much the same as all the others around the nation (if actually a little smaller). Nonetheless, let us hope that a new animal exhibit has halted the slide at this particular collection (no pun intended). And yet it all looked so promising only a few years ago. Merlin doesn't have any other zoos as such, Chessington surely is the testing ground of their ambitions in this area.

CHESTER ZOO
Upton-By-Chester, Cheshire CH2 IEU
MAP REF: 35/C3
SIZE: 123 ACRES
OPENED: 1931
OWNER: NORTH OF ENGLAND ZOOLOGICAL SOCIETY
SPECIES: 422

As BRITAIN struggled to find its feet after World War Two Chester Zoo expanded rapidly driven by its founder George Mottershead and whilst it would be true to say that there was an element of being in the right place at the right time he undoubtedly showed remarkable foresight and application. Much hyperbole surrounds the so-called 'zoo without bars' syndrome and actually the infant Chester Zoo was far from such an ideal. The truth is that Mottershead eschewed architectural sympathies to use practical and cost effective building materials whilst at the same time providing more spacious enclosures than traditional urban zoos. He provided a combination of zoo and park situated just perfectly for the huge working class populations of Lancashire and the West Midlands as they sought to leave their streets behind in their newly-acquired cars. Amazingly some of Mottershead's constructions stand up to scrutiny even under today's criteria such as the Lion enclosure, the Sea Lion Pool and particularly his Tropical House. Others, such as the Parrot House and his Monkey House found their appearance less conducive to modern-day sympathies and have been replaced. Mottershead died on the 5 May 1978 at the age of 83.

The death of George Mottershead was the end of an era for the zoo and one which coincided with a difficult following decade for zoos in the UK. Dr Michael Brambell was now in charge having left London Zoo where he had been Curator of Mammals. Mottershead had not built with longevity in mind (quite the opposite in fact) and much of Chester's infrastructure was looking worn. Within a framework of declining attendances revitalization was started and the march towards today's successes started. Brambell deserves enormous credit for this and today's Chimpanzee House and 'Europe on the Edge' aviary are from his tenure. Probably his most significant contribution was to change the whole axis of Chester Zoo by virtue of moving the entire visitor entrance area from one side of the zoo to the other.

In 1995 Gordon McGregor Reid took over as Director (he had been Chief Curator) and the pace of change became almost breathtaking. Today Chester Zoo is regarded as the UK's top zoo with good reason. The zoo is fortunate to benefit once more from George Mottershead's foresight in the shape of swathes of extra land (over 600 acres) bought up around the zoo in years gone by. Indeed Chester has long-term plans to significantly expand over the next twenty years. Recent years have seen record attendance after record attendance and Chester has, for a few years now, been Britain's most popular zoo.

Under the stewardship of McGregor Reid it rather seems that some major exhibit or other opens every year. 'Spirit of The Jaguar' is perhaps the only one of these to have architectural aspirations-possibly because it was funded by the motor car company of that name. It truly is a cathedral to *Panthera onca* showing that species in both arid and rainforest habitats, certainly there are houses dedicated to the whole felidae around the world that are less than half the size. 'Realm of the Red Ape' is another huge edifice and home to both species of Orang Utan as well as satellite exhibits as notable as Crocodile Monitor and Belanger's Tree Shrew. I might also add that this vast structure, turning in at a cost of some £5.6 million places practicality and husbandry well before aesthetics – whisper it quietly, but it is quite ugly!

Quite honestly Chester hasn't ever concerned itself with architectural niceties and a strong horticultural tradition has always served to mask that fact, even if the Chimp's conical accommodation was a marked departure from the pseudo-agricultural. Another recent development that was right in line with the 'barn philosophy' was 'Twilight Zone', yet does any visitor ever bother with the external appearance when the inside nocturnal walk-through is so utterly atmospheric? The orientation here is basically towards bats and three species (Seba's Short-tailed, Rodrigues Fruit and Livingstone's Fruit) are housed here. The committed chiroptophile may find some frustration in the sense of bats rather than the view of them but the excitement of the general visitor is quite palpable.

Recent years have seen the old Pachyderm House reinvigorated and doubled in size whilst proclaiming itself to be the 'National Breeding Centre' for Asiatic Elephants. Gone are the Hippos, rhinos, tapirs and African Elephants of George Mottershead's day, to be replaced with three separate areas for one species and a variety of substrates. The outer paddock (once thought enormous) has been doubled in size. Other types of animal do live here on an Asiatic zoogeographic basis, in vivaria and aquariums, but the height of the Great Indian Hornbill aviary will take some beating anywhere. And if Chester's policy has long been towards larger enclosures then recent individual exhibits for Andean Condors, Spectacled Bears, Black Rhinos and Cheetahs (amongst others) have served to emphasize the trend.

Some of Chester's older buildings have not yet gone the way of the bulldozer and are still put to good use. I'm sure the 1952 Aquarium is much smaller than the zoo would ideally like but it has made the most of its circumstances by focusing on endangered smaller species. Enthusiasts should make a special note of the Omani Cave Fish and Anderson's Salamanders seen here as they are both zoo rarities. Chester's Monkey House was in urgent need of attention and one of old Chester's worst exhibits, to be honest it was little different to those of London and Belle Vue in the 19th century. In 1997 it became 'Monkey Islands' with only four greatly enlarged indoor habitats and lushly planted outer islands which have surprisingly withstood the attentions of the Mandrills, Sulawesi Crested Macaques and Lion-tailed Macaques that use them. Black-headed Spider Monkeys have a less decorated, hot-wired, grassy enclosure which has the advantage of a better view of the monkeys. 'Islands In Danger' is a conversion of a rather rickety old Tropical Bird House into a combined rare bird and Komodo Dragon house. Britain's only Birds of Paradise, the Red species are kept and bred here.

There is much more to Chester Zoo than space here really permits, for instance a penguin enclosure that was amongst the first to take temperate species off concrete and place them in tussock grass or a new butterfly house which looks as if there is a solid, long-term commitment to the propogation of these insects; but if you will permit me a slight indulgence I would like to end my account of Chester with some personal, but relevant nostalgia. In 1964 a six year old boy looked inside a new exhibit at Chester Zoo in wide-eyed wonder at what he perceived to be 'the jungle'. This exhibit was Mottershead's brand new Tropical House and of course, I was that little boy. Now officially entitled 'Tropical Realm', I'm glad, almost relieved, to say it has lost none of its charm and is still easily the best exhibit of its kind in the country. Back in 1964 this house seemed vast and it still does. A few things have changed, the small nocturnal section has gone, we've lost one wing of the reptile area and I doubt that I will see another male Mountain Gorilla in captivity (touted as such at the time, then they became Eastern Lowland, then the *graueri* taxon which is a subspecies of Mountain Gorilla!). Other aspects have changed for the better – an area for Buffy-headed Capuchins has been added, the old Mountain Gorilla indoor quarters are really more suited to hornbill enclosures (for Rhinoceros and Great Indian species) and the reptile collection places more emphasis on rarer, endangered species such as Philippines Crocodiles and Caiman Lizards. There are rare birds too, such as the Congo Peacock and further hornbills. And it always was a fairly simple idea – take a huge barn, heat it up and fill it with plants and animals, above all make it awesome. Of course, today's Chester has much more conservational relevance but the Mottershead philosophy is still much intact as seen in the 'Natural Vision' project which is anticipated to increase the zoo's size by as much as 200 acres and may well prove Chester to be the finest zoo in the world if it all comes about.

CHESTNUT CENTRE, OTTER, OWL & WILDLIFE PARK

Castleton Road, Chapel-En-Le-Frith, Derbyshire SK23 0QS
MAP REF: 36/C3
SIZE: 50 ACRES
OPENED: 1985
OWNERS: PRIVATE
SPECIES: 27

THE CHESTNUT CENTRE was the first in what was to become a small chain of otter and owl dominated wildlife collections. In recent years owner Roger Heap has added the New Forest Owl and Otter Centre and Battersea Park Children's Zoo to the group. The concept was fairly simple - take a woodland walk in the bottom of a small valley in breathtaking surroundings and dot it with a few owl aviaries and otter enclosures. Basically the formula remains the same after almost 25 years of operation.

In 1993 the Chestnut Centre brought itself to the notice of the UK zoo world by importing the first Giant Otters (from Germany) ever to be seen in the UK. A wonderful enclosure was built for them that converted an old pond into an almost-believable darkwater Amazonian river tributary. Sadly the hoped-for breeding of this species never occurred and a new young pair also from Germany has recently been acquired. These wonderful animals are worth the journey to the Chestnut Centre on their own. Three other otter species are shown in the zoo guide – Asian Small-clawed, European and American but none of the last of those species was there upon the occasion of my visit. The Short-clawed species has bred and proliferated into a number of different groups and enclosures, mostly provided with shallower dabbling pools as it is the belief of the owner that this species prefers such a situation. A few other mammals have been added to the collection in recent years in the shape of the Common Fox, Scottish Wildcat, Pine Marten and Polecat.

Around a dozen species of owl are kept at the Chestnut Centre with all the usual suspects present such as Spectacled Owl, Great Grey Owl, Burrowing Owl and Snowy Owl. The five British species are represented. One unusual aviary resident is Aharoni's Owl which is thought to be some naturally occurring hybrid between the European Eagle and Savigny's Eagle Owl, occurring in south west Eurasia. Whether or not the Chestnut Centre can get the new Giant Otter pairing to give us a UK first breeding or not is a question for both the Centre (I would imagine) and the enthusiast, but Giants or not, the centre will always be worthwhile for its combination of natural beauty and captive wildlife.

COLCHESTER ZOO

Maldon Road, Stanway, Colchester, Essex CO3 0SL
MAP REF: 37/D4
SIZE: 60 ACRES
OPENED: 1963
OWNERS: PRIVATE LIMITED COMPANY
SPECIES: 275

THERE IS NOTHING more exciting than a brand new zoo, particularly if it is top class, but it is possibly even more satisfying to see the transformation of the poor and mediocre into something worthwhile. Colchester Zoo was a child of the sixties with ever-changing stock, poor labelling and often unattractively housed. Of its era it certainly wasn't a bad place, but when the Tropeano family bought the zoo in 1983, time was definitely overtaking it. Those last 26 years have seen Colchester become quite a major player on the UK zoo scene with the largest collection of mammal species for instance. Would Zuckermann and Mottershead have ever conceived of such a thing? A charitable arm (Action For The Wild) was started in 1993 and a wildlife sanctuary is being created in South Africa. The zoo is also very active within EAZA and Managing Director Dominique Tropeano has done a great deal of important work as chair of the Committee on Technical Assistance and Animal Welfare in improving 'slum' zoos of Eastern Europe.

Colchester, in appearance, is quite unlike any other UK zoo. The 'original' zoo below Stanway Hall has been transformed into a veritable maze of modern, glass-fronted enclosures. An enthusiast can easily get lost amongst the Giant Anteaters and Pallas' Cats, the Fosas and the Binturongs. Look out for the Silvery Langurs, the only ones in Western Europe. There are more familiar zoo animals too, such as both Amur Tigers and Amur Leopards. And of course a collection of this size must have its Lions. If you like your collections full of animals and exhibits, then this is the place for you. It might also be interesting to see how long it would take to go around Colchester Zoo reading all the labels, because it is packed with information.

By and large exhibits and whole orders of animals are intertwined at this zoo, the owners believe that the likes of reptiles and fish, even birds, are often quickly passed over by visitors if presented in their own taxonomic houses. The policy here is to place such exhibits strategically in and amongst zoogeographical exhibits and as such they receive more attention. There is, however, a rather unusual row of birds of prey aviaries including Andean Condor and Bateleur Eagle. Why 'unusual'? Well, these are glass and timber fronted (rather than wire) creating a harmonious blend with the mammal enclosures nearby. There is also a walk-through waders aviary as well as a vulture aviary with some four species of these birds.

Colchester was the first to bring Gelada Baboons back to the UK in the nineties, these monkeys naturally belong in meadows and they have one here, but with the addition of a simple, but large, climbing frame which they use well. There is a strong primate collection at this zoo with the endangered Buffy-headed Capuchin, L'Hoest's Guenon, Cherry-crowned Mangabey and Lion-tailed Macaque being notable. A colony of Common Chimpanzees occupies a veritable labyrinth of enclosures and Orang Utans have a brand new house as I write (2009). An indication of the size and scope of the 'Tropeano era' is that the new Orang House had to be almost levered into the zoo such is the lack of available space despite several land acquisitions over the years.

Reference to extra land takes us onto the expanded 'new' Colchester Zoo and two major developments stand alongside each other forming a gateway to the African area. These two developments are barnlike structures built in the timbered manner of traditional Essex barns and which are now the favoured style of housing at the zoo. First of these is the Elephant House and its group of five African Elephants including Kito born at the zoo using the latest ground-breaking artificial insemination techniques. Alongside this house is another very similar, but larger, building by the name of 'Spirit of Africa'. Large ungulates such as Giraffes, White Rhinos, Greater Kudu and Damara Zebra are stabled here with a spacious, sandy, moated paddock as their external accommodation. Inside the house a zoogeographical mix includes reptiles, insects and fish with housing for Pygmy Hippos and Patas Monkeys as well. Not too far away are Mandrills, Warthogs, Red River Hogs, Striped Hyenas and Cheetahs all in grassy, open enclosures.

'Zoo-spotters' may also care to take notice of the UK's only Slender-snouted Crocodiles at Colchester although sadly the UK's only Rocky Mountain Goats have left the collection. One reptile species that isn't mixed in with other exhibits is the Komodo Dragon exhibit again, timbered, with a retractable roof which will be a useful husbandry tool. Many reptiles benefit from natural sunlight and certainly it is a part of Komodo Dragon husbandry. One also wonders what original owner Frank Farrar would make of his old elephant paddock now given over to Patagonian Sea Lions! Actually this huge project required the removals of many tons of earth (as you can imagine) to give enough depth for a pool that includes an underwater, walk-through tunnel thought to be amongst the longest in Europe and 500,000 gallons of water.

It would appear now that Colchester Zoo is in the enviable position of having been modernized and has replaced all of the old zoo; yet don't think the work will stop, in fact knowing Dominique Tropeano he'll probably start again!

COMBE MARTIN WILDLIFE & DINOSAUR PARK
Combe Martin, Devon EX34 0NG
MAP REF: 38/B4
SIZE: 25 ACRES
OPENED: 1986
OWNER: PRIVATE LIMITED COMPANY

FOUNDED IN 1986 by Robert Butcher in the grounds of a derelict Higher Leigh Manor as a small zoo with the addition of model dinosaurs, adding animatronic dinosaurs some years later as part of a rather theme-parkish approach to attracting visitors. Recently the title 'Botanical Gardens' has also been added to the mix and indeed the park does inhabit lush surroundings mostly forested. Then again, 'Tomb Of The Pharaohs' is also to be 'enjoyed' which gives an idea of the rich mixture here.

The zoological collection at Combe Martin isn't large but most of what does exist is rather well done. Much of the collection lies in a dark, verdant woodland valley that most certainly has the feel of the tropics about it. The topography of the valley is used to create a series of aquatic exhibits, of which the top one is for pinnipeds in the shape of South African Fur Seals (which have bred here) and Californian Sea Lions. Below these animals are African Penguins and if the first two exhibits seem a little incongruous in a woodland setting, a quite excellent otter enclosure (for Asiatic Short-clawed Otters) does not. Descending further the visitor encounters a strange Wolf enclosure with a sizeable pond in the middle. Combe Martin makes quite a big deal about Wolves and offers a Wolf Education and Research Centre for visitors as well. The Wolves, supposedly of pure European stock have a rather strange enclosure around a large pond. Also in this area of Combe Martin are a good set of primate cages with Entellus Langurs and White-faced Sakis as two notable inhabitants. There are African Lions, a Butterfly House and a Meerkat enclosure touted as the largest in the UK. Be aware of the fact that last admission is at 3pm although the enthusiast will not struggle to see everything here in a couple of hours.

COTSWOLD FALCONRY CENTRE

Batsford Park, Moreton-In-The-Marsh, Gloucestershire GL56 9AB
MAP REF: 39/C4
SIZE: 2 ACRES
OPENED: 1988
OWNERS: PRIVATELY OWNED
SPECIES: 58

OVER THE LAST twenty years or so, falconry centres have proliferated over the length and breadth of the nation. Many of these add little to aviculture and follow much of a standard format. A few genuinely push our knowledge and the conservation of birds of prey forward. The Cotswold Falconry Centre is such a place. Formed in 1988 and situated in Batsford Park as one of the varied attractions within the country estate, the centre takes the breeding of birds of prey very seriously indeed. In 2006 the Yellow-headed Caracara was bred for the first time in the UK at this establishment. Indeed this is only one of five species of caracara kept here. For this writer, the keeping of vultures, eagles and other larger raptors beyond the usual hawks and owls signals a real sign of professionalism and the Cotswold Falconry Centre can boast Secretary Birds, Chilean Eagles and African White-backed Vultures as part of a comprehensive collection. As is usually the case these days, owls are not ignored either, with a series of unusually tall aviaries for these birds. The rare and unusual Ashy-faced Barn Owl from Hispaniola can be observed here. It is somewhat refreshing to encounter an individual approach to a raptor collection and a concerted professional approach to captive breeding as well.

COTSWOLD WILDLIFE PARK

Bradwell Grove, Burford, Oxon OX18 4JW
MAP REF: 40/C4
SIZE: 86 ACRES
OPENED: 1970
OWNERS: PRIVATELY OWNED
SPECIES: 257

ONE OF OUR most beautiful collections as befits a zoo based in the heart of the Cotswolds, this establishment opened in 1970. It was a time when a number of country estates looked upon wildlife to attract visitors. A few chose safari parks but Bradwell Grove (the estate) suited a zoological garden much better. Cotswold quickly reached what was considered at the time an optimum size and for many years additions were comparatively few and change imperceivable. The place always looked nice and felt good, so no-one really minded. Recent years have changed that aspect and there is a momentum about the place these days that has seen a number of new exhibits and species at the park.

Quite a few establishments tried to blend animals into a walled garden setting. No-one succeeded to the extent which Cotswold has done and the walled gardens here are gems – zoos within a zoo, which would be quite an attraction in their own right. Rarities such as Great Blue Touraco, Ground Cuscus and Striped Possum can be observed here and the Great Indian Hornbill bred for the first time in the UK here too (in 1982). Other avian 'firsts' include Scheepmaker's Crowned Pigeon and Black Stork, the park has also just acquired the rare Trinidad Piping Guan. A wonderful greenhouse-style Tropical House works at just the right scale. There is a walk-through aviary but the likes of Humboldt Penguins, Meerkats and Asiatic Short-clawed Otters are the real crowd pleasers. To the east the visitor moves past parrots, callitrichids and lemurs (including Greater Bamboo Lemurs, possibly the world's rarest) to a new (2007) walk-through Madagascan exhibit, where Collared Lemurs, Alaotran Gentle Lemurs and a Crowned Sifaka mix with some of the more usual species.

Another block of exhibits utilizes the courtyard and outbuildings of the manor houses, with a recently refurbished Reptile House taking top honours here. Morelet's Crocodiles have bred in this house, a UK first for a rare taxon. This is also one of the diminishing band of UK collections to exhibit venomous snakes, and when the Cotswold Wildlife Park opened an Invertebrate House in 1978 it was one of the country's first such buildings, albeit almost 100 years after London first came up with an Insect House!

For all the interest and quality of the above exhibits, the archetypal vision of Cotswold Wildlife Park is perhaps the White Rhinos on the lawn in front of the great house; a situation which had deteriorated over the years to one ageing animal with ageing accommodation. Both circumstances are being resolved as I write.

Recently, the zoo opened a new Wolf wood, with the canids viewed from a boardwalk, and nearby are the rarer (in zoos) White-lipped Peccaries, as well as Brazilian Tapirs. Visayan Warty Pigs have recently joined the collection. There are Lions, Amur Leopards, a pheasantry, Siamangs, an owl walk and more. All in all, a choice collection in a glorious setting. A top UK zoo in fact.

CRICKET ST. THOMAS WILDLIFE PARK

Cricket St. Thomas, Somerset TA20 4DD

MAP REF: 41/C4
SIZE: 45 ACRES
OPENED: 1967
OWNERS: PRIVATE LTD COMPANY
SPECIES: 75

YET ANOTHER beautiful country estate decided to make animals its attraction in 1967 when Cricket St. Thomas Wildlife Park opened its doors. The estate's owners, the Taylor family, founded the park in conjunction with one Major Ogilvie and most of the zoo was set in the picturesque valley of Purtington Brook. In common with virtually all zoos of the period, there was little in the way of collection planning and the park grew in an ad-hoc manner. The need was even felt to have a baby Asiatic Elephant housed in miniscule conditions – a scale also represented by an Aquarium, a Nocturnal House and a Reptile House, all long since gone. A certain emphasis was placed on the natural beauty of the location and the small river that runs through it, but enclosures and houses came and went, sometimes in the blink of an eye, in the courtyard area. The figurehead of the park (although not open to the public) was the Georgian mansion which became known to millions as Grantleigh Manor through its use in the popular television series 'To The Manor Born'.

Disaster befell Cricket St. Thomas when, in the mid-nineties, a partnership was struck with TV 'personality' Noel Edmonds to rebrand itself as 'Crinkley Bottom at Cricket St. Thomas – Britain's first TV Theme Park'. It is difficult to describe the garish mayhem created in just a few words, so I won't try! Fortunately, the park came to its senses after just a couple of seasons, but in some ways the damage had been done. It was probably a relief to everyone when Warner Holidays bought the park in 1999. Although a large hotel was built on the site, some decorum and standard was at least restored and adjustments of a positive nature made to the animal collection. The wooded area of the valley opposite the hotel was utilized rather more, creating one of the largest and most effective lemur walk-through exhibits in the country. (Red-fronted, Red-bellied, White-fronted, Ring-tailed and Black and White Ruffed species) Enclosures for Amur Leopards and otters were created (the latter changed to Bush Dogs in recent years). Species such as Cheetah and African Wild Dog were added to the attractive ruminant paddocks around the river. On the negative side, a rather pleasant Tropical House was dismantled. A few primate species are maintained – some callitrichids, Sulawesi Crested Macaques and a nice moated exhibit for Black-headed Spider Monkey.

Although the lazy meadows of Cricket St. Thomas remain much the same around the valley, a great deal of change has happened. Doubtless the size and scope of the collection in future will be tailored to the economic demands of a commercial ownership.

CURRAGHS WILDLIFE PARK

Ballaugh, Isle Of Man IM7 5EA
MAP REF: 42/B3
SIZE: 40 ACRES
OPENED: 1965
OWNERS: ISLE OF MAN GOVERNMENT
SPECIES: 89

THIS SURPRISINGLY large collection would probably be untenable within the macro-economic structure of this oft-overlooked island were it not for the fact that it is owned by the local government. And given the fact that tourism on the Isle of Man has very much declined (it was at one time a fairly popular destination from Scotland and the North of England) the Curraghs Wildlife Park does very well to attract around 50,000 visitors per year. The park is situated in a marshy area and parts of the park are now designated as areas of Special Scientific Interest. In 1989 a zoogeographic layout was formulated, and sensibly, a certain emphasis was placed on wetland species. There isn't too much here in the way of animal houses, in fact the nature of the terrain would preclude the building of sizeable houses. As it is there is a boat-like construction known as 'The Ark' which contains a few small mammals and a tall shed recently built for a colony of Rodrigues Fruit Bats has an outside flight cage, this in turn connects to 'Life On Islands', an unusual walk-through aviary with some stand alone vivaria. Potoroos, Gough Island Moorhen and Cuban Hutias are three of the species in here.

The largest animals on view are Brazilian Tapirs (which breed here), Capybaras (which also breed here) and Fishing Cats. Crab-eating Macaques, Marsh Mongoose, Raccoons and three species of otter (Asiatic Short-clawed, European and North American) give further evidence of an aquatic orientation. Amongst the waterfowl and waders Straw-necked Ibis and Australian White Ibis stand out, particularly as these two species are often found together in the wild. Taxa such as Red Panda, European Lynx and Grivet Monkeys are perhaps not representative of wetland species but do, in fact, nicely pad the collection out. Most enclosures are wooden framed and mostly in good order, as indicated above circumstances are not conducive to bricks and stone. The grounds are lightly wooded.

In its own strategic plan Curraghs Wildlife Park makes the statement that 'few national governments maintain a facility to participate in the work of zoos worldwide in rectifying the damage to the natural world caused by people.' This much is true sadly.

DARTMOOR WILDLIFE PARK

Sparkwell, Nr Plymouth, Devon PL7 5DG
MAP REF: 43/B4
SIZE: 30 ACRES
OPENED: 1968
OWNERS: PRIVATE LTD COMPANY

SITUATED ON the slopes above the tiny village of Sparkwell for almost 40 years Dartmoor Wildlife Park trundled along under the idiosyncratic stewardship of one Ellis Dawe. And when I make reference to a more 'unique' style of ownership I can point to Mr Dawe's headstone installed in his garden whilst its subject was quite clearly alive and kicking! Ellis Dawe lost no time in making some fairly brash comments about other zoos whilst ironically time overtook his rather 'homemade' establishment. Eventually he attracted some unwelcome publicity from anti-zoo factions, most of this was unfair and incorrect because Dartmoor actually had some spacious and rather decent enclosures. But there is no smoke without fire and it would be true to say that many exhibits were decidedly past their 'sell-by' date.

A new era was to arrive in 2007 when the Mee family purchased the wildlife park having had little or no experience with zoos. This kind of thing has happened plenty of times before of course but on this occasion television got hold of the story and lifted this small collection into the public spotlight. It came as a surprise to the new owners (but not to me I might add) that many enclosures were badly detoriated and much of any new impetus has been by way of restoration. As I write it takes a discerning eye to see that things are a great deal different – the meadows running splendidly down from the house would make a fabulous 'savannah' but are still populated by a mixed bag of deer, domestic animals and a solitary Brazilian Tapir. There are still big cats in large, grassed enclosures – African Lions, Tigers, Jaguars, and these are at least safe from a public perspective now. Smaller cages hold Vervet Monkeys (now vanished from larger zoos), a Serval and Raccoons. There are Asiatic Short-clawed Otters.

Speaking personally I always found it rather frustrating that easily the best building at Dartmoor Wildlife Park was the restaurant/shop – a stout stone-built affair that would make a splendid animal house. This is now one of the better restaurants in a UK zoo but also serves to highlight the new owner's dilemma – with so much to resolve do they improve the visitor infrastructure or do they enlarge an essentially small animal collection in a modern manner? It would appear that the former course of action has initially been chosen and I think it is the wrong one. Visitors, after all, follow lemurs and Leopards not cake and ice cream.

THE DEEP

Quayside, Hull, Humberside HU1 3UF
MAP REF: 44/D3
SIZE: 9000 SQUARE YARDS
OPENED: 2002
OWNERS: CHARITABLE TRUST
SPECIES: 180

LIKE MANY OTHER parts around Britain Hull has sought to revive and regenerate its waterfront in the last two decades. The most conspicuous sign of this is probably the angular shape of The Deep touted as 'the world's only submarium'. The shape itself represents the bow of a ship and a submarium is apparently a unique mix of aquarium, interactive electronics and film. Part funded by the Millennium Commission (£21.5 million out of £45.5 million), it opened in 2002 to massive acclaim with attendances running at almost three times the projected 300,000 visitors.

In plain language, The Deep represents Britain's attempt to rub shoulders with the major players of the world's aquarium circuit and in that respect probably has only two British competitors in the shape of Plymouth's National Marine Aquarium and Blue Planet near Ellesmere Port. Having visited many of the world's leading aquariums I can honestly say that The Deep's combination of animals and flashing lights is quite unique. I will be quite honest and state from the onset that I am not very keen on this combination and I am not surprised that it is not replicated elsewhere. On the other hand, I would not say that The Deep is without merit – some aspects of this aquarium are indeed world class. Best of these aspects for me is 'The Twilight Zone' added to the aquarium in 2005 and one of the few significant nocturnal areas in the aquarium world. Japanese Spider Crabs, Wolf Eel, Pacific Giant Octopus and Spotted Ratfish are just a few of the fascinating inhabitants but for me the real stars are the Deep Sea Isopods – huge relatives (8" or so in length) of the everyday woodlouse and seen in few aquariums it must be said.

'Endless Ocean' is the name for The Deep's major community tank and at almost 40 feet in depth it relies on that factor to make it significant because it is not particularly long or wide. The usual shoals of Lookdowns and Golden Trevallys are always a pleasure but there are six species of shark in here too in the shape of Nurse, Zebra, Sand Tiger, Whitetip Reef, Spotted Wobbegong and the UK's only Grey Reef Shark. The other notable inhabitants here are Green Sawfish, again they are generally uncommon and found only in major aquariums.

Other displays include those for local fish and a large coral reef exhibit which is open-topped to chest height making sure any adult has to view from a bent-over position and with totally inadequate fish identification systems. Recently The Deep converted one area of small tanks to the theme of 'Slime' and whilst the first assessment is one of theme-park kitsch it really is rather good. One may expect some amphibians and worms therefore but not Brazilian Tiger Slugs and the first living Hagfish I've ever seen. Good stuff, which taught me not to be quite so pre-judgemental.

Those parts of The Deep that are given over to living, breathing zoology are really rather good and it is to be regretted that they are interspersed with too much technology. Doubtless these arcades are touted as 'educational' and however much this may be the case, I believe that they subtract a great deal of gravitas from a worthwhile institution.

DEEP SEA WORLD

Forthside Terrace, North Queensferry, Fife KY11 1JR, Scotland
MAP REF: 45/C2
OPENED: 1994
OWNERS: DEEP SEA LEISURE PLC
SPECIES: 196

NORTH QUEENSFERRY is a strange little town living in the shadow of the gargantuan Forth Railway Bridge. For over 15 years now it has been the home of Deep Sea World, Scotland's premier aquarium, and if the town is dominated by the huge bridge then the aquarium appears even more dominated, situated, as it is, in an abandoned quarry looking up at the huge rust-red skeleton of the monolith. The quarry is known as Battery Quarry and was created to obtain whinstone used not only in the Forth Bridge but as far afield as the London Underground and even Russia. It really is the most unusual situation for any kind of zoo or aquarium and in visiting hundreds of such places around the world I cannot think of a more eccentric setting, in effect it is as if a multi-storey car park has been plonked in the bottom of a great big hole.

Deep Sea World bills itself as "Scotland's Shark Capital" and the underwater safari (as the aquarium calls it) via a perspex tunnel is quite rightly the aquarium's pride and joy, it is unusual inasmuch as it is a temperate exhibit showing marine life from around the Northern Atlantic, maintained at around 12 degrees C. No less than 11 species of shark and ray are kept in the 4.5 million litre tank mostly of the smaller varieties such as Smooth Hounds and dogfish but also the Piked Spurdog *(Squalus acanthias)* which is less commonly seen. Angel Sharks are also kept here, a benthic species where one can easily see the affinity sharks have with rays. Commendably Deep Sea World is working with Blue Reef in Hastings to breed these species (breeding marine species of all kinds is very much in its infancy and a problem to be seriously addressed by all aquariums). As these sharks are not easy to keep let alone breed, this is quite a challenge. More contentious is the keeping of Sand Tiger Sharks at Deep Sea World. Firstly these sharks are normally regarded as inhabitants of tropical waters but, as previously mentioned, at this aquarium they are maintained at lower temperatures. Yet the Sand Tigers thrive here with 'Tinkerbell' the largest at over 10 feet – a look at the natural distribution of the species sees it occur in the Tasman Sea, Patagonian coast and as far north as Boston on the eastern seaboard of the USA. Hardly balmy waters then.

Also to be seen on the underwater safari are Pollock, Conger Eel, Cuckoo Wrasse and the spectacular, almost aluminized, form of the Gilthead Bream plus various flatfish and many different types of invertebrate.

By contrast with the walk-through tank the rest of Deep Sea World is rather uninspiring. Basically one long hall has been given over to a little bit of everything that can be in a public aquarium but the emphasis is on a little bit – nicely done of course, but I was reminded of the recent adage about all style and no content. So it is that we have an 'Amazonia', a 'Lake Malawi', a 'Coral Reef', the inevitable piranhas and a less predictable 'Krakatoa'. A small variety of tree-frogs and reptiles are on show and supervised handling of the creatures is still allowed in the tidal pool area (which in itself is becoming unusual).

In 2005 an area was constructed to the side of the aquarium for the rescue and rehabilitation of seal pups brought in by the S.S.P.C.A. Britain's populations of Common Seals and Grey Seals are of global importance so both the direct action concerned and the public awareness created are to be highly commended. In addition Deep Sea World gets involved in a number of projects such as beach cleaning events and Project Seahorse as well as a variety of in-house exhibitions which apportion important ecological messages.

It is perhaps unfortunate that Deep Sea World has not, as yet, chosen to do anything about its rather depressing setting in the bottom of a quarry looking out over a cocoa-brown, glorified pond. Something rather spectacular could be done with it and I would be amazed if much thought had not already been given over to the subject. As it stands those who appreciate the idiosyncratic (in a variety of forms) will love Deep Sea World even if the committed aquarist might find it a little superficial in places.

DESFORD TROPICAL BIRD GARDEN
Lindridge Lane, Desford, Leicestershire LE9 9GN
MAP REF: 46/C3
SIZE: 6 ACRES
OPENED: 1984
OWNERS: PRIVATE
SPECIES: 84

THE SLEEPY VILLAGE of Desford lies not far from the M1 in Leicestershire and just outside the village in a small wooded valley surrounded by farmland is the Tropical Bird Gardens. A stream runs through the gardens and good use is made of it for a kookaburra aviary, nearby is a small aviary for Guanian Toucanets – amongst a selection of only a few non-psittacines kept here. Free flying parrots are all over the place and something of a novelty these days. Much of the rest of the collection are housed in simple wooden aviaries, in fact I would be interested to know about winter accommodation due to the predominant lack of indoor quarters. There is a small walk-through aviary as well. As with all collections housed in woodland there is rather a gloomy and damp feel to the place despite one or two interesting psittacines (Black Lory, Crimson-bellied Conure etc) and some useful avicultural notes on the labelling. It might be rather more accurate to call Desford a bird forest rather than a bird garden and certainly a visit in wet weather may well prove uncomfortable!

DRAYTON MANOR ZOO
Drayton Manor Theme Park, Tamworth, Staffordshire B78 3TW
MAP REF: 47/C3
SIZE: 15 ACRES
OPENED: 1967
OWNERS: PRIVATE LTD COMPANY
SPECIES: 135

THERE ARE a handful of visitor attractions which really found their commercial feet by becoming full-blown theme parks. Drayton Manor in the heart of the Midlands is one of these. A small zoo has existed at the park since 1967 but until recent times had become something of a sideshow. This circumstance repeated itself at all the theme parks with zoos in the UK to be quite honest. By the early nineties all the parks were faced with something of a choice – change, rearrange or close. I'm glad to say that all theme parks chose the former options although Drayton Manor was probably the last of these establishments to do anything significant. The result is a compact little zoo with much to commend it these days.

Drayton Manor Zoo has always done rather well with reptiles. Former curator John Foden was the first person in the UK to breed the False Water Cobra *(Hydrodynastes gigas)*. A result of all this is a rather neat Reptile House with around 25 separate vivaria presented in straight lines. All the bases are covered in here from crocodilians (West African Dwarf Crocodile) to large constrictors (Green Anaconda) to various chelonians. Elsewhere another fine exhibit is the one for Brazilian Tapirs where a fairly significant stream has been tailored to the enclosure, providing the water feature that these animals need. Not surprisingly therefore, the species has bred here.

The zoo keeps an aged male Chimpanzee and, again, accommodation for this animal has been totally upgraded resulting in an unusual outdoor area formed largely from wooden boardwalks. It is unlikely the species will return to Drayton when this animal dies. Other primates are found in a range of monkey cages, for instance Lar Gibbons, Black-headed Spider Monkeys and Patas Monkeys (now uncommon in the UK), with some callitrichids in the small mammal house. At the very entrance to the zoo Rhesus Monkeys can also be seen and this is another species which was once the mainstay of the UK zoo scene and has now largely disappeared.

Any zoo that can keep Tigers is plainly to be considered seriously and Drayton keeps the Sumatran subspecies. Black leopards and a clever enclosure for Fishing Cats utilising a stream are other felids to be found here as well as a whole host of Scottish Wildcats. Until recently Patagonian Sea Lions could also be found here but the penguin accommodation (Humboldts) has now been extended into their area. With regard to birds, parrots dominate the collection and have a significant range of aviaries known as 'Parrot Walk' to themselves. birds of prey and owls are also well displayed.

An unfortunate aspect of the theme park zoos is the entry situation as theme parks charge significantly more to get in than zoological collections and therefore these zoos disenfranchise themselves from people who don't want fairground rides or a fifty pound bill to enter. Recent years have seen Drayton open in winter for a much more modest admission fee and it is hoped that this can continue because this small zoo is well worth making the effort to visit.

DRUSILLAS PARK
Alfriston, East Sussex BN26 5QS
MAP REF: 48/D4
SIZE: 11 ACRES
OPENED: 1923
OWNERS: PRIVATE LIMITED COMPANY

IT MAY COME as a surprise to some that Drusillas has been around for over 80 years. In all that time it has never really sought to market itself as much more than a children's zoo and for most of that time Drusillas was owned by the Ann family. They sold the zoo in 1997 to Laurence and Christine Smith who, in all fairness, have taken the zoo forward whilst still aiming fairly and squarely at the children's market. It will disappoint the zoo enthusiast to take one look at Drusillas map and find that around half of the area is given over to a mini-theme park even if it is a rather low-key one. On a more positive note the collection, mainly of smaller species, is maintained at a high level and kept quite separate from the 'fun'. If I stated that Servals and Sulawesi Crested Macaques are probably the largest species on display then this will give some indication of the nature of the zoo. Of course the proliferation of some E.E.P. species has enabled small zoos such as this one to partake in responsible breeding programmes and play a conservationally relevant part, the downside of which is that the zoo's callitrichids and lemurs are the same as might be observed anywhere else. Yet it is important that there are quality homes for rare species which have proliferated. I'm sure it matters not to the general public which species of fruit bat is on exhibit within a zoo, so quite frankly it might as well be an endangered species such as the Rodrigues even if this is somewhat predictable for the seasoned observer. Of course prairie dogs, Meerkats, penguins, coatis and owls are actually all nice exhibits, and well done at Drusillas as are Canadian Beavers and Asiatic Short-clawed Otters – but you just knew they would be there didn't you?

Given the youthful nature of the clientele at Drusillas one particularly useful exhibit is 'Pet World', which aims to show the correct care and maintenance of virtually every pet suitable for children. It should engender respect as well, indeed this is true for all of the animal collection here although I am of the opinion that this may well be undermined by the sheer amount of frivolous entertainment also served up on this small site.

DUDLEY ZOO

2 The Broadway, Dudley, West Midlands DY1 4QB
MAP REF: 49/C3
SIZE: 48 ACRES
OPENED: 1937
OWNERS: NON PROFIT ZOOLOGICAL SOCIETY
SPECIES: 175

IT IS SAID that when Dudley Zoo opened on the 12th May 1937 an estimated 250,000 sightseers descended on the town with only 50,000 allowed access to the zoological gardens. Not a drink nor a cake nor a slice of bread was left unsold in the immediate area. Today's zoo has to be content with visitor numbers of around 150,000 for the entire year. The new zoo of 1937 was indeed state-of-the-art utilizing the modernistic architecture of Berthold Lubetkin as did London Zoo and Whipsnade in the same decade. To this day a great deal of Lubetkin's work can still be seen at the zoo and for all its historical importance has undoubtedly been an architectural albatross around the neck of the zoo for many years. As useful animal homes Lubetkin's work has now been discredited, it wasn't the first time or last time that architectural design had bludgeoned the zookeeper into the ground but it has caused Dudley Zoo more than its fair share of headaches over the recent decades. But a creaking infrastructure of housing hasn't caused Dudley's fall of attendance; for the first forty years of its existence Dudley Zoo stood more or less alone as a significant tourist attraction. Today there is a museum just around the corner, a huge shopping centre just across the way and the likes of Cadbury World (yes, I know) not too far to the east. West Midlands Safari Park isn't that far away either. There is some tough competition from the natives and at times the current Dudley Zoo has struggled to hold on.

Over the last thirty years I can hardly think of another zoo that has had as many false starts, rebirths and unfulfilled plans as Dudley. We are in fact lucky that the zoo is still here at all due to the situation whereby the commercial ownership of the seventies (Scotia Holdings) intended to close the zoo for good in December 1977. A combination of the local council buying off Scotia and the stewardship of Bristol Zoo averted total disaster. The zoo is now under the control of a non-profit zoological society. Nor is the last thirty years a story of inertia, there have been a number of initiatives and mini-eras that have built new exhibits and threatened to reassert the zoo as a midlands major once more. As I write, various plans are in the wings as they have been so often before.

DUDLEY ZOO

The major rebranding of Dudley Zoo in the recent past has placed equal emphasis on historical tradition via the 13th century castle at the top of a very precipitous hill. The zoo infact curls all the way around the hill and it is no surprise that the feature was chosen as a defensive vantage point all those centuries ago. At the bottom of all this lies the very centre of Dudley, in fact in some places you can see right up the high street from the zoo. I'm a fan of urban zoos so rather than bemoan the commercial industrialized landscape I would sooner embrace the magic of a few serene, zoological acres overlooking it all. The zoo also owns and utilizes a few acres of flat land at the very bottom of the hill itself including the wonderful thirties-styled entrance gates (now sadly out of use).

One of Dudley's more significant recent moments came about when a remnant of a previous reinvigoration campaign in the early nineties was overhauled. Originally opened as a strange hybrid of tropical house and ecology exhibit, the second of these was quickly replaced by new Chimpanzee accommodation feeding into a vast grassy paddock for the apes. 2007 saw true and proper conversion of the house into a rainforest experience after years of watching it desiccate into a dust bowl. Asiatic Short-clawed Otters and free-ranging White-faced Sakis plus callitrichids are the order of the day now. It looks, feels and smells (yes!) much better and has a new name of 'Monkey Tails'. The otters too tell a story in that they were part of the same 'new generation' as the Tropical House (then called the Geochrom) in as much as a rather splendid enclosure was designed for them near the old Bird House. It was in fact so good that it won a 1991 UFAW award. Time moves on however, and although the enclosure still looks well the otters did not breed there, hence a change of location to the 'new' Tropical House. I hope they can find a good use for the old enclosure, it should easily be possible.

As I write Dudley has a brand new Lion enclosure underneath the balcony of the old Lubetkin Bird House running on down quite a slope in the grassed paddock/high fence style. African Wild Dogs have taken up residence in the Lion's old enclosure. Nearby is the now ubiquitous lemur walk-through exhibit replacing a rather nice waterfowl area which I liked but clearly the public didn't! Amongst the more usual species in here is the very rare Crowned Lemur. Also brand new is the conversion of the Lynx exhibit into a rather strange children's crawl-in, pop-up exhibit via a rather amateurish-looking glass case. Odd, and rolling back rather too many years I managed to undertake the experience myself hoping that I would gain a new perspective on the felidae. I didn't.

Perhaps the epicentre of Dudley Zoo is a block of cream-coloured classic Lubetkin enclosures for Polar Bears, Lions and Tigers. Only the circular Polar Bear enclosure was entirely fashioned out of concrete, the cat enclosures ran off into the hillside. Whatever the vagaries of time and the nasty taste its remnants can occasionally impart, one cannot fail to be impressed by these enclosures. Today the Polar Bear enclosure is unused with new ideas floating by every few years as to a modern usage. The enclosures on either side are currently used for Sumatran Tigers and some elderly Himalayan Black Bears. Snow Leopards (with a fabulous view of downtown Dudley) and Bush Dogs live not too far away. That Lynx exhibit is here too and, all in all, this area is classic Dudley – yesterday, today and hopefully tomorrow.

So what exactly represents the best of Dudley Zoo today? Well I would say they have the finest Red Panda enclosure I've ever seen – it simply melts into a wooded hillside, even a veteran of such things, like myself, cannot discern where it ends. Simple but very effective is the Humboldt Penguin exhibit where the shape of the old castle moat is used to create a real, grassy incline which must give these birds a daily physical workout replicating nature. I do also like the flamingo pond just inside the entrance, in all probability it isn't very good for breeding but the waterfall, giant rhubarb plants and clipped lawn create such an attractive first impression.

Dudley has always been a general collection with no particular speciality – and it remains that way today despite some downsizing over the years. Giraffes and Bornean Orang Utans inhabit housing which is just about acceptable, the Reptile House with its old-style barren vivaria is badly in need of replacement and full of rather too many common species particularly Red-eared Terrapins. Brazilian Tapirs, Babirusas and White-handed Gibbons all do okay for themselves in terms of accommodation. There is a wooden Primate House which suits smaller species well and Patagonian Sea Lions make good use of a long, shallow pool that in its day housed a Killer Whale on one side and Bottle-nosed Dolphins on the other side! It is amazing to contemplate now that it is merely adequate, and no more, for a small group of pinnipeds (although scaled-down a little it must be said – only a little mind you!). There are monkey meadows using the latest hot-wire style (Sulawesi Crested Macaques and Black-headed Spider Monkeys) and a few blocks of aviaries (overall the bird collection is rather diminished). The aquarium closed long, long, ago.

I like and respect Dudley Zoo a great deal; they always keep going and in tough times have never thrown in the towel. On a murky November day with all of mankind whizzing about its business hundreds of feet below whilst the visitor is enveloped in zoological calm the zoo has a unique atmosphere. I wish them well with the latest new horizon and sincerely hope that this one takes them back to where they deserve to be.

DURRELL WILDLIFE CONSERVATION TRUST

Les Augrès Manor, Trinity, Jersey JE3 5BP
MAP REF: 50/C4
SIZE: 42 ACRES
OPENED: 1959
OWNERS: A CHARITABLE TRUST
SPECIES: 142

THE BRITISH have done small zoos better than anyone and no small zoo is better than the one on Jersey. Now known simply as Durrell this is more than a zoo, more an epicentre of conservation sending shockwaves around the world, jolting scientists into action. It was founded by, and is now named after, Gerald Durrell who sadly died in 1995. More than anyone else Durrell touted a conservational role for zoos and this has now been universally accepted as the primary mission for all manner of collections. Pure rhetoric would never have been enough for Jersey Zoo however, and over the years the organisation has initiated a number of programmes at both in situ and ex situ level which can point directly to species such as the Mauritius Kestrel, the Pink Pigeon or the St Lucia Whiptail Lizard and say 'Durrell saved that taxon from extinction'. The International Training Centre has imparted knowledge and expertise to over 1500 students since 1978 and these students have taken the Durrell mantra around the world, forming perhaps the most effective conservational tool in the longer term. Jersey Zoo made a difference and now Durrell continues the fight; pound for pound no zoo has ever made a larger contribution.

So what of the zoo itself? Well I'm pleased to say that Durrell has never looked better and Gerald Durrell would be greatly impressed by his legacy. Jersey Zoo of the sixties and seventies was bound by some of the zoo traditions of the time in terms of exhibition values and in the last thirty years concrete, wire and bars have been replaced by newer, softer, techniques. And whilst it is true that ultimately virtually any exhibit can be improved almost at the very moment it is finished, then Durrell has 'greened' itself slowly and surely to become arguably our most attractive zoo. Basically the zoo nestles in a valley below Les Augrès Manor; over the last decade the valley has been both naturalized and extended. In some areas it is difficult to grasp quite where enclosures begin and end amongst the verdancy. This is intentional. Such rarities as St Lucia Amazon Parrots, Alaotran Gentle Lemurs and Meller's Duck now seem to actually live in the forest as do callitrichids with such species as Pied Tamarin and Black Lion Tamarin being Durrell specialities. In fact the conservational programmes I mentioned above unsurprisingly dominate the collection here in terms of species. Madagascar is particularly well represented, and if Britain is now the lemur centre of the zoo world then Durrell is probably responsible for this. I doubt that we would have seen such rarities as Black and White Ruffed Lemurs and Red Ruffed Lemurs proliferate in the UK zoo community had not Jersey become involved with the two species. Aye-ayes started here too and I spent most of my life thinking I would never see one (or that the species might not even exist any more). The first European captive breeding occurred here in 1992 and so far nine have been born whilst the husbandry and breeding protocol of the species was positively pioneered.

All of the above species thrive at Durrell under discreet, possibly even modest, accommodation in architectural terms. That most beautiful of fruit bats, the Livingstone's Fruit Bat, is housed in a long, unglamorous, poly-tunnel that works the bats' flight muscles and provides a blueprint for a more attractive tropical house to come. Nor should we forget the Rodrigues Fruit Bat which has seen a zoo-based breeding plan, initiated at Durrell, increase a fragile population of fewer than 100 individuals to over 5000 animals. Yet there are heavyweight exhibits delightfully presented in the modern zoo style as well. 'Cloud Forest' mixes Spectacled Bears, Coatis and Black Howler Monkeys in outdoor accommodation that has beautifully overgrown itself and with the added frisson of indoor bear viewing. Nearby is 'Jewels Of The Forest' where somehow in a comparatively small space the very essence of an Asian rainforest stream has been created for the likes of the ultra-rare Blue-crowned Laughing Thrush, the Palawan Peacock Pheasant, Nicobar Pigeons and Hooded Pitta. Sumatran Orang Utans occupy a two-island moated exhibit with good, tall, indoor housing and the Lowland Gorilla outdoor enclosure still looks good even if the indoor area is a little cramped (one of the zoo's highest priorities).

The major animal house at Durrell is the Gaherty Reptile House built in 1976 and named after a Canadian benefactor. Unusually for the time and still rather too unusually today, the off-show breeding accommodation comprises around two-thirds of the capacity. The 'shop front' vivaria are large apart from a few latter-day terrariums for the likes of Mallorcan Midwife Toad (another Durrell speciality) and various poison arrow frogs. They contain a mixture of everyday 'public' species together with rarities such as the Lesser Antillean Iguana *(Iguana delicatissima)* or Montserrat Mountain Chicken (yet another species receiving Durrell 'intensive care'). The off-show area is particularly interesting, not only for the work with critically endangered species such as the Round Island Boa, Flat-tailed Spider Tortoise and the Mauritius Accidental Gecko, but for the front-line breeding and husbandry techniques which often sees taxons new to herpeculture assimilated or 'cracked' then passed on to other institutions whilst Durrell breaks new ground with other species.

As you can gather, Durrell is a remarkable place, yet for all its good work it is bound by the constraints of its island home. Of course the reputation of Durrell couldn't be higher on Jersey itself and over half of its membership still comes from outside the island, yet the organisation still needs a thriving tourist economy – which is currently in serious decline for a variety of reasons. It could be that in order to fulfil its destiny, Durrell may have to look, in part at least, elsewhere in the world for the funding that it needs to undertake and expand the work it does so superbly.

EAGLE HEIGHTS WILDLIFE PARK

Lullingstone Lane, Eynsford, Kent DA4 0JB
MAP REF: 51/D4
SIZE: 49 ACRES
OPENED: 1996
OWNERS: PRIVATE
SPECIES: 60

SITUATED IN rolling countryside just on the outside of the M25 motorway which circumnavigates Greater London, is Eagle Heights Wildlife Park. Until very recently it was Eagle Heights Bird of Prey Centre but very gradually and bit by bit animals other than birds of prey have been introduced. Most remarkable amongst these are Cheetahs and if the rest of the animals are staples such as Meerkats, Asiatic Short-clawed Otters and Coatis, then some intention has been signposted with *Acinonyx jubatus*. Unusually these days, huskies are also to be found here, reminding this writer of his childhood when this breed of dog was to be found all over the zoo world. At a time when the Maned Wolf EEP is desperately in need of participants, it does seem to be a rather indulgent move today. A small Reptile House will not challenge the herpetologist in terms of rare and endangered species by and large but on the occasion of my visit there was an impressive Panther Chameleon *(Furcifer pardalis)*.

As might be expected however, the collection at Eagle Heights is still mostly about Birds of Prey and uniquely the majority of the collection is housed indoors in the manner of a traditional bird house. Whilst the viewing may therefore be at close quarters I found the room rather oppressive to be honest. There are some interesting species here however, Palm Nut Vultures and White-eyed Kestrel (*Falco rupicoloides* – an African taxon) particularly took my eye. There are some outside aviaries and most of the owls are in these, some sturdy brick-built aviaries house the larger eagles such as Martial Eagle and Bald Eagle.

Needless to say flying displays are something of a highlight here and they fly some big birds too which look impressive wheeling around the valley that Eagle Heights looks down upon. Clearly the centre takes its responsibilities to falconry seriously as can be ascertained by the fact that they run a national accreditation course in Birds of Prey Care and Management through the Open College Network.

EDINBURGH ZOO

134 Corstorphine Road, Edinburgh EH12 6LR, Scotland
MAP REF: 52/C2
SIZE: 80 ACRES
OPENED: 1913
OWNERS: ROYAL ZOOLOGICAL SOCIETY OF SCOTLAND
SPECIES: 180

SCOTLAND'S SECOND most-visited paid tourist attraction is Edinburgh Zoo which has occupied one side of the steep and lofty Corstorphine Hill since 1913. This makes it Britain's third oldest zoo still in existence, a somewhat surprising fact although failures were common in 19th century zoo Britain and many now-forgotten places came and went, indeed Edinburgh Zoo is actually that city's second attempt at such a fine establishment. As with all our older zoos the last twenty years have been dynamic ones on this Scottish hillside. And the pace has quickened in the last five years. Edinburgh is the only place in the UK where the visitor can observe Koalas. Such species as Japanese Serow, Bawean Deer, Wolverine, Lesser Kudu, Musk Deer and Darwin's Rhea are names to quicken the pulse of the zoo connoisseur and have been reintroduced to these islands by this zoo.

Of course rare animals are wasted without the infrastructure of a good zoo around them. Edinburgh Zoo identified a number of shortcomings over twenty years ago, a few years ago it even contemplated leaving Corstorphine Hill, I'm glad they decided against it. Although the steep gradient will always be a challenge to a pushchair or a pensioner the opportunity to build enclosures into the hillside or wind exhibits around natural contours creates a number of design opportunities that add enormous character. The latest of these is 'Budongo Trail' – a £5.65 million Chimpanzee facility. No ersatz-immersion here or half-hearted attempts to blend unconvincingly into a 'natural' landscape. No efforts to convince us that we are in steaming rainforest whilst a force eight easterly whistles around our ears! This is a bold zoo building presenting three differently climate-controlled and substrated indoor enclosures as well as a large outdoor area with endless climbing possibilities. In the US I'm constantly informed that Jane Goodall has given the nod of approval to a whole host of Chimpanzee enclosures many of which are overwhelmingly average. Well if Goodall can get to see 'Budongo Trail' she may well set herself a whole new yardstick! An outstanding exhibit.

Primates do rather well at Edinburgh, 'Magic Forest' is one of the finest exhibits I've seen for callitrichids with wonderfully planted cages both inside and out. The visitor is left with the impression that he or she has stumbled across some kind of overgrown tropical temple inhabited by tiny monkeys. 'Living Links' is from 2008 and features Brown Capuchins and Squirrel Monkey in the latest style of hot-wired grassy paddocks. Funding of some £1.6 million for this development came from the Universities Scottish Funding Council and the exhibit is also a research facility in conjunction with the University of St Andrews illustrating well that conservation is still not the be-all and end-all purpose of animals in captivity. The Monkey House is perhaps more traditional but personally I have little issue with that and these days it includes a rather 'choice' selection including Purple-faced Langurs (the only ones of the nominate subspecies in captivity), a female Aye-aye and Owl-faced Monkeys (a European zoo speciality).

Edinburgh is most famous for its penguins of course, having bred the first King Penguin in captivity as long ago as 1919. 'Penguin parade', a bizarre ritual where the penguins (usually Kings and Gentoos) go for a little stroll, still happens, and strikes me as a rather entertaining, harmless little interlude. These days the penguins temporarily depart a lengthy enclosure built twenty years ago, but still one of the few where genuine 'porpoising' can be observed. Rockhoppers, in addition to the Kings and Gentoos, already mentioned are also kept here.

One or two of Edinburgh's exhibits have been hewn from the hillside and appear almost as natural rocky concaves. A good example of this is the Sea Lion pool at the very foot of the hill and I've always liked it, nearby the old Polar Bear enclosure has been converted into an aviary for a young pair of Steller's Sea Eagles and they look superb in here. Further up the incline, a set of carnivore enclosures set up against the hillside look more contrived and have been largely taken over by Wolverines. Nonetheless they have solidity about them that will appeal to the urban zoo enthusiast (of which I am one). Until fairly recently the Edinburgh Zoo made comparatively little use of the upper levels of Corstorphine Hill and the zoo experience diminished the further your legs drove you. Your reward for all the effort may have been as little as Soay Sheep and Highland Cattle, even ponies! Eventually the zoo woke up to the potential of this extra space and the walk will be rewarded with Gelada Baboons, Amur Tigers, Asiatic Lions, Maned Wolves and

Giant Anteaters in newish enclosures. A wooden boardwalk has been taken out over the Grevy's Zebra paddock and there is no better view of these equids in a British zoo – you might even spot the Lesser Kudus!

In 1989 Edinburgh gave up on elephant keeping, a move followed by London, Bristol and Dudley meaning that no truly urban zoo in the UK keeps these animals anymore. In Scotland's capital Giraffes and White Rhinos have followed, fortunately the rot stopped there as Indian Rhinos have joined the collection even if their accommodation in the old Elephant and Giraffe enclosure is a salutary reminder of why the former types left the zoo! It isn't bad as such, merely uninspiring and of course I would be foolish if I did not realise that the zoo knows this more than I do. Of more concern at Edinburgh is something of a move away from smaller animals and at this moment the bird collection is smaller than it has ever been with the reptile collection almost non-existent (the aquarium is long gone with the building forming part of the impressive entrance facility). Hopefully this is a temporary circumstance. The Edinburgh Zoo has extensive and exciting plans for the future not least of which is a possible rainforest exhibit in Glasgow (currently one of the largest cities in Europe without any significant wildlife attraction). Today's economic crisis has thrown elements of doubt over these plans but experience shows that bad times pass just as surely as good ones and I remain confident that major developments will occur before too long.

ESCOT

Escot Park, Ottery St. Mary, Devon EX11 1LU
MAP REF: 53/C4
SIZE: 220 ACRES
OPENED: 2002
OWNERS: PRIVATE

Escot is a Georgian country house situated in manicured parkland almost upon the A30 in Devon. In fact, the estate was split in two by the extended road in 1990. Scattered around the gardens are a few wildlife attractions that just about warrant inclusion in this book. Possibly the most unusual element of Escot is that it is the home of the Seahorse Trust and of course there is no reason why an inland facility could not maintain seahorses. As I write (summer 2009) a new home for these fish is being fashioned in the old courtyard, of course a small room can hold quite a number of specimens. Also noteworthy is a lengthy Asiatic Short-clawed Otter enclosure and there are exhibits for Red Squirrels and Wild Boar. Perhaps more importantly, Escot is working with European Beavers and a two acre enclosure is home to a wild-caught unrelated pair from Germany. However viewing of the beavers is only by appointment. Falconry displays are given through the summer months. A very pleasant feature at the bottom of a sloping site is a water meadow full of native plants; this should also include a small waterfowl collection but flash floods in

2008 lead to dams being washed away that have not yet been repaired. Escot is a lovely spot and largely unknown even locally (as much was admitted to me by an employee) but they need more animals. At the moment it represents rather steep value-for-money, although it undoubtedly is one of those spots for the 'perfect zoo site' fantasy.

EXMOOR ZOOLOGICAL PARK
South Stowford, Bratton Fleming, Nr Barnstaple, Devon EX31 4SG
MAP REF: 54/B4
SIZE: 14 ACRES
OPENED: 1982
OWNERS: PRIVATE
SPECIES: 190

A FEW MILES AWAY from Combe Martin Wildlife Park is a purer animal experience in the shape of the Exmoor Zoo which has evolved from a bird garden through a variety of names. There are no gimmicks or noisy sideshows here just a small zoo full of interesting animals, mostly of smaller kinds but also the likes of Cheetahs, Ostriches and Sitatunga.

Exmoor Zoo basically comprises two halves; the first of these to be encountered is a myriad of enclosures, cages, small houses and aviaries plus a small lake. Many of the expected current day zoo species are to be found here such as Meerkats, Yellow and Banded Mongooses, Asiatic Short-clawed Otters, Black-tailed Prairie Dogs and Crested Porcupines. It really is a case of animals to the right of you, animals to the left of you… but all well kept and spotlessly clean. There are a few less common species such as Black Howler Monkey, Diana Monkey and Tayra, and a good collection of callitrichids with Black Tuft-eared Marmosets, two species of Silvery Marmoset (*argentata* and *melanura*), Emperor Tamarin and Golden-handed Tamarin amongst others. The current burgeoning UK population of Azara's Agouti started at Exmoor. Around the fringes of this part of the zoo open meadows house a variety of lemurs, plus Maned Wolves and the brand new 'Exmoor Beast' exhibit (melanistic Leopards). Overseas readers may not be familiar with persistent rumours in these parts of wild big cats proliferating on the wilds of Exmoor. Suffice it to say that it is quite a story in the UK.

The other part of the zoo is rather more open, spreading out over undulating countryside. There are cranes (Sandhills recently arrived), Blackbuck and the Cheetahs and Sitatunga mentioned above. So far virtually all has been mammals but there is a reasonable bird collection as well with Northern Ground Hornbills, Palm Nut Vultures and Yellow-shouldered Amazons being just a few of the highlights. A small reptile collection is kept in the visitor centre with Blue-tailed Monitors *(Varanus doreanus)* as an unusual treat – a recently repromoted subspecies of Mangrove Monitor *(Varanus indicus)*.

A species count of almost 200 is remarkable for any small zoo let alone one that does not include fish or invertebrates. As small zoos go this is my kind of place.

EXPLORIS

The Ropewalk, Castle Street, Portaferry BT22 1NZ, Northern Ireland
MAP REF: 55/B2
OPENED: 1987
OWNERS: ARDS BOROUGH COUNCIL

THE CONSERVATION village of Portaferry on the shores of Strangford Lough was considered to be the ideal place to situate an aquarium specializing in marine life from around the Irish coast in 1987. So popular did it prove that it was extended, re-opened by Prince Charles and renamed Exploris in 1994.

Four major areas can be seen at Exploris. The 'Strangford Lough Hall' concentrates on the juveniles of species of fish such as Cod, Pollock and Coley found in the inlet together with the likes of Shannies and Common Spider Crab. A variety of aquaria is presented in the 'Irish Coast Zone' some surrounded by artificial rock, others by timber whilst others are open-topped in the current fashion. The strange appearance of the Lumpsucker, wonderful Common Cuttlefish and the frankly disarming Wolf-fish are just a few of the inhabitants. At 250 tonnes the 'Open Sea Tank' has some suitably sturdy windows holding all that sea water back and is so large as to house a sunken vessel – a perfect habitat for Conger Eels. Dogfish, Ballan Wrasse, adult Cod and Sea Bass are amongst other inhabitants. In 2000 an attractive pebbled seal pool was added outside the front of the main building. This acts purely as a rescue and rehabilitation facility for two native species of seal so do not expect to find animals on show at all times.

Northern Ireland's only aquarium does a good job in portraying local species in an exciting way without resorting to the glamour of tropical forms. As befits a local authority facility it is both professionally presented and popular.

FLAMINGO LAND THEME PARK & ZOO

Kirby Misperton, Malton, North Yorkshire YO17 6UX
MAP REF: 56/C3
SIZE: 100 ACRES
OPENED: 1961
OWNERS: PRIVATE LIMITED COMPANY
SPECIES: 154

DID THE SIXTIES UK zoo boom start with Flamingo Land? Well possibly not, but one could easily select it as such for a number of reasons. Situated in the middle of wide open Yorkshire countryside (it briefly subtitled itself 'Yorkshire Zoo') between York and Scarborough, the new zoo certainly targeted car owners. It was unashamedly commercial and indeed became the figurehead of a whole host of related animal attractions in the north and midlands. In those days it was called Flamingo Park and it quickly became famous as the first zoo in Europe to keep dolphins along the lines of the American oceanaria. By 1968 the zoo had even brought in a Killer Whale, again the first of its kind to be kept in captivity in Europe. The banner of voracious commercialism flew over Flamingo Park through Associated Pleasure Parks and later, Scotia Developments. As time moved on more and more non-zoological attractions were added. Eventually the zoo was sold to Robert Gibb (a director of Scotia Developments) in 1978 and the metamorphosis to theme park became unstoppable.

That the change brought in more paying customers is beyond argument, but in amongst it all the zoo element started to recede into the background. By the early nineties the zoo and its collection were creaking – long gone were the dolphins and whales, elephants and giraffes. Little happened to the infrastructure of the zoo in those years and like all the theme-park zoos, there was pressure either to close the zoo or make major improvements. The latter course was selected (as it was at others of its kind), one cannot help but feel that Disney's Animal Kingdom in the US focused a few minds on the essential attraction of animals.

It is the current decade that has seen Flamingo Land (as it became known) press on with redeveloping the zoo. Common Hippo (in a substantial new pond) and White Rhino were added, Giraffes returned. Lions were placed in a new 'Forgotten City Lion Reserve' and the one-time Elephant House (later camels) was converted into a rather dark and gloomy Chimpanzee House with outdoor island. The old Dolphinarium is now for Californian Sea Lions (not a new development in fairness) with the small aquarium underneath now determined to be 'Creatures of the Deep'. European Lynx have taken the space formerly used by the Lions, Amur Tigers remain adjoining. Much of the new architecture uses the brash, often unconvincing, artificial rockwork frequently seen in theme parks as is now the case with all the big cats here. Not enormously to my taste, but a big improvement, I will concede. The old Reptile House remains but is now termed 'Little Monsters' World Wildlife Attraction and Education Centre' (I know!). Perhaps it is in that re-christening that the zoo problem still remains at Flamingo Land. The 'fun' encroaches much more than at Chessington or Drayton Manor and there is less individual definition of theme park and zoo. A watersplash ride by name of the 'Lost River Ride' snakes around the Lion exhibit and a waterbird aviary – the theme park has swallowed-up the danger of a big cat to adorn itself with extra frisson. I can no more condone this blend than I could a Chimps' tea party and if this is to be the way of things I must consider quite seriously if it was a good idea for Flamingo Land to even keep its zoo. True, most of the zoo is well away from the thrills and spills and most of the improvements are acceptable, even good in the case of the Hippos, but there is a lowest common denominator about the fun, the food and family aspiration which is almost dispiriting at Flamingo Land, and reflects on the animal collection rather too much. If we ever stood for zoos to be taken seriously (and they need to be) then it is difficult to laud such a brash, commercial blend which in turn places so little emphasis on education and conservation.

FOLLY FARM ADVENTURE PARK & ZOO

Begelly, Kilgetty, Pembrokeshire SA68 0XA, Wales
MAP REF: 57/B4
SIZE: 30 ACRES
OPENED: 1989
OWNERS: PRIVATE LIMITED COMPANY

FOLLY FARM has grown from a themed 'farm' experience to become Tenby's major visitor attraction over the last twenty years. It is now a combination of farm, old-style funfair and zoo offered at a remarkably low entrance price. Given these factors its popularity comes as no surprise. Our concern is quite obviously the zoo side of things and, as is usually the case, this is not intertwined with the funfair (or indeed the farm). The zoo currently occupies around half of the whole site and plainly has plenty of room to expand further.

An open grass paddock and fence approach determines the basic nature of this zoological park but, wisely, Folly Farm doesn't have an issue with spacious cages enabling Ocelots, Fosas, Greater Vasa Parrots and Marsh Mongooses to be exhibited. The latter species is now quite rare in zoos. An indication of Folly Farm's intent came in the shape of a recent addition of a bachelor group of Giraffes housed in the typical agricultural barn method of today with a huge outdoor enclosure shared with Chapman's Zebras. The Giraffes are subspecific hybrids, or 'zoo' Giraffes as they are often termed. Folly Farm does a quite excellent job in explaining the purpose of this, indeed the labelling in the Giraffe House is, on the whole, top class. Other paddocks contain Eastern Bongo, Kafue Flats Red Lechwe and Reindeer amongst others.

Those who believe that biggest is best concerning zoo enclosures will applaud two huge ponds (almost lakes in fact) for Brazilian Tapirs (which breed here) and Capybaras respectively. I'm not too sure about the unusual Ring-tailed Lemur island in the middle of the Capybara lake however, its bare, unnaturalistic appearance is rather out of keeping with the surroundings. Alongside these two lakes are solid, typically 'zoo' walled enclosures for Meerkats, Black-tailed Prairie Dogs, Mara and Raccoons (with odd, American mining ephemera as enclosure decoration for the latter). Also quite recent is a fenced, therefore hot-wired, enclosure for Barbary Macaques with a bizarre pink, presumably Moorish (or Foreign Legion) castellated house which does nothing at all for the overall aesthetic.

In general terms Folly Farm is doing rather well for itself. On two separate visits I have found it to be overflowing with visitors. It is perhaps unfortunate that the zoological collection is rather burdened by a name which suggests a less than serious intent. That the zoo appears solid and serious is the clear answer to that and I await future developments with interest due to the rapid expansion of the collection in recent years.

GALLOWAY WILDLIFE CONSERVATION PARK

Loch Fergus Plantation, Kirkudbright, Dumfries & Galloway DG6 4XX, Scotland
MAP REF: 58/B2
SIZE: 27 ACRES
OPENED: 1990
OWNERS: PRIVATE
SPECIES: 71

AS THE ADDRESS would indicate this small zoo lies within a man-made coniferous forest although much of the zoo lies in clearings which means it is surrounded by forest rather than being in it. For the most part the collection is housed behind larch pole fences or cages constructed from the same materials. There are contradictions within the collection too which see a vast field for Maned Wolves for instance whereas the Lowland Anoas occupy a strange series of small wooden corrals (although they breed here so it is clearly the aesthetic in question and nothing else). Other larger mammals to be seen would include Brazilian Tapirs and Dholes although it is the smaller mammals which unsurprisingly dominate. Red Pandas have bred here, which isn't the easiest of achievements; Palm Civets, Bat-eared Foxes and Siberian Weasels can be seen too. Recently a new Caracal Lynx enclosure was constructed with the help of staff from Chester Zoo. Amongst the more predictable elements are lemurs, Meerkats and Asiatic Short-clawed Otters. Aviculturally Galloway is not very strong but there is a free-flight aviary on an Australian theme for Australian Masked Plovers, Ruddy Shelducks, Black-crowned Night Herons and Common Kookaburras.

All in all there are a surprisingly large number of animals here, possibly too many in truth and maybe it is time to concentrate on more enclosure quality of the Caracal Lynx kind. The feeling here, as I see it, is that they want to be a big collection but have probably moved a little too fast in getting there. Time for consolidation methinks.

GREAT YARMOUTH SEA LIFE

The Promenade, Great Yarmouth, Norfolk NR30 3AH
MAP REF: 59/D3
OPENED: 1988
OWNERS: PRIVATE LTD COMPANY

IT IS VERY difficult to actually review most Sea Life centres for the simple reason that they mostly work to the same, presumably successful, formula – touch tanks, jelly fish, seahorses (conservationally bred of course), a main walk-through tank etc, all nicely presented but sanitized and without identity. It's as if McDonalds had moved into the zoo business, and 'business' is generally an unacceptable word for zoos and aquaria – but rest assured for Merlin Entertainments, business it is. There are variations – Merlin own the famous old Brighton Aquarium for one, Weymouth Sea Life Park is rather unique in this country and now they own the London Aquarium as well, but for the most part you wouldn't really know one Sea Life Centre from another.

So it is at Great Yarmouth with a custom building situated a few yards from the resort's long and yellow beach alongside the main promenade which runs along the front (surprise, surprise). I made a note of Gold-banded and Snake species of pipefish, which are both attractive and unusual aquarium species. 'Island of the Gods' made such an impression on me that I can't actually remember what it was and for the rest it was 'Fisherman's Wharf', 'Deep Sea Wrecks', *Pterois volitans*, Thornback Rays, 'Kingdom of the Seahorse' etc, etc...

More recent is the £200,000 Humboldt Penguin enclosure. The Humboldt species is the *Spheniscus* of choice for the Sea Life chain which makes sense because it is a) an endangered species b) the most undemanding penguin species in captivity. Given that Amazonia (a small tropical house) is a few yards away on the Great Yarmouth seafront then there is a good couple of hours of animal viewing around these parts although neither Amazonia or Sea Life will over-excite the connoisseur.

HAMERTON ZOO PARK

Hamerton, Nr Sawtry, Cambridgeshire PE28 5RE
MAP REF: 60/D3
SIZE: 29 ACRES
OPENED: 1990
OWNERS: PRIVATE LIMITED COMPANY
SPECIES: 131

THAT THE ZOO fraternity has pulled together in breeding cooperation over the last twenty years or so is undoubtedly a good thing. Yet diversity of zoo collections set against maintaining zoo populations without the infrastructure of the worldwide animal trade is problematic. Sometimes it is the smaller collections that add much needed variety or even bloodlines to existing populations by virtue of an enthusiastic, knowledgeable or determined individual. The maverick zoo man is still needed, maybe even more so in an age when a bureaucratic approach can often be injurious to collections. Such a man is Hamerton Zoo Park owner Andrew Swales and whilst his zoo is quite clearly a part of co-ordinated studbook programmes there is a definite whiff of something different about the collection here.

Started in 1990 as the Hamerton Wildlife Centre, from the onset the zoo always included a few taxa that were rare or not found at all in other UK zoos. A real marker came in 1995 when Hamerton brought in the first Aardwolves to be seen in a British zoo in that century, nor was it long before a first UK breeding for the species followed. The Aardwolf is a shy and retiring animal, insectivorous to boot. It is therefore not easy to keep nor will it ever displace Meerkats or dolphins in the public eye – but it is a zoo enthusiast's dream and they are still be found at the park. Collared Lemurs have also thrived at Hamerton and are rarely seen, Jaguarundis too – a fragile zoo population but Hamerton has always played its part. Now the zoo has Oncillas, the UK's only specimens of this diminutive American small cat. Jackals are also now rare in zoos and the Black-backed species can be seen here. Also on view now are a group of Mountain Viscachas, not seen in British zoos since an elderly specimen basked under a heat lamp at Chester ten or more years ago. A UK first zoo breeding was also achieved with these. There are birds too, indeed they were the first love of the owner, a fact reflected in choice residents such as Yellow-knobbed Curassow (also known as Daubenton's), Argus Pheasant, Himalayan Snowcock, Hooded Vulture and Palm Nut Vulture, although Double-wattled Cassowaries were probably not envisaged twenty years ago!

The impression so far then is probably one of interesting smaller species and, in all fairness this is largely true, but Meerkats can only ever do so much for visitor numbers. The addition of Tigers to the zoo's inventory achieved a great deal a few years ago, and whilst a male white Tiger may not do much for the purist the cat more than pays his way. He is housed with a more commonly coloured female Bengal in both an unusual indoor-but-outdoor shed as well as a large grassy enclosure which includes a public viewing tunnel. Much effort has also been put into a Cheetah breeding programme and the zoo currently holds no less than eleven individuals housed in six separate enclosures (some of which are off show).

It is probably true that the infrastructure in and around the zoo is reaching its capacity especially with the forthcoming addition of Giant Anteaters and Red River Hogs. This is because Hamerton Zoo Park was fashioned from the corner of a huge farm field all those years ago and the provision of services such as water and electric was never easy. It is also an exposed site although hedges and bushes are now starting to mature. Most of all Hamerton is not well served by roads despite being within a few miles of both the A1 and A14. The hamlet of Hamerton scarcely exists at all to be fair and the overall profile is a decidedly rural one. Collections have always come and gone on the British zoo scene and most of the departures are not missed, Hamerton has fought hard to remain true to zoo ideals in the face of various pressures, I'm more than glad to state that it is here to stay.

HAREWOOD BIRD GARDEN

Harewood House, Leeds, West Yorkshire LS17 9LQ
MAP REF: 61/C3
SIZE: 4 ACRES
OPENED: 1970
OWNERS: HAREWOOD HOUSE TRUST
SPECIES: 96

THIS BEAUTIFUL bird garden occupies four acres of land running down to a large lake beneath the magnificence of the 18th century Harewood House. Started in 1970 in an era (still not over) when many a Lord or an Earl was trying to find a way of making a country estate viable by virtue of tourism, the Earl of Harewood came up with the then-popular notion of a bird garden. Many (most?) competitors have since fallen by the wayside but Harewood's bird garden continues to thrive with over a quarter of a million visitors annually. Although the serenity of the setting can lull the observer into supposing that things have remained quite unchanged at this establishment this is actually not at all correct; at one time a veritable indoor zoo threatened to overtake part of the stable courtyard, there was once a small tropical house and the walk-through aviary keeps visitors outside today. The bird collection is smaller too, fluttering in at around 90 species these days, in the main the collection contains little that cannot be seen elsewhere fairly easily with the possible exception of Palm Cockatoos, Great Argus Pheasant, Papuan Hornbills and Stanley Cranes. An overview of the collection would reveal no birds of prey (although Red Kites can be seen wild on the estate) and only a few softbills although the beautiful Purplish Jay can be observed.

Penguins in the shape of Humboldts can be seen with underwater viewing and the lake cries out for flamingos in which case Chileans can be seen in an enclosure designed in conjunction with the Wildfowl and Wetlands Trust which has already obtained breeding results for the first time in twenty years. Harewood also works with the World Pheasant Association and about a dozen pheasant species are maintained.

Possibly due to such a beautiful setting and nicely maintained grounds Harewood does not feel the need to push any boundaries these days which is a shame, the fact remains that there are less birds here than ever so the pleasure of a visit is currently tinged with the disappointment of creeping regression.

HASTINGS BLUE REEF

Rock-A-Nore Road, Hastings, East Sussex TN34 3DW
MAP REF: 62/D4
OPENED: 1990
OWNERS: BLUE REEF GROUP

ORIGINALLY ONE of the Sea Life chain of aquatic attractions for some years this aquarium was known as Underwater World and was independently owned. In 2007 the aquarium became part of the group which not only owns the Blue Reef aquariums but also Blue Planet near Chester and Deep Sea World at Queensferry, Scotland. The old Underwater World placed special emphasis on local marine life which all fitted in rather neatly with the whole area that the aquarium is situated in, in the form of a heritage village devoted to Hastings's unique fishing industry (there is no harbour for instance). A much more general theme has been adopted by the new owners placing much more emphasis on the same tropical species as can be observed at other Blue Reef aquariums.

HAWK CONSERVANCY TRUST

Sarson's Lane, Weyhill, Andover, Hampshire SP11 8DY
MAP REF: 63/C4
SIZE: 22 ACRES
OPENED: 1966
OWNERS: CHARITABLE TRUST
SPECIES: 65

WHEN SCHOMBERG wrote 'The Penguin Guide to British Zoos' 40 years ago the Hawk Conservancy Trust was Weyhill Zoo Park, a small general collection with no direction. A few years later in 'Animals On View' Anthony Smith deemed it to be Weyhill European Wildlife Park with obvious consequences for the animals to be found there. Three decades on and we now find a specialist birds of prey collection which is one of the leaders in this new burgeoning area. Chief Executive Ashley Smith is the son of the founder Reg Smith and has seen the collection move towards a serious conservational role with a charitable trust overseeing the work at Weyhill (launched 2002).

In some ways the Hawk Conservancy has the best of both worlds – it is rural (a necessity for falconry really) yet is very conveniently situated close to the A303, a fast dual carriageway headed for the West Country. Almost sixty taxa of Birds of Prey and owl are kept here with African Harrier Hawk, Andean Condor, White-bellied Sea Eagle and Mauritius Kestrel amongst the most noteworthy. I was particularly impressed with a large vulture aviary holding the now critically-endangered Oriental White-backed Vulture.

Weyhill is heavily involved in the vulture conservation project in Pakistan.

A brand new aviary pays particular heed to the Hawk Conservancy's location not too far from the Salisbury Plain and currently holds two male Great Bustards which are surplus to the reintroduction scheme for the species in this area of the UK reflecting the conservationally responsible policies of the Trust.

HIGHLAND WILDLIFE PARK
Kincraig, Kingussie, Invernesshire PH21 1NL, Scotland
MAP REF: 64/C1
SIZE: 260 ACRES
OPENED: 1972
OWNERS: ROYAL ZOOLOGICAL SOCIETY OF SCOTLAND
SPECIES: 35

OF THE MAJOR arterial roads of Great Britain, there can be few that rival the scenery around the A9 as it heads north through the Cairngorms to Inverness. Just off this road and in the middle of an epic of granite, pine and heather, is the Highland Wildlife Park, started by one Neil Macpherson in 1972. He was fortunate to receive the help of a local landowner (Sir Andrew Forbes Leith) and the local tourist development board to make his vision a reality, but basically the idea was to combine the extant and extinct fauna of Scotland in a captive environment that was part safari park and part zoo. The concept was a perfectly valid one and remained the same until recently. In 1986 the park, which had seen a slight but nonetheless regular diminution of visitor numbers, was acquired by the Royal Zoological Society of Scotland, headquartered at Edinburgh Zoo.

The casual visitor to Scotland would find it nigh impossible to view important native species such as Pine Marten, Scottish Wildcat and the magnificent Capercaillie. At the Highland Wildlife Park it is possible to view them all as well as larger animals (of which more later), but attendances which had declined to around 60 to 70,000 people per year, indicated that the allure of native fauna was not all that it might be. A policy was formulated which embraced a general Palaearctic zoogeography and gave scope for attractions such as Amur Tigers and Polar Bears to raise the profile of the collection. As I write, the policy is well underway and has been embraced with the dynamism now typical in the collection planning of this society.

Clearly the open spaces of the Highland Wildlife Park make perfect sense for hoofed animals and it is in this area that the connoisseur will truly identify and savour the new dimensions to the collection. Perhaps this is most noticeable on the rocky outcrops and hillocks of the part where Goral, Turkmenian Markhor, Blue Sheep and Afghan Red Sheep seem perfectly at home and the UK enthusiast can appreciate taxa absent from these shores for too long. Takin are recent additions to both this collection and the British zoo scene as a whole. It is the Mishmi subspecies on show here, and if public access to their semi-forested enclosure is rather too difficult they do seem to suit their surroundings. Of course the park has always shown Reindeer. It was compulsory. But now there are two taxa with the much rarer Forest Reindeer *(Rangifer tarandus fennicus)* of Finland now on show as well as the semi-domesticated nominate subspecies.

The Highland Wildlife Park is in fact quite difficult to access other than by car even though, surprisingly, a railway station exists only 7 miles away. Indeed the motorist finds himself straight into the drive-through, having paid his admission, with Kiang as the first exhibit. Of all the safari park experiences, the one at the Highland is my favourite – true, there is a sense of genuine tension if a lion or a tiger ambles really close in a traditional safari park but mostly I am distinctly underwhelmed by the repetition of it all. Maybe that is the key to this place – that the European Bison, Bactrian Deer and European Moose living in the main reserve are so different from the other identikit African species, or maybe it is a sixth sense that they seem to belong here. I can't quite put my finger on it, I must admit, but there is a 'something' here – that's for certain.

There are monkeys at Highland Wildlife Park now as well. A Palaearctic simian? Well, only Japanese Macaques could come close to qualifying for that description and that is what they have housed around the old waterfowl lake. Plans are afoot to give these 'snow monkeys' a hot tub, replicating the popular image of a population in the wild which warms via hot springs. Time will tell whether these captive-bred individuals will enjoy the same 'treat' or not. Japanese Serows have recently been added to the macaque exhibit. In 2008 Amur Tigers arrived and are housed in a large forested enclosure not too far away from European Beavers which arrived in the same year. Most of the other usual Eurasian suspects are here too – Wolves in a large sloping paddock with plans to move into pure subspecies in the future, Wild Boar, European Otters, and European Lynx. Birds are perhaps under-represented but there are Common Choughs as well as the Capercaillie mentioned earlier. These huge members of the grouse family have an interesting set of breeding aviaries which enables the hens to move from aviary to aviary, but not the male birds. In the late spring this all gets rather fraught and a visit at this time is well worth it to see the birds' courtship displays. Usually the park has Black Grouse and Red Grouse on display as well. The grouse family are not easy captive subjects.

One other aviary has an unusual design as well and it is the one combining Snowy Owls with Arctic Foxes. Of course these two are sworn enemies in the wild but a clever and discreet use of wire mesh at the wildlife park ensures that only the birds can reach certain parts of the cage - and can nest away to their hearts content.

Red Pandas are recent additions to the park's inventory and there is talk of Edinburgh's lone female Polar Bear (the only one on public display in the UK) moving up to the Highland Wildlife Park. This represents a long term commitment to the most charismatic of Palaearctic species. This wildlife park has always been a magnificent spot; they would have had to build an animal dungeon for it not to be such is the breathtaking scenery, but in the last few years things have got even better with the new collection protocol. I hope they can attain improved attendance figures for the simple reason that this quality establishment deserves it.

HORNIMAN MUSEUM AQUARIUM

100 London Road, Forest Hill, London SE23 3PQ
MAP REF: 65/D4
SIZE: 200 SQUARE YARDS
OPENED: 1903
OWNERS: CHARITABLE TRUST

AMONGST THE SUBURBS of South London lies one of the capital's best kept secrets in the shape of the Horniman Museum. This free-of-charge facility with its recognisable facade was left to the local populace by tea-trader Frederick J. Horniman in 1901, he had been actively filling the building with curiosities for the previous thirty years or so. It is an interesting place with a sizable Natural History Gallery, ethnological displays and the Music Room, full of every conceivable type of musical instrument. In 1902 a small aquarium was added to the attractions here and a £1.5 million total overhaul presented to the public in July 2006. At 200 square yards in size obviously this isn't a huge aquarium but works within the framework of a number of themed areas such as 'Guyanian Rain Forest', 'Mangrove Swamp', 'Fijian Coral Reef' plus native coastal and freshwater species. There is even a parlour tank full of anemones and gobies which seeks to replicate the beginnings of glass aquariums in the mid-19th century. The Horniman Aquarium specializes in the display and propagation of living corals. This is a recent development in aquariums and until the seventies the only corals found in captivity existed near actual coral reefs at places such as the Waikiki Aquarium, Hawaii and the Noumea Aquarium in New Caledonia. Advances in lighting techniques (the ultraviolet spectrum is important) and biologically balanced aquarium systems have brought about a remarkable change which is perhaps not instantly perceivable due to the quality of some imitation corals over the years. It is still not an everyday circumstance to see these living creatures, the time and skill being something of an indication that an aquarium has serious intentions.

HOWLETTS WILD ANIMAL PARK

Bekesbourne, Kent CT4 5EL

MAP REF: 66/D4
SIZE: 90 ACRES
OPENED: 1975
OWNER: HOWLETTS & PORT LYMPNE ESTATES LTD
SPECIES: 54

FAMOUSLY Howletts Wild Animal Park and its sister collection at Port Lympne are the creation of the maverick zoo man John Aspinall who died in 2000, leaving these two collections and The Aspinall Foundation as his zoological legacy. Volumes have been dedicated to Aspinall's idiosyncratic policies, theories and way of life, it would be beyond the scope and size of this book to analyse the man in any detail here, suffice to say that he is a very significant figure in UK zoo history. His way was a determination to pursue his own course and for many years the John Aspinall collections refused to be a part of the organised zoo community whilst at the same time making a conservational contribution that was far beyond that of most of their peers. Today much of the arrogance of Howletts has gone with its founder leaving a zoo which is much more a part of the mainstream than it was years ago, the work carries on apace however, some of it still way in advance of the rest of the zoo community. An example of this would be the purchase and preservation in the Congo and Gabon of approximately 1 million acres of forest ostensibly for the reintroduction of Western Lowland Gorillas but clearly supporting entire ecosystems as well.

Howletts itself comprises of an ancient estate set around a Georgian mansion acquired by Aspinall in 1957 and opened to the public in 1975. That this idyllic setting should be given over to wild animals including some of the most important groupings in the zoo world is perhaps a dream that many readers would have. Yet for all this utopia there has always been a demand that the animals come first. And not necessarily in a cloying, sentimental way either. Much of the animal husbandry here is guided towards attempts to reverse world trends in declining species and eroded habitats. So it is that Howletts can boast groups of Western Lowland Gorillas and Clouded Leopards that are the most numerous in captivity. The visitor will see gorillas and elephants aplenty yet may be fortunate to catch the faintest glimpse of the beautiful Clouded Leopard. Most of the zoo's specimens of this species are kept well away from the public in the hope of perpetuating breeding success with this, perhaps the most difficult of all felines in captivity. This is often the way of things at Howletts.

Do not expect great tributes to zoo architecture here in the Kent countryside. The animal accommodation could be best described as 'functional' yet it is always spacious and of course tailored to the best needs of its inhabitants. And the visitor will find little respite from the weather on a rainy day at Howletts – only the animals get to go indoors! The functionalism of Aspinall animal husbandry is best epitomized by the 'Gorillariums' which turned conventional zoo wisdom with gorillas on its head back in 1968 when first devised. At the time tiled 'bathrooms' were thought to be best for apes with a concrete floor, all the better for spraying down. Disease was the enemy and hygiene forged the blueprint for enclosures. Aspinall changed all this, for him boredom was the real enemy of the great apes in captivity and his cages were floored with deep straw litter for unlimited foraging as well as numerous slides, ropes, climbing frames and other instruments of similar entertainment. The Gorillas thrived in this environment and before long his breeding record with the species overtook and considerably surpassed anyone else's.

Howletts is very strong in a number of specialised areas, which could be summarized as felines (big and small), ungulates, African Elephants, Western Lowland Gorillas and monkeys. There are other mammals of course, but hardly any birds or reptiles. Ratels trundle around their enclosure (a first UK captive breeding here in 1972), there are Red River Hogs, Wolves and Black Rhino. But if I were to point the seasoned zoo enthusiast in any particular direction it would have to be the langurs. The large, active groups of Javan Brown Langur and Spectacled Langur are worthy enough but the real connoisseur's touch are the Grizzled Langurs, Mitred Langurs and Banded Langurs (the latter two being subspecies of *Presbytis melalophos*). These are the only ones of their kind outside of their native Indonesia and they have bred quite well at Howletts.

The Aspinall clan is directly represented by son Damian these days but he and various family relatives still largely push the collections along guidelines established by John Aspinall. The famous man's hubris was almost irreplaceable and may not ever be seen again, and yes, there is a slight sense that the pace of the collection has slackened a little, nonetheless Howletts is a zoo to be primarily judged on its contribution which is formidable indeed.

HUNSTANTON SEA LIFE SANCTUARY

Southern Promenade, Hunstanton, Norfolk PE36 5BH
MAP REF: 67/D3
SIZE: 1000 SQUARE YARDS
OPENED: 1988
OWNERS: MERLIN ENTERTAINMENTS
SPECIES: 110

OPENED BY UK wildlife personality Terry Nutkins in 1988 Hunstanton Sea Life Sanctuary was a needed facility to aid the large seal populations of this part of the East Coast. Unfortunately the word sanctuary is used rather too often by all of the Sea Life group. One definition of the word 'sanctuary' is 'to leave undisturbed and safe' – by that criteria no publicly visited facility can ever be a sanctuary therefore. Anyway, enough of semantics, the fact remains that Asiatic Short-clawed Otters and Blacktip Reef Sharks are hardly needing any kind of sanctuary having been imported for purposes of display! Like the Sea

Life Sanctuary at Oban in Scotland which started the whole Sea Life phenomenon off, Hunstanton is part indoors, part outdoors. In addition to the seals (Common and/or Grey), Humboldt Penguins and those Asiatic Short-clawed Otters are outdoors. Inside we visit themes all too commonly seen at Sea Life Centres in the shape of sharks, crabs, touchpools and 'North Sea'. In other words a little bit of all sorts. Summer displays tend to 'do the rounds' amongst the various Sea Life Centres so that each can have a 'new' attraction having been somewhere else the previous summer. Clearly Sea Life have taken us way above and beyond the concept of the old seaside aquarium in a most professional manner but it's like seeing a good local pub taken over by Brewers Fayre – it all looks much nicer but has the rank taste of uniformity in the name of the balance sheet. Not really for me I'm afraid.

ILFRACOMBE AQUARIUM

The Old Lifeboat House, The Pier, Ilfracombe, Devon EX34 9EQ

MAP REF: 68/B4
OPENED: 2001
OWNERS: PRIVATE
SPECIES: 75

THIS SMALL aquarium situated in the Old Lifeboat House rather moves the agenda away from the familiar seaside aquarium with its traditional fisherman's catch many of which will not make it much beyond one summer season in the tanks. With over 70 species on view the Ilfracombe Aquarium takes an ecological approach as its theme in order to trace the journey of a young, native trout from an Exmoor stream right out to the Atlantic Ocean. This is done via various stages of the river, which eventually reaches the calmer waters of the Taw Estuary. At this juncture various exhibits examine coastal life via rock pools and a reproduction of harbour life just around the corner. Finally the open ocean is represented with just a nod towards the land once more via fauna from the Lundy Marine Reserve out in the Bristol Channel. The enthusiast may well find most of the aquarium's inhabitants such as Cuckoo Wrasse, Thornback Rays and Lesser-spotted Dogfish to be fairly familiar but the imaginative way in which their lifestyles are explained, lifts this aquarium above most of its type.

ISLE OF WIGHT ZOO

Yaverland Seafront, Sandown, Isle Of Wight PO36 9AA
MAP REF: 69/C4
SIZE: 4.5 ACRES
OPENED: 1955
OWNERS: PRIVATE

AROUND THE Isle of Wight are a number of Victorian fortresses often known as 'Palmerston's Follies' after a somewhat neurotic governmental defence ploy of the 19th century. The Isle of Wight Zoo is situated behind one of these fortress walls on the very front of Sandown Bay, it was started as a minor concern in 1955. Jack Corney bought the zoo in 1976 and his daughters run the zoo to this day. In the last dozen years or so the zoo has placed emphasis on big cats and lemurs, although Jack Corney's original speciality was reptiles and a decent collection of these plus a large collection of bird-eating spiders remains to this day, although the intention is to go towards Madagascan herpetological species in the future. Lions, Leopards and Jaguars can be found here but the real speciality is with Tigers of which there are numerous specimens. Four years ago the 'Tiger Sanctuary' was developed based on natural habitats of the Kanha National Park in India, it certainly took this small zoo to a new level of exhibitry. Broadcaster Chris Packham referred to it as 'truly world class'. Ultimately the Isle of Wight Zoo will have to hone its policy with Tigers due to the amount of inter-racial hybrids at the zoo (including some with South Chinese blood, the rarest Tiger subspecies of all). At one time this zoo was rated amongst the country's poorest but it has managed to successfully pull itself well away from that level, a story which is always heartening to see.

KINGSLEY BIRD & FALCONRY CENTRE

Sprinks Lane, Kingsley, Staffordshire ST10 2BX
MAP REF: 70/C3
SIZE: 4 ACRES
OPENED: 2006
OWNERS: PRIVATE
OPEN: WEEKENDS ONLY

KINGSLEY BIRD and Falconry Centre occupies a precipitous site in the glorious Churnet Valley – a small valley not dissimilar to the one occupied by the Chestnut Centre only a little larger with space for a steam train line and a canal. The centre had previously been a small zoo in effect, called Chernet Valley Wildlife Park. Under the new ownership of Gareth Lord and his wife, the speciality is now birds of prey.

Around fifteen aviaries and an otter enclosure (yes, Asiatic Short-clawed) are dotted around a very steep wooded hillside which looks out over the valley. Only the reasonably agile should attempt the trail in all fairness but for those that can make it around, the result is a collection with one or two unexpected twists and turns. Of course Great Grey Owls, Harris' Hawks and European Eagle Owls are almost compulsory fare for any collection these days but we mustn't forget the effect these magnificent species have on the general public. However, at Kingsley there are also Black Kites, Ferruginous Hawks and the American subspecies of Barn Owl to tempt the more jaded zoo palate. The collection also includes an African Red-necked Buzzard *(Buteo auguralis)* – said by its owner to be the only one in the country.

The owner is also interested in unusual colour morphs of British birds so if cinnamon Song Thrushes, leucistic Starlings, and 'black' (actually chocolate brown) Barn Owls attract your curiosity then here they are. As yet this is a collection in transition but signs are that at Kingsley Bird and Falconry Centre the owners would like to do something a little different than other falconry centres.

KNOWSLEY SAFARI PARK

Prescot, Merseyside L34 4AN

MAP REF: 71/C3
SIZE: 560 ACRES
OPENED: 1971
OWNERS: PRIVATE

IT IS PARTICULARLY satisfying to find a zoological collection on the Knowsley estate because this was once the home of a legendary naturalist and his menagerie, aviaries and glasshouses. Upon becoming the 13th Earl of Derby in 1834 his lordship (the owner of Knowsley) gave full reign to his passions for fauna and flora, and by the time of his death in 1851 he had accumulated one of the largest private collections that these islands had ever seen. A number of species were named after him including Lord Derby's Eland and Lord Derby's Parakeet. His achievements were many but particularly noteworthy was the first captive breeding of the Budgerigar in 1848. The now famous artist Edward Lear was also employed here from 1830 to 1837 and made extensive visual records of the collection. The 14th Earl (who became Prime Minister in 1852) disposed of the collection and it was the 18th Earl who brought back to Knowsley a serious collection of animals in 1971. It might be rather an obvious thing to say but I would add that the safari park is some distance away from the areas around the house where the 13th Earl kept his animals over 150 years ago.

I often consider safari parks to be rather unchanging places – a set formula, lots of breeding from those species that do well in such places and an unashamedly commercial aspect once the visitor has parked up and got out of his car, but a little look back at

KNOWSLEY SAFARI PARK

Knowsley's past threw up one or two surprises. Thirty years ago one would have found Bottle-nosed Dolphins at Knowsley, the building still remains although speaking personally I find the Sea Lion show that has replaced the Dolphins to be similarly anachronistic with its cartoon-styled surroundings and anthropomorphized 'fun'. Sea Lions have always been around the park but at first the rest of the collection was all African animals. Various newcomers have eventually eroded this theme from Brow-antlered Deer to American Bison and Emu to Pere David Deer (a particularly fine group). Amur Tigers once lived in a drive through enclosure but proved to be a too devious and wily bunch prone to attacking the tyres of warden's vehicles! These tigers now have a rather uninspiring fenced compound which cars and buses can drive past. One copse of woods is given over to largely Asian animals and here a sizable group of Nilgai can be observed, these largest of Indian antelopes are by no means the omnipresent zoo animals that they once were. Cheetahs have gone from the collection and from other safari parks too, indeed the paucity of endangered species in all parks is a cause for some concern on the whole. These are just the places for African Wild Dogs or Grevy's Zebra and we should see these endangered species in all safari parks.

At Knowsley there are nine drive-through areas – the Lions are in a wooded area, there is a large group of Olive Baboons together with the Common Zebra that have proved over aggressive to young White-bearded Gnus and were removed to the monkey area. White Rhinos breed at Knowsley and look well in the open spaces, they live with a variety of species, most notably Common Eland and Forest Buffalo. Speaking of buffalos, the ardent zoo-spotter may care to take note at this country's uncommon Cape Buffalo (a group of 5 females) housed with the Pere David Deer.

At the very end of the safari trail things begin to look up somewhat – lots of well labelled information, a chance to take in some air and properly contemplate your surroundings. Yes, as you might imagine the drive-through has ended and Knowsley's African Elephants and Reticulated Giraffes inhabit enclosures rather more typical of zoological parks with animal houses and fences, moats and hot-wire – all the good stuff we know and love. Until fairly recently the group of African Elephants were walked to their hilltop enclosure but now everything is operated under protected contact and the paddock has been enlarged to accommodate this. It is surprising to see the herd (if not the bull) separated from the visitors only by a hot-wire 'bed' and a flimsy wooden fence. (Personally I'd think rather long and hard about this arrangement, a more sturdy metal surround would provide a significant safeguard). The true reality of the situation is however, that this is now a significant breeding group with no less than two calves to date. Some more animal exhibits are sprinkled around the visitor area which, as is usually the case in safari parks, borrows much from theme park culture. Fortunately three excellent exhibits for Meerkats, Short-clawed Otters and Red River Hogs are just about spared the mayhem of the fairground. There is also a small farm for children, and a reptile and invertebrate room is secreted away in the bowels of that ghastly Sea Lion House.

To me safari parks are an enigma. Quite clearly for herd animals they are ideal yet even so the circumstances are suitable only for a few selected species because, despite the space, the mix has to be right. But beyond even that when the customer steps out of his car the whiff of commercialism is overwhelming and it is difficult to take any scientific aspirations seriously. One cannot help but feel that an opportunity is being lost and I think the 13th Earl of Derby might just have agreed with me.

THE LAKE DISTRICT COAST AQUARIUM
South Quay, Maryport, Cumbria CA15 8AB
MAP REF: 72/C2
OPENED: 1997
OWNERS: PRIVATE

THE BOLD sandstone walls of Maryport's somewhat convoluted harbour-front serve as a vestige of an industrial past and underline its current austere economics, barren and underused as they are. A somewhat bleak town looks down on the harbour from its hilltop vantage point – only a few miles away from the grandeur of the Lake District, the town is many miles from sharing in that area's tourist bonanza. The Lake District Coast Aquarium is a small attempt to make some redress and to try and attract some of the millions of visitors from the interior out to Cumbria's generally rather unspectacular coastline.

Constructed as a purpose built aquarium with the aid of regional funding, the aquarium specializes in the sealife of Britain particularly the Solway Firth and the Irish Sea (which are of course local to it). I was reminded somewhat of the Anglesey Sea Zoo which is not surprising given that they both specialize in local species. The Lake District Coast Aquarium takes its sea water directly from the local harbour. This is particularly interesting in view of the fact that Maryport is on a river estuary (the Ellen) and therefore the aquarium can only remove water from the incoming tide when freshwater is displaced. For around half the year additional chilling of the water is required to maintain it at a maximum of 16°C. In fact aquarium owner Mark Vollers is something of an expert on aquarium design and the aquarium manages to maintain a high standard of water under simple and efficient means. Some 45 different exhibits are on show going from freshwater displays of local fish to harbour walls and rock pools. Such oddities as Sea Toads (actually crabs), Greater Sand Eels and Fifteen-spined Sticklebacks prove that there is interesting sealife beyond Clownfish and Lionfish.

The most impressive area is known as the shipwreck and features half a dozen tanks set amongst sturdy timbers of an old fashioned sailing vessel. I particularly enjoyed the John Dories in this area and wondered why I don't see more of this in native species in aquariums.

Maryport does not have a great deal to shout about but it does have a fascinating small aquarium, one of the new generation of new seaside aquariums that have taken that particular genre to an improved level and not necessarily in the Sea Life style.

LAKELAND AQUARIUM

Lakeside, Newby Bridge, Cumbria LA12 8AS

MAP REF: 73/C3
OPENED: 1997
OWNERS: PRIVATE LIMITED COMPANY
SPECIES: 191

FORMERLY KNOWN as the Aquarium of the Lakes the aquarium was acquired by the Spanish leisure chain Parques Reunidos in 2008 This company also owns Blackpool Zoo and the Bournemouth Oceanarium. Although basically still based around local water life there has been a move to one or two more general themes under the new ownership.

The Lakeland Aquarium is situated in the small community of Newby Bridge towards the southern end of Lake Windermere (England's largest lake). There is a boat terminus and a stop for a re-opened steam train line. The aquarium occupies a substantial brick building with faint architectural overtones of the Victorian era despite a fairly recent vintage.

The old theme here was of a Lake District waterway making its way to the Irish Sea, under the new ownership a theme of 'lakes of the world' has been adopted under separate categories of Africa, America etc. Thankfully the local element has been retained including the walk-through for Lake Windermere species with the likes of Barbel, Bream, Sturgeon and Crucian Carp – ducks too, in the shape of Common Pochard. These waters have to be maintained at a maximum of 12°C, not always easy to do in indoor aquariums. Even more temperature sensitive is the Arctic Char, another Windermere resident rarely seen in captivity and kept separately (and cooler) at the Lakeland Aquarium. In fact the appearance of the Arctic Char in this lake is something of a mystery with the most likely theory being that they are remnants of the last Ice Age. One of the former displays was the 'Riverbank at Night', a display of local small mammals now replaced by a rather more predictable rain forest exhibit which is just another pocket jungle à la everywhere else. The otters at Lakeland always were Asiatic Short-clawed so nothing spoiling in that respect now.

Lakeland Aquarium is a decent and professional place but it has lost something in becoming a typical 'bit of this, bit of that' aquarium so beloved of the chains. Go there, give it some time, even if you don't like it nothing is wasted in countryside such as this but I'm still tempted to say that the aquarium has lost, not gained, by bringing in the marmosets.

LAKELAND WILDLIFE OASIS

Hale, Milnthorpe, Cumbria LA7 7BW
MAP REF: 74/C3
SIZE: 5 ACRES
OPENED: 1992
OWNERS: PRIVATE LIMITED COMPANY

LAKELAND WILDLIFE OASIS is situated right on the A6 just south of the town of Milnthorpe but is still remarkably easy to miss given the totally inadequate signage and modest size of the establishment. The zoo is basically comprised of an indoor complex and a small outdoor zoo separated by the centre's car park.

All manner of small thematic areas are crammed into the main building which also includes the restaurant. Initially portents are rather promising with a tiny aquarium and a variety of museum-style exhibits seeking to explain the basics of life on Earth. However, it soon becomes apparent that rather too much has been attempted and the result is rather a jack-of-all-trades. Most of this building is comprised of greenhouses and so, quite naturally, the visitor soon comes to a small butterfly area with the pleasant addition of a Splendid Sunbird and some vivaria for invertebrates. Next is a tropical hall with rather a D.I.Y. feel about it, and a variety of reptiles and birds as well as some rather odoriferous tree shrews. In keeping with the general hotchpotch, a kind of sub chamber involves information on whales and a small tank containing a Short-eared Elephant Shrew.

A more traditional zoo occupying a couple of acres can be found outside, a good half of the acreage is woodland. It is in this woodland that the best parts of Lakeland Wildlife Oasis can be found. Although forested areas tend to engender rather dark and moody enclosures it is nonetheless a truism that some species prefer these circumstances. Clearly here it is working as some rather newly installed Fosas have already started to breed, Red Squirrels likewise. A 'South American Safari' has recently been created with a walk-through cage area populated by Squirrel Monkeys, Common Marmosets and Ypecaha Wood Rails. Rather less impressive is a dark and damp walk-through aviary with some truly miserable pheasant cages to one side. Green Peafowl, Demoiselle Cranes and Waldrapp Ibis are all interesting birds but I wasn't going to linger long in here. Meerkats behind breezeblock walls and a waterfowl pond, which is little more than a hole in the ground, complete the collection which can be visited in just over an hour. I'm left to reflect that Lakeland Wildlife Oasis needs to focus on its purpose rather more, at this moment it is neither fish nor fowl – not strong on education or conservation nor on any particular group of animals. Rather than ineffectively and inadequately explaining planet Earth why not take one particular ecosystem (rainforests spring obviously to mind) and concentrate on that? The term 'roadside zoo' is used in the U.S. to explain a certain level of a rather unacceptable zoological collection, well Lakeland is literally a roadside zoo and is absolutely acceptable in its standards yet rather uninspiring in its aspirations.

LEEDS CASTLE AVIARY

Leeds Castle, Nr Maidstone, Kent ME17 1PL

MAP REF: 75/D4
SIZE: 1 ACRE
OPENED: 1988
OWNERS: CHARITABLE TRUST
SPECIES: 90

LEEDS CASTLE is one of the most impressive medieval castles in the world enclosing the River Len to sit in the middle of a veritable lake; in its grounds lies The Aviary which pays tribute to the avicultural legacy of The Hon. Lady Baillie who was once the owner of this historic site, she bequeathed Leeds Castle to the nation upon her death in 1974. Lady Baillie specialised in waterfowl, Australian finches and Australian parakeets. The aviaries you see today at Leeds Castle were created in 1988 as a memorial to her; they are actually located to the side of the original aviary site, which is now a garden.

A total of 48 different metal-framed flights are maintained in The Aviary together with two open enclosures for cranes and storks. Together with the paved walkways and manicured islets of greenery the impression is a very orderly one. An ornamental function was never going to be an adequate usage however and there is serious intent in the bird collection here. First UK breedings for Von Der Decken's Hornbill, African Crowned Hornbill and Fischer's Touraco have all occurred here. Equally important in these times of bird importation bans are the breeding of toucans such as the Toco and Channel-billed species.

The collection of psittacines is also quite strong here including Red-vented Cockatoo, Cuban Amazon and Queen of Bavaria's Conure, but perhaps no species is more important than the Blue-crowned Laughing Thrush, a critically endangered species from China thought to number less than 200 in the wild. Leeds Castle maintains the European Stud Book for this taxon. We can therefore identify another of the smaller collections determined to play a larger part and which is undertaken with some élan at this tidy place. It is perhaps also worth mentioning that the substantial waterfowl collection here has mostly been disbanded in the last year or so.

LIBERTY'S OWL, RAPTOR & REPTILE CENTRE

Crow Lane, Nr Ringwood, Hants BH24 3EA
MAP REF: 76/C4
SIZE: 2 ACRES
OPENED: 1990
OWNERS: PRIVATE
SPECIES: 72

'LIBERTY'S' WAS ORIGINALLY opened as 'The New Forest Owl Sanctuary' on the site of an old pig farm, converting the former breeding pens to aviaries. This enabled an absolutely enormous collection to be built up, in fact the collection became too large and rather ran away with itself. The new ownership re-branded and re-opened the centre in 2005. Although improvements have been made I remain unconvinced that this site is itself uplifting enough for a public display as the wired-over concrete pens, which are dimensionally adequate for the most part, create a very austere impression. An ex-airforce aircraft hanger adjoins the bird zoo and has a small reptile house built inside it. As yet it is early days for the new owners so they must yet be given time but as far as I am concerned changes do still need to be made despite the large collection of owls which still remains.

LINTON ZOO

Hadstock Rd, Linton, Cambridgeshire CB21 4NT
MAP REF: 77/D4
SIZE: 16 ACRES
OPENED: 1969
OWNERS: PRIVATE
SPECIES: 105

LEN SIMMONS bought Linton Zoo in January 1972 and so began the long haul of transforming a typical sixties zoo boom hotchpotch collection into a modern day zoo. A priority on the windswept Cambridgeshire meadows was to plant flowers, shrubs and trees and these have now matured, a look at the fields surrounding the zoo gives an impression of the way it once was.

Linton isn't a huge collection but as the years have gone by the owners have concentrated on making the very best of what they have – with new things added from time to time. Recent changes have been made to some of the big cat enclosures to rival the rather beautiful one for Amur Tigers which has been there for some time. African Lions, Snow Leopard and a mixed pair of Black Leopard and 'normal' Asiatic Leopard; a major development in 2002 was the Rare Lemur Breeding Centre which works by virtue of individual indoor exhibits linking to a common outside enclosure. For the most part the lemur mix of Sclater's, Crowned, White-collared, Red-bellied, Red Ruffed, Western Grey Gentle and Mongoose seems to work quite well.

The aviaries here are beautifully planted and a real testament to the horticultural abilities of Linton Zoo as mentioned above. One aviary in particular is rather different to the others and is rather like the framework to a large barn but wired-over instead of timbered, it is therefore possible to breed Southern Ground Hornbills in here. Often these birds are kept clipped and flightless in other zoos. Although they don't use a cavity as do other hornbill species they are still tree nesters so I would have thought that full flight was essential for captive breeding. It seems to be the case here at Linton. An even more unusual recent breeding was that of the Elephant Beetle *(Megasoma elephas)*, a large brown beetle from South America sharing the same subfamily as the Rhinoceros Beetles.

After a number of years with Grevy's Zebras Linton has recently changed to the Hartmann's Mountain Zebra which along with the Brazilian Tapirs are really the only ungulates here. The policy here has been one of steady consolidation, there is further room for expansion and perhaps a little more indoor viewing would not go amiss but overall the Simmons family have every right to be proud of their small zoo.

LIVING COASTS

Beacon Quay, Torquay, Devon TQ1 2BG
MAP REF: 78/B4
OPENED: 2004
OWNERS: CHARITABLE TRUST
SPECIES: 51

ADVERTISED AS Torquay's coastal zoo, Living Coasts is nothing short of a world class zoological attraction and one of Britain's very best zoos. Living Coasts is owned by the Whitley Wildlife Conservation Trust which also owns Paignton and Newquay zoos and emerged in 2004 out of partnership with the local council as part of a scheme to regenerate Beacon Quay. This most northerly part of the Torquay seafront has, since 1857, housed a spa with swimming pool and ballroom becoming the entertainment complex Coral Island in the 1960s, an aquarium called Aqualand was also situated here until the 1990s. After demolition in 1997 a number of ideas were considered for the site before the all-in-one marine zoo that is Living Coasts finally won the day.

Basically this zoo consists of one gigantic aviary split into a number of thematic and distinct areas, some of these exhibits can be viewed at lower ground level in the form of underwater viewing areas. Almost immediately upon entering Living Coasts the attention of the zoo enthusiast is grasped by Britain's only dedicated alcid exhibit appropriately titled 'Auk Cliff'. This area is home to Tufted Puffins, Pigeon Guillemots, Common Guillemots and Red-legged Kittiwakes. Instantly the connoisseur will gauge how unique this place is from that small list alone. An aptly planted area for small waders is equally enticing with Ruffs, Black-tailed Godwits and Avocets amongst others. Other parts contain sea ducks such as Black Scoter, Long-tailed Duck and no less than three species of eider duck. Caspian Terns might surprise the observer with their size by comparison with the Common Terns that also live here. Bank Cormorants from Africa can also be seen (the only ones outside of that continent).

The above paragraph is a real zoo enthusiast's diatribe, but to be a financial success Living Coasts has to attract the everyday tourist for whom Redshanks hold little allure. Chief amongst these attractions are penguins in two displays – Gentoos and African with Macaronis on their own. Seals had to be included too, but yet again no concessions to Californian Sea Lions or Common Seals, here we have South American Fur Seals with their distinctive pointed noses. And in an effort to cram as much value-for-money into the site a mangrove area has recently been installed in the bowels of the Living Coast beneath the outdoor exhibits as has a local coasts display.

All of these zoological wonders in their naturalistic mini-environments overlook the Atlantic ocean with the framework of the towering aviary making Beacon Quay something of a beacon once more. Considering the fact that this is basically one very large exhibit I easily spent a couple of hours here, nor have I visited in winter when many of the ducks are in full colour winter plumage. I'll definitely do that one day and so should you.

THE LIVING RAINFOREST
Hampstead Norreys, Thatcham, Berkshire RG18 0TN
MAP REF: 79/C4
OPENED: 1996
OWNERS: CHARITABLE TRUST

THE LIVING RAINFOREST produces a nice little guide book which tends to talk in general terms about rainforests and their importance; on the back cover is a picture of a rainforest in some tropical part of the world. It is this picture that rather illustrates the problem with the Living Rainforest in that there is no way that a couple of rather squat greenhouses in rural Berkshire can represent the cathedral-like state of the real thing and its unending diversity. Despite good intentions here (this is a non-profit charitable organisation promoting the planet's most vital habitat) one is distinctly underwhelmed by it all. There are African Dwarf Crocodiles and Goeldi's Monkeys, Red-billed Toucans and Golden Mantellas, Carpet Pythons and Red-bellied Piranhas but for those of us who constantly visit zoos and museums it is all rather predictable. Even if this were a tropical house within a zoo rather than a single attraction I wouldn't particularly rate it highly. The message at the Living Rainforest is vehemently and well put, it is just that I wonder if it can be at all effective at such a diminished level.

LOCH LOMOND AQUARIUM SEA LIFE

Ben Lomond Way, Balloch G83 8QL, Scotland
MAP REF: 80/B2
OPENED: 2006
OWNERS: MERLIN ENTERTAINMENTS

ONE OF THREE inland sites for the Sea Life chain of aquariums sees the brand installed in a huge circular stone 'bunker' at the Loch Lomond 'Shores' Shopping Centre and whilst much of the chain tends towards repetition, there is often some local flavour to at least one or two exhibits. At Loch Lomond, exhibits entitled 'Deep Loch', 'Luss Water' and 'Falls of Falloch' illustrate various facets of local freshwater and marine life via species such as trout, Pike and Char, although it might be added that the 'Falls of Falloch' runs into an indoor otter exhibit (the whole aquarium is indoors) – unfortunately for zoogeography these otters are Asiatic Short-clawed! The rest of the aquarium follows the usual Sea Life themes via 'Bays of Rays', seahorses, jellyfish, 'Nemo's Kingdom' and of course the ubiquitous walk-through tank, known here as the 'Tropical Ocean Tunnel'. I might also add that the Sealife experience is no longer a cheap one, with adult prices well into double figures these days and thus comparable with our major zoos even if the visitor experience is considerably less!

LONDON SEA LIFE AQUARIUM

County Hall, Westminster Bridge Road, London SE1 7PB
MAP REF: 81/D4
OPENED: 1997
OWNERS: MERLIN ENTERTAINMENTS

THE LONDON AQUARIUM opened with tremendous fanfare in 1997 at that time it was owned by the Japanese company Shirayama Shokusan who own the Country Hall site where the aquarium is situated. It would be safe to say that enthusiasts were slightly underwhelmed. Certainly it wasn't in the very top tier of world-class aquariums even if it was sizable for the UK. However, along came the London Eye and anything situated next to that icon of the current age cannot fail to attract visitors. In 2008 Merlin Entertainments, of Sea Life Centre fame, purchased the London Aquarium with the intention of making changes. As this is a rather larger concern than the average Sea Life Centre there was considerable conjecture on the subject.

Surprisingly Merlin Entertainments have turned the London Aquarium on its head. This is because the visitor now tours the aquarium from the lowest level up through all three levels. It is a tour of the world's aquatic environments via the so-called 'ocean conveyor'. Initially this is portrayed via temperate aquaria themed as 'Atlantic Depths' and 'Tidal Reach'. Species such as Wolf Eel, Common Octopus and the under-exhibited John Dory can be found here.

The 165,000 gallon 'Reef Tank' houses Europe's largest group of Cownose Rays and a large Green Turtle (marine turtles have become rare exhibits in the UK), it has been converted to a walk-through experience by the addition of an acrylic tunnel. Largest of all the exhibits at the London Aquarium is the 'Pacific Tank' with large shoals of Golden Trevallys and Monos amongst a number of species including four of shark (Zebra, Nurse, Brown and Sand Tiger). At one time the Sea Life chain was opposed to the keeping of large species of shark in captivity but doubtless this complaint will now slowly fade away. 'Seahorse Temple' and 'Nemo's Coral Caves' take us to familiar Sea Life themes and the 'Tropical Rain Forest' is largely unchanged with Mangrove, Amazonia and Lake Malawi as the subjects. The rather low-key but nonetheless interesting 'River Thames Story' has been slightly truncated sadly.

So is the makeover an improvement or not? Overall I would say that Merlin have improved the London Aquarium but it is not the world-class aquarium that Britain still lacks. Welcome to the world's largest Sea Life!

LONDON WETLAND CENTRE (WWT)

Queen Elizabeth's Walk, Barnes, London SW13 9WT

MAP REF: 82/D4
SIZE: 104 ACRES
OPENED: 2000
OWNERS: WILDFOWL AND WETLANDS TRUST
SPECIES: 46

THE CREATION OF The Wetland Centre alongside the Thames in South West London from four redundant Victorian reservoirs was a unique undertaking which was more about creating a habitat for wildlife than a captive collection. Indeed the centre itself states that there is no other equivalent development on this scale in any other capital city in the world. There is a captive collection however, and the fourteen naturalistic habitats created for it are very well done if somewhat limited. For instance 'Northern Forests' includes a pond entitled 'Pine Forest' with Smew and Goldeneyes whilst Carolina Wood Ducks, Hooded Mergansers and Buffleheads live in the 'Broad-leaved Forests' area, a lodge designed as a North American Beaver trapper's log cabin is also included. I found the 'Islands' area to be the most interesting area with 'Hawaii' containing Nene and Laysan Ducks, 'Falklands' has Black-necked Swans and Greater Magellan Geese, 'Australia' is represented by the unusual Freckled Duck and even more unusual Magpie Goose.

It would seem that the captive collection at Barnes is smaller than at any other Wildfowl and Wetlands Trust Centre yet at the same time is probably the best presented. Clearly the emphasis here was to provide a refuge for wildfowl in the middle of one of the world's great conurbations which is reason enough of course. However, even non-twitchers will gain a great deal from the quality on show here.

ZSL LONDON ZOO
Regent's Park, London NW1 4RY
MAP REF: 83/D4
SIZE: 36 ACRES
OPENED: 1828
OWNERS: ZOOLOGICAL SOCIETY OF LONDON
SPECIES: 755

LONDON ZOO IS the most important zoo in the world and it is still one of the great zoos of the world as well. Until the Zoological Society of London formulated the idea of a zoological garden as a scientific resource captive animal collections had either been a status symbol for royalty and other wealthy individuals or, at the other end of the spectrum, street level curiosities. The Menagerie du Jardin des Plantes in Paris may well claim earlier roots but, as the name indicates was not really devised as a scientific zoo rather an attempt to rehouse the huge amounts of exotic animals in the city of the time (1793). Perhaps the Paris Zoo deserves the title of 'the first modern zoo' because of the scientific interpretation of the collection there but equally there is little doubt that it was London that took the baton of living zoology and ran with it.

Having established the importance of the London Zoo by its origins alone then it saddens me to say that there are many enthusiasts who would question my definition today of it being a great zoo. It is true that old sparring partners of years gone by such as San Diego, Zoo Berlin and New York's Bronx Zoo now have much bigger collections than London. Over the last thirty years the Zoological Society of London (ZSL) has had to come to terms with the restrictions of a 36 acre site in a royal park. All of the zoos mentioned above have much more room even if I think London has perhaps gone a little too far in removing some larger mammals. Nor do I see at San Diego and Zoo Berlin the open spaces and lawns which London seems quite happy to maintain. Yet I find myself falling into the same trap as the detractors. London Zoo still has some excellent exhibits, perhaps not enough for 'greatness' but when I add the Institute of Zoology, the library, the expertise, the *in situ* work and the influence of the society there can be little doubt that it is still great indeed.

Following the well-documented dramas of the early nineties, when closure was narrowly averted, the last decade has been quite a successful one for the ZSL with attendances increasing to over one million once more, a number of new exhibits are helping to bring this about.

Two years ago the area of the zoo immediately below the entrance was opened up by creating 'Gorilla Kingdom' which retains a few parts of the previous Sobell Pavilions as satellite exhibits for White-naped Mangabeys, Diana Monkeys, Black and White Colobus and Brush-tailed Porcupine as well as a small walk-through aviary. Obviously it is all based on an African theme running through to a larger African Aviary ('African Safari') nearby which did a rather good job of tidying up the eastern side of the old Stork and Ostrich House. This is not the only conversion of old facilities in recent times. The Bird House has almost been turned upside-down and is largely a walk-through tropical experience known as the Blackburn Pavilion after its benefactor David Blackburn, whilst the Cotton Terraces have been tweaked a little to become 'Out Of Africa' with African Wild Dogs amongst the Warthogs, Okapis and Giraffes. Casson's heavyweight and blunt Elephant House (1966) is now known as 'Zoo World' – a rather amorphous concept where some birds and small mammals occupy cages in the old elephant stalls and the conservational role of zoos is explained. The outer enclosures now house Bactrian Camels and Britain's only Bearded Pigs. Pygmy Hippos find themselves in the converted, old Sea Lion pool in summer months.

It can be identified therefore that a number of the old buildings have found new uses and for the most part this works well. I am less convinced about the temple to small mammals that was the Charles Clore Pavilion when refurbishment came along in 2006. Operating on two levels, one diurnal, the other a subterranean nocturnal house, 'the Clore' (as aficionados termed it) started in 1967 with more mammal species in it than any other UK zoo had in its entire grounds! Even at the time it was perhaps a little cramped and, as the years went by things were changed in line with modern-day sympathies – enclosures were knocked together and connected, breeding groups of species were encouraged. Indeed far from running at capacity a number of enclosures were often unsatisfactorily empty. The redevelopment of 'the Clore' a few years ago saw the heart of the building ripped out and replaced with a small, multi-specific rainforest whilst other useful enclosures became classrooms. What was special had become rather ordinary and I cannot find any zoo enthusiast that likes the new development much at all. There are still elements of 'the Clore' that stand up to scrutiny and 'zoo spotters' will appreciate such species as Panay Cloud Rat but on the whole I am reminded of the adage about style rather than content.

Of all the new buildings I am perhaps happiest with the new invertebrate house built as part of the tsunami of national development that was the Millennium Fund and which accounted for half of the cost (£4.4 million). Originally called the 'Web of Life' this building now goes under the name of B.U.G.S. (Biodiversity Underpinning Global Survival) and in keeping with that has probably retracted to a more invertebrate-orientated policy although there are quite a few fish in there and an occasional bird or callitrichid. Basically built around a central exhibit/research/services block, by clever use of ramps the public is taken up and down to a number of levels including a small aquatic section. I can think of no better invertebrate house in Europe. Old favourites such as a cockroach-infested kitchen sink came over from the former Insect House joining rare and conservationally important species such as Weta Crickets, White-clawed Crayfish and Giant Fregate Beetles. London was the first zoo ever to have an Insect House in 1881 and in the last twenty years or so has initiated a number of very important captive breeding programmes with Partula Snails or Wart-biter Crickets: it is therefore totally appropriate that London Zoo should have such a state-of-the-art facility.

Some old parts of London Zoo remain basically unchanged, the Snowdon Aviary (which for all its shortcomings I've always liked), the Lion Terraces (due for replacement in the near future), the Parrot House (now reduced to a few external aviaries), the Lubetkin-conceived Penguin Pool without penguins (which live elsewhere in the zoo) is maintained as an important piece of architectural history. The Reptile House looks much the same from the outside but has never looked better internally due to the exceptional presentation of the vivariums which are decorated in a rich style almost unimaginable only a decade or two ago. Particularly noteworthy is the venomous snake collection, which is one of the few areas of today's inventory to compete with the taxonomic variety of the zoo's yesteryears. To the south and west of the Reptile House are new, modern, stand-alone, exhibits for Galapagos Tortoises and Komodo Dragons. The latter have become famed in recent years due to a parthenogenetic birth at the zoo.

For over a decade now London Zoo has touted a potential new aquarium in London's docklands going under the name of Biota! I believe that this could be a big success and would possibly give this country its first world-class aquarium. Yet the project is probably at this moment as far away as it has ever been, in the meantime the zoo's 1924 aquarium struggles on under antiquated and deteriorating conditions. Many tanks have been screened off and much capacity lost yet a great deal of vital work is successfully undertaken here with small unglamorous freshwater types of goodeid or pupfish. If Biota! does ever happen I would not like to think that it would be at the expense of those wondrous dark rooms under the Mappin's Terraces. And it was the Mappin's Terraces that were to symbolize London's return to health when they were re-opened for bears in 1995. Sadly the Sloth Bears have now moved on to Whipsnade but in all fairness their exhibit on the Mappins was an untidy one and the new Australian exhibit 'Outback' installed in their place looks much better.

With attendances slowly increasing once more and a steady progress being made in overhauling old houses and exhibits, the future for our most important zoo looks quite bright. We should not see the traumatic days of almost twenty years ago, when the famous old place nearly closed, ever again. Yet I do believe there is frequently a lack of aspiration and that too often the zoo is now a follower and not a leader. Only when this mindset is adopted will London Zoo become once more a tourist 'must-see' in the manner of a Berlin or a San Diego.

LONGLEAT SAFARI PARK

Longleat Park, Warminster, Wilts BA12 7NW
MAP REF: 84/C4
SIZE: 296 ACRES
OPENED: 1966
OWNERS: PRIVATE
SPECIES: 87

WHO WOULD have thought that the circus fraternity with their beastwagons and exhibitionism would spawn the ultimate concept of an open zoo? It was one man of course in the shape of Jimmy Chipperfield and it was his idea to bring the African game reserve to colder climes, although the concept hasn't quite overwhelmed the zoo world in the manner which many predicted it would at the time. I don't think I would be too unkind in suggesting that profit was the main motivation rather than welfare, after all only a few basic species were required and animal housing was kept to a minimum. The 7th Marquess of Bath quickly saw the lanes around his country estate jammed with cars and coaches proving that the concept was a more than viable one. And whilst the public swallowed the notion that safari park animals were, in essence 'free', there has been a certain cynicism in informed quarters about the commercial outlook of these places that still exists to a degree. I have some sympathy with this viewpoint in that safari parks should be the perfect places for breeding ungulates but almost every rare species found in them has originated from traditional zoo breeding programmes. At Longleat there is a drive-through deer enclosure but sadly the deer are everyday species kept for public feeding rituals. Doubtless too, good reasons were offered for the departure of the African Elephants a few years ago but it is difficult to identify any real validity for the argument beyond a financial one.

Longleat is, of course, famous for its Lions and with the dramatic decline of the African population of the species safari parks could well make a useful contribution. There are Giraffes, White Rhino, Ostrich and many of the commonly seen grassland species from the same continent, although Longleat departed from an African-only policy long since. So it is that Wolves, Brazilian Tapirs and a fairly motley group of Tigers (whites, half-whites, subspecific mixes etc) can also be found here. A large but rather barren free-flight aviary for Chilean Flamingos, Sacred Ibis and others occupies some of the area previously given over to the African Elephants.

The combination of animals in Longleats' sizeable lake is rather idiosyncratic too. The Californian Sea Lions porpoise alongside the visitor boats in an unusual display, whilst Common Hippopotamus also have access to this body of water (fenced in as you can imagine). A small island is home to an elderly male Lowland Gorilla; but leaves me fairly unimpressed with either the nature of the island or the rather shabby accommodation. Pets Corner manages to mix a few zoo animals in amongst the usual domestic types and recently a fruit bat flight was added to this area.

The highlight of Longleat Safari Park is its setting and the wonderfully ornate house and gardens nearby, sadly I find the animal side of things to be rather unremarkable, indeed over-hyped. Over three quarters of a million visitors per year do not agree with me, doubtless persuaded in part by the park's television profile on 'Animal Park'.

LOTHERTON HALL BIRD GARDEN
Lotherton Lane, Aberford, Leeds LS25 3EB
MAP REF: 85/C3
SIZE: 7 ACRES
OPENED: 1974
OWNERS: LOCAL AUTHORITY

IT WILL COME as a surprise to many to learn that Leeds' largest collection of birds is not actually at the well-known Harewood Bird Garden. No, on the very eastern fringes of Leeds there is a collection which, in species terms at least, is half as big again at around 150 species. What's more one of the UK's largest avian collections is actually a free of charge public facility courtesy of the local council. Over the years many public parks have acquired an odd aviary of two and continue to do so, one of the determining aspects of this book was the size and level at which they should be included. Amongst all the parks here is the collection that grew and grew until it was decided that the bird garden should be set on professional lines in the early 80s.

At this juncture one should perhaps cast aside visions of northern industry and green parks juxtaposed to each other. Lotherton Hall is actually a 1000 acre estate set amongst agricultural fields almost 10 miles out of the city. It was bequeathed to the council in 1968 by Sir Alvery Gascoigne. This is not a country known for its free zoological attractions outside of museums so it will come as little surprise to find that I rate Lotherton as the best of these. That there is little competition is true but that should not detract from one of our better bird gardens.

Over the years the bird garden has transformed itself from some rather ramshackle constructions into a number of rather stoutly built brick aviaries. Nothing impresses more than the African walk-through aviary at more than a 100 feet across and almost 30 feet high supported by two mighty columns almost in the manner of a mesh big top. At first seemingly planted sparsely it does in fact represent a wadi which in nature would be dried up apart from the rainy season. Grey-necked Crowned Cranes, Blue-winged Geese, Sacred Ibis and a large flock of Little Egrets are amongst the inhabitants. Approaching this construction in size is the Condor Aviary which is certainly tall enough but without the other dimensions necessary for the Andean Condors to use the height I feel.

Lotherton seems to be strong in two distinct areas. Firstly there is a good collection of touracos with species such as Hartlaub's, Schalow's and Red-crested amongst others, even Western Grey Plantain-eaters, an untypically coloured member of the same family. Waterfowl are plentiful too and I do like the almost ornamental way they are displayed making for good viewing and easy identification. There are meadows for the likes of Marabou Storks (with breeding platform), White-naped Cranes, Sarus Cranes and Black Storks. Spix's Guan is also fairly unusual in captivity and can be found breeding here. Hornbills (Southern Ground and Trumpeter), Southern Helmeted Curassow and Noble Macaw are all noteworthy species. True, there are a few gaps in the collection and what 'commercial' bird garden could afford not to have penguins? Yet complaint is churlish when everything is so nicely done and costs not one penny to see. There has been a steady progress at Lotherton Hall Bird Garden over the years and possibly we should not expect more from the ratepayers of Leeds, even I would urge them to start making a charge in order to get those penguins (and maybe even pelicans!).

MACDUFF MARINE AQUARIUM

11 High Shore, Macduff, Banffshire AB44 1SL, Scotland

MAP REF: 86/C1
OPENED: 1997
OWNERS: LOCAL AUTHORITY

A PURPOSE BUILT roundhouse on the Banffshire coast is the stout home of the Macduff Marine Aquarium. The aquarium needs to be robust, as winter storms take no prisoners in these northerly parts. This is a modern facility which looks beyond the old seaside aquarium concept to portray various types of local marine habitat. 'Deep Reef and Sea Floor' contains the likes of Squat Lobster, Common Octopus, Norway Lobster and Thornback Ray whilst 'Coastal Habitats' would include Atlantic Salmon, Sand Eel, Grey Mullet and Grey Gurnard. There are various crabs, blennies and gobies in 'Shallow Waters' as well as Lumpsucker and Long-spined Sea Scorpion. Moon Jellyfish are displayed separately; for certain these delicate sea creatures do not mix with other species. Uniquely for the UK, Macduff Marine Aquarium maintains a tank with living kelp. This seaweed is in fact quite hard to maintain in the aquarium and requires natural sunlight. Virtually all kelp seen in aquaria is imitation. This tank is the largest here at 30 feet in diameter containing 90,000 gallons of seawater and fish such as Cuckoo Wrasse, Pollock, Turbot, Cod, Conger Eel, Wolf Eel and Haddock. I always applaud any local authority maintained wildlife facility in these islands for the simple reason that they are quite rare. In the case of Macduff the Marine Aquarium is small but very nicely presented, even microscopic sea life has not been forgotten and can be viewed in the 'Sealab'.

MANCHESTER MUSEUM VIVARIUM
Manchester University, Manchester M13 9PL
MAP REF: 87/C3
OPENED: 1966
OWNERS: UNIVERSITY OF MANCHESTER

A SMALL living collection has been displayed and maintained at the Manchester Museum since the mid-1960s. In those days it was okay but I used to wonder what the point of it was when Belle Vue Zoo, just a couple of miles away, had such an excellent new Reptile House. Belle Vue has been gone for over thirty years now but that absence didn't add much lustre to the little herpetological corner up in the eaves of the local museum. By the turn of the millennium all this had been swept away however and the Vivarium totally rebuilt in a different location within the same building. Although still small the exhibits here are some of the nicest I've encountered, most definitely a case of quality over quantity. In fact in 2002 the 'Amazonian Rainforest' vivarium received the UFAW zoo exhibit award. Its moss-covered, bromeliad-festooned, tree trunks and tannin-coloured waters are the finest I can recall – just perfect for frogs I would have thought. And it is frogs that are the real speciality here with curator Andrew Gray working both *in situ* and *ex situ* with Costa Rican species in particular. The star species in many ways is the Splendid Leaf Frog *(Cruziohyla calcarifer)* with a first captive breeding for this impressive species and the only other specimens in a couple of other UK zoos as I write. Other exhibits are a little more general illustrating Madagascar or a desert environment for instance. Support graphics are first class with the use of models or artifacts recalling Emmen Zoo in Holland (although the curator has never been there!). Manchester has had two zoos and an aquarium in its history but nothing of significance for over twenty years. The Vivarium at the local museum may be tiny but it is certainly significant in both appearance and the work it undertakes.

MANOR HOUSE WILDLIFE PARK

St Florence, Tenby, Pembrokeshire SA70 8RJ, Wales

MAP REF: 88/B4
SIZE: 12 ACRES
OPENED: 1982
OWNERS: PRIVATE
SPECIES: 20

ACTUALLY I'm not sure that the above name is the official title of this zoo anymore as their leaflet defines it to be 'Anna Ryder-Richardson's Manor House Wildlife Park'. Ryder-Richardson is a television presenter who bought this rather tired and worn-out rural zoo in 2007. Not surprisingly the new owner was able to use her media contacts in order to attract television to her new project. A one-off programme (there will be others in future) followed the rather predictable storyline of rescue and renovation with Ryder-Richardson's lack of basic zoological knowledge causing rather a stir amongst seasoned observers. The latter didn't cause me too much concern provided that a poor place could become better.

As I write Manor House is in its second season under the new regime. The most noticeable change is in the sprucing up of the place – new signage has been installed (not exactly error-free) and the rather dreary 18th century house from which the park takes its name has been cleaned up. A poor Reptile House has been closed, as has the model railway. The walled gardens with their assortment of mis-matched cages and enclosures have also been closed and a few other aviaries dismantled. The 'outer' zoo with large grassy paddocks for American Bison, Damara Zebras, Przewalski's Horse, Bactrian Camels, Llamas and a Brazilian Tapir remains intact.

Clearly just closing things down is not the future of Manor House and a lemur walk-through (erroneously touted as Europe's largest when it isn't even Britain's largest) for the Ring-tailed and Red Ruffed species is the most prominent contribution. In a somewhat naïve marketing strategy the park now claims that it is 'uncaging' the animals and 'Valley of The Apes' is a new island and water exhibit for a pair of Siamangs. Of course by 'uncaging' everything, birds become disenfranchised (a small group of Chilean Flamingos are just about the sum total), reptiles more or less impossible (they have Sulcata Tortoises) and many small mammals difficult. And here we have the rub, there are simply very few animals at Manor House now. Even I found it difficult to extract much more than an hour from my visit.

Tenby is quite an intense zoological experience – within these pages you will find Folly Farm Amusement Park and Zoo plus Silent World Aquarium, both of these are ten minutes away from Manor House by car. Folly Farm in particular represents value for money (it costs less to enter than Manor House), it could be that the general public agree with me and Manor House will struggle to succeed with its current strategy.

MARTIN MERE WETLAND CENTRE (WWT)
Burscough, Ormskirk, Lancs L40 0TA
MAP REF: 89/C3
SIZE: 530 ACRES
OPENED: 1975
OWNERS: REGISTERED CHARITY
SPECIES: 110

FOR MY MONEY the most attractive of all the Wildfowl and Wetlands Trust establishments is Martin Mere situated in the flatlands of North West Lancashire. In just over 30 years, soggy agricultural land (there was, in medieval times, a huge lake here) has been transformed into a wooded oasis and attractive gardens. Of course much of the site remains as marsh, reedbed and water meadow for the large numbers of wild waterbirds that visit here. In recent times I have thought it ironic that a wetland trust should be focused so centrally on wildfowl when all manner of animal life has evolved to live in wetland habitats, and it would seem that the WWT is coming around to that way of thinking too – hence the 'new' name of Martin Mere Wetland Centre. Wildfowl still dominate but there is a move towards other forms of waterlife as we shall see.

All the WWT centres have a multi-purpose visitor building as their introduction – good quality food and decent book selections make them fairly unusual for wildlife attractions in this country. Martin Mere's had to locate solid ground for its construction due to the origins of the site. Not too far away from the log-built visitor centre are new enclosures for Asiatic Short-clawed Otters and European Beavers, both of these are very nicely presented in what can only be termed 'zoo-style'. I heartily approve. And tall lightweight fences have also cropped up around some of Martin Mere's enclosures too, this is because cranes are now becoming a feature of WWT collections and here in Lancashire the Demoiselle, Grey-necked Crowned and Common species can be observed. It would be nice to see a progress towards rarer taxa in the future. Together with a 'Pond Zone' (which is largely educational) these are the only moves towards a more generalised theme at the moment but doubtless it is a policy which will proliferate.

There are actually only about 20 less species of waterfowl at Martin Mere than at the famous parent collection Slimbridge, and where Martin Mere really scores is in the definition of that collection. Mallard are the very devil to prevent from integrating into captive wildfowl collections, fortunately there aren't too many here, but it is the smaller pens for one or two individual species that are maintained so well and really serve to highlight species. Black Spur-winged Goose, Freckled Duck and Pink-eared Duck are amongst the rarer species to be readily identified and a barren, pebbled, habitat for Flying Steamer Ducks (the other three species of steamer duck are flightless) superbly replicates their coastal home on the very tip of South America.

The larger walk-through areas take a zoogeographical theme through all the continents (not Antarctica obviously) and less predictably there are also two smaller walk-throughs for Asian and European endangered waterfowl respectively. Flamingos are not waterfowl of course but have always been awarded 'honorary' status by the WWT and they have the Greater and Chilean species at Martin Mere as well as Crested Screamers. To be blunt, recent visits to Slimbridge have left me a little disappointed whereas a long-overdue visit to Martin Mere left me utterly delighted. Read into that what you will.

MARWELL ZOOLOGICAL PARK
Colden Common, Nr Winchester, Hampshire SO21 1JH
MAP REF: 90/C4
SIZE: 98 ACRES
OPENED: 1972
OWNERS: MARWELL WILDLIFE
SPECIES: 109

THE SIXTIES and seventies saw an explosion in the number of wildlife attractions in the UK. A number of these were started purely as money making enterprises; others had at least some integrity in that their owners wanted to run a zoo – to surround themselves with animals but not a great deal more than that in truth. A few had serious intent – Jersey (started in 1959 but was still, in essence, a sixties zoo), the Norfolk Wildlife Park under Phillip Wayre, Blackpool, Colwyn Bay and others. To this select band can be added Marwell Zoological Park which opened in 1972. Inspired by the Catskill Game Farm in New York State, Marwell was the dream of John Knowles, who had experienced considerable commercial success in the poultry industry and who envisaged an 'open' zoo along the lines of Whipsnade specializing in ungulates. As might be expected the infant zoo park had its trials and tribulations but quickly established itself as a worthy and important addition to Britain's zoo community.

Occupying a gentle valley surrounding the Tudor splendour of Marwell Hall, it says much for the concept and planning of the layout that the zoo seems both spacious and manageable for the visitor at the same time. Grassy paddocks dominate but there are a number of animal houses and traditional zoo enclosures as well, although these never seem to intrude into the essential rurality, a feeling encouraged by surrounding woodlands.

Mention was made earlier of Marwell's ungulate speciality but gradually over the years many other species have been added to create a more rounded zoological experience. If anything followed immediately in the wake of the hoofstock it was the larger felidae – at the moment Amur Tigers, Amur Leopards and a quite excellent recent Snow Leopard enclosure represent this group of animals with Sand Cats (in a Desert House), Servals and Ocelots representing the small cats. As with many UK collections, the last twenty years have been particularly busy and vibrant ones, including a rather unique lemur walk-through whereby the public is enclosed for the most part also a Tropical House that was once installed in the now-defunct Windsor Safari Park. Owls, parrots and cranes form the backbone of a bird collection that is in truth overshadowed by the mammal collection, but not before Marwell had a first UK breeding for Secretary Birds (1988), and this species is still to be found at the zoo. African Penguins occupy a modern pool around a dozen years old.

Primates have slowly proliferated here, from a large group of Pottos, through various callitrichids, including free ranging Golden Lion Tamarins, up to Diana Monkeys, King Colobus, Sulawesi Crested Macaques and gibbons. An Australian Walkabout, small Reptile House and a new Siamang enclosure are recent additions.

Yet we must return to the ungulates for our most lasting impression of green and leafy Marwell. Not many zoos can boast of all three zebra species and large herds of Nyala, Roan Antelope, Scimitar-horned Oryx and Sable Antelope are not only impressive but of significant conservational importance. The epicentre of the Somali Wild Ass in the UK is here. Giraffes and Okapis proliferate and the White Rhino seems to be just as appropriate in this corner of Hampshire as it does on the African savannah. Talking of Africa, Marwell's latest development is 'African Valley', a huge 30 acre meadow for Giraffes, Ellipsen Waterbuck, Grevy's Zebras and Ostrich. Warthogs and Babirusa represent the pig family and there is a large group of pig-like Collared Peccaries too. Pygmy Hippos can be observed either grazing in a large meadow or submerged in the heated waters of their suitably 'atmospheric' Aquatic Mammal House. After many years of absence from the UK zoo scene, Marwell recently brought in Takin, the Mishmi subspecies *(Budorcas taxicolor taxicolor)* to be exact, and were rewarded with a UK first breeding in June 2006.

Apparently the precise moment of Marwell's conception was a chance meeting between founder John Knowles and zoo director Walter D. Stone (of the Franklin Park Zoo in Boston) in a bar in Boston, Massachusetts. Over 46 years on from that encounter we should perhaps raise our own glass to fortune itself because one of our best zoos emerged from it.

THE MONKEY SANCTUARY

Murrayton, Looe, Cornwall PL13 1NZ
MAP REF: 91/B4
SIZE: 10 ACRES
OPENED: 1964
OWNERS: MONKEY SANCTUARY TRUST

OPENED BY Leonard Williams in 1964 as a sanctuary for Humboldt's Woolly Monkey – a species found fairly frequently as unsuitable pets at the time. In fact he was the first person to breed the species in captivity in the UK and it is only fairly recently that the diet of Woolly Monkeys has been shown to be a way to their captive success.

Williams' husbandry of the primates was rather radical as well in as much as he provided much more space and variety of surroundings for the monkeys than was the case in traditional zoos of the time. Indeed he even allowed limited, supervised, unprotected encounters with the animals long before the idea was universally embraced with other species.

Today Woolly Monkeys are still the main species at Looe although some rescued Brown Capuchins and Barbary Macaques have been added to the collection. Unfortunately the sanctuary has adopted a rather peculiar, almost anti-zoo policy in recent years (Leonard Williams died in 1987) and one symptom of this is to promote a non-breeding policy (that is one important welfare element missing then). Beware that the sanctuary is not open on Fridays and Saturdays apart from Easter and May Bank Holidays.

MONKEY WORLD APE RESCUE CENTRE
Nr Wareham, Dorest BH20 6HH
MAP REF: 92/C4
SIZE: 74 ACRES
OPENED: 1987
OWNERS: PRIVATE LTD COMPANY
SPECIES: 15

STARTED IN 1987 by Jim Cronin, Monkey World is a zoo where the animals come first. It could rightly claim the title of 'sanctuary' but would not shrink away either from the fact that it is a primate zoo, initially based on rescued animals yes, but increasingly part of the mainstream zoo community with some of its residents part of European breeding programmes.

Sadly Jim Cronin died in 2007 and now Monkey World is run by his wife Dr Alison Cronin and her devoted staff. Jim Cronin was once a keeper at Howletts (amongst others) and there is a certain Aspinallesque quality to Monkey World whereby enclosure aesthetics are sacrificed for welfare considerations. The result is large enclosures, sometimes quite ugly ones, but a situation in the middle of some Dorset woodland probably makes this aspect less noticeable. Surprisingly some gibbons, of which Monkey World now owns five species (Siamang, Mueller's, Agile, Lar and Golden-cheeked), have rather narrow functional long cages. Decent enough for brachiation maybe, but at odds with other primate accommodation here.

Monkey World's highest profile has been with Chimpanzees and Orang Utans, particularly the former species of which the zoo has the largest number outside of Africa. These are kept in three main groups but breeding is not encouraged unlike the group of Bornean Orangs (the centre also has one Sumatran). Most of the apes have been rescued from tragic or unlikely circumstances, indeed a brand new addition is an Orang Utan nursery.

The monkeys include Common Marmosets, Woolly Monkeys, Common Squirrel Monkeys and a group of elderly Stump-tailed Macaques retrieved from a laboratory where they had been used for asthma research. More recently over 80 Capuchins of various types have been rescued from a 'research' facility in Chile and are housed in four different enclosures. Apart from any ethical aspect, husbandry of the animals had been poor and they deserve their retirement at Monkey World where care will be of the highest order. A few years ago an area known as 'Malagasy' was added to the park which comprises of the now ubiquitous lemur walk-through, inhabited by a group of the Ring-tailed species.

A number of establishments around the country hide behind the term 'rescue centre' and use the word 'sanctuary' as an excuse for poor conditions whatever the species and whatever the motivation. The opposite applies at Monkey World where the highest standards mostly prevail (not forgetting those gibbons) – I wish that all animal 'rescuers' were this good!

THE NATIONAL BIRDS OF PREY CENTRE
Newent, Gloucestershire GL18 1JJ
MAP REF: 93/C4
SIZE: 15 ACRES
OPENED: 1967
OWNERS: PRIVATE LIMITED COMPANY
SPECIES: 68

STARTED AS THE Falconry Centre by Phillip Glazier, the centre was bought from him by his daughter, Jemima Parry Jones in 1983 and it was under her that an international reputation was established. Indeed it is highly likely that no zoo or similar establishment in the world could beat a total of 60 different bird of prey taxa bred in confinement. Parry Jones has her own formula for this, one important element of which were aviaries completely roofed over in a shed style – they were not, or are not, pretty, but they worked pretty well. Things continued to progress and evolve until 2003 when the owner decided to move to the USA complete with many of the outstanding birds from the collection. The National Birds of Prey Centre was sold to Keith Beavan and possibly in the general public's eyes things continued much the same as before. For the zoo connoisseur however, it was a backward step with many of the special species missing and one or two of the aviaries converted into other, more commercial usage. It just wasn't the same and I felt the same as when I first saw the 'new' Birdland in Bourton-on-the-Water, almost twenty years before. However, as I write (early 2009) the wheel has turned a full circle and Jemima Parry Jones has bought the place back. An interim organisation entitled 'The International Centre For Birds Of Prey' has followed the 'raptor lady' as she toyed with new ideas and fresh locations for her birds so we cannot yet say if Newent will embrace the new title or not. And it would certainly be unfair to review the centre of the recent past. Falconry in all its forms has proliferated beyond belief in the last couple of decades, not all of it has been on true and proper foundations. To see one of our very best places diminish did not help and Jemima Parry Jones is most welcome back to these shores. I have every confidence that she will restore Newent (as aficionados call it) back to its former glory and I have little doubt that the large inventory of breeding species will increase still further.

NATIONAL MARINE AQUARIUM
Rope Walk, Coxside, Plymouth, Devon PL4 0LF
MAP REF: 94/B4
OPENED: 1998
OWNERS: REGISTERED CHARITY
SPECIES: 324

THE NINETIES finally brought the new aquarium era to the UK, and whilst there are some who believe that from a global perspective the giant aquaria of some nations never really arrived, the National Marine Aquarium's appearance was a most conspicuous one. Overlooking Plymouth Sound this glass and concrete structure costing an initial £14.9 million, could, in truth, be a smart, new, public building suiting a number of potential purposes anywhere in the land. It took 18 months to build and opened in May 1998. A couple of major additions have since expanded the aquarium further.

As might be expected from the National Marine Aquarium's location and name all the exhibits here concern seawater and for the living systems this is drawn from a 14.5 metre deep bore hole not far from the aquarium itself in Plymouth Sound. The major exhibits are Atlantic Reef, Mediterranean Sea and Coral Seas. Each of these has its strengths but the most interesting is the Mediterranean. In truth fish from this region are becoming uncommon in aquaria outside the area of the sea itself, so the various breams, wrasses, mullets, even Barracuda are worth a good look. Not only that, but at 10.5 metres deep this particular tank is claimed as the deepest in Europe. Maintained at 18°C, it has a curious curved viewing window that really does pull the observer into the exhibit. Atlantic Reef is overlooked by a skylight providing shards of natural sunlight – some familiar fish here such as Whiting, Pollock and Cod, all displayed behind Britain's largest aquarium window. The third of these three important exhibits is Coral Sea, containing the usual colourful selection of tropical fish and, quite unusual in these islands, a sea-turtle in the shape of a Loggerhead.

There are other smaller areas too, such as Shallow Water, a recently refurbished area of tidal zones and rock pools. As with most other aquaria in this country, seahorses are popular at Plymouth with 8 species, in addition there are over 70 sharks in ten species, with Sand Tigers the largest. The aquarium seeks to create a seamless interaction with the local marine environment and has a scientific approach as befits a charitable community project. There is a politically correct approach here which I've no doubt has absolute, intentional integrity, yet I can't help but feel that there is an element of deception about it.

We still do not give the public in this country the full experience of what an aquarium can be; at the National Marine Aquariums there are no birds, no mammals and, quite frankly, almost a shortage of living exhibits per se. It is all very nicely done with a gravitas about it that one or two majors in the US would do well to adopt, but the favourable comparisons almost stop there and it remains to be seen if the UK can ever build a truly world class aquarium – after all we invented the genre.

NATIONAL SEA LIFE CENTRE BIRMINGHAM
Brindley Place, Birmingham B1 2JB
MAP REF: 95/C3
OPENED: 1996
OWNERS: PRIVATE LTD COMPANY

BIRMINGHAM HAS more miles of canal than Venice so maybe the placement of a Sea Life Centre in the middle of England has at least some connection with water. This particular Sea Life Centre is announced to be the 'National' one (it seems no-one needs any permission to call something 'national' at all) and was purpose built in the very epicentre of the canal system of the city. The aquarium is roughly the same size as any other Sea Life Centre in truth but seems to be very popular and the summer months will inevitably find a queue of people waiting to enter. More than other centres in the group, the building operates on a number of visitor levels and therefore appears to be larger than it actually is. This particular centre has a largish freshwater part under the name of 'Amazonia', a Mangrove Swamp, Otter Sanctuary (just what are Asiatic Short-clawed Otters being saved from?) and a Seahorse Breeding Centre. I might add with regard to the latter that the Sea Life Centres and ex-Sea Life Centres do perform quite an important task in breeding seahorses although the improvement of technical skills probably has a greater effect than the numbers bred. Sea Life Centres are relatively expensive places to visit, there is certainly some truth in the fact that if you've seen one then you've seen them all (with the possible exception of Weymouth and London).

NATIONAL SEAL SANCTUARY

Gweek, Cornwall TR12 6UG
MAP REF: 96/B4
SIZE: 45 ACRES
OPENED: 1975
OWNERS: MERLIN ENTERTAINMENTS LTD

THE CORNISH SEAL SANCTUARY actually started on the northern coast of Cornwall in 1959 and moved to Gweek in 1975. Although not far from the sea the sanctuary overlooks the mouth of the Helford River and basically consists of six regimented, somewhat functional pools at the bottom of a grassy hillside (some with underwater viewing). As a rescue and rehabilitation centre the sanctuary concerned itself only with the indigenous Common and Grey species of seal. Gradually Californian Sea Lions and a few penguins were added to bring in the visitors before Merlin Entertainments (owners of the Sea Life chain) bought the centre and re-named it the National Seal Sanctuary. Clearly the conundrum here has always been to provide visitors with a lengthy experience, the worthy work of the sanctuary notwithstanding, and the result is that Patagonian Sea Lions and Asiatic Short-clawed Otters have been added. 2005 saw the Cornish Coast Experience installed, which is a 'rock pool experience' educationally presented (rather ironic really, one wonders how many real rock pools are not too far away!). The prize catch here however is a Hooded Seal who was rescued twice in effect, with the result that this rare zoo species now has a permanent home at Gweek. It would be churlish to complain about elements of the National Seal Sanctuary however, because whatever the motivation behind the place, clearly a great deal of good and important work goes on here.

NATIONAL WETLAND CENTRE WALES (WWT)

Llwynhendy, Llanelli, Carmarthenshire SA14 9SH, Wales
MAP REF: 97/B4
SIZE: 45 ACRES
OPENED: 1991
OWNERS: WILDFOWL AND WETLANDS TRUST
SPECIES: 74

FOLLOWING SIX YEARS of construction Sir David Attenborough opened the Wildfowl and Wetlands Trust's Welsh centre in 1991. Covering over 450 acres in total the site is situated on the Burry Inlet and, as always with the WWT has been sited on an important natural wetland habitat. The captive collection occupies about a tenth of the overall area and as such is the smallest WWT centre. As with the other WWT sites a visitor centre is really the focal point. At Llanelli a particular advantage of the small visitor centre is that the public can enjoy the restaurant facilities and the picture windows looking out over the so-called 'top pond' all at the same time. As usual, a high standard of books are also available for purchase.

The customary collection policy of zoogeographical pens is adhered to at Llanelli in the shape of Asian, European, Australian and South American but there are some less predictable areas too such as the 'Tundra Pen', 'Goldeneye Pond' and 'Island Pen'. To be honest the collection here has nothing that cannot be seen at other WWT centres but nonetheless species such as Freckled Duck, White-winged Wood Duck and Andean Goose are always a pleasure at close quarters. Only one kind of flamingo is found here and that is in the shape of a large breeding flock of Caribbean. A wider spectrum of wild wetland life is to be seen in areas such as the marsh garden and butterfly garden but as yet Llanelli has not moved into animals such as otters and cranes which are starting to become a feature of other WWT centres. Duck rearing facilities have also been seconded to Slimbridge in a policy of centralisation common to most, if not all, of the centres.

Each of the WWT centres has its own subtle, in some cases major, differences from the others. Llanelli is as undulating as any centre for instance and probably more wooded too, as with all the centres a true nature lover cannot fail to be impressed.

THE NATIONAL ZOO OF WALES
Colwyn Bay, Conway LL28 5UY, Wales
MAP REF: 98/3B
SIZE: 37 ACRES
OPENED: 1963
OWNERS: ZOOLOGICAL SOCIETY OF WALES
SPECIES: 85

UNTIL 2008 this was the Welsh Mountain Zoo of course and if not quite atop a mountain it certainly inhabits the top of a very steep hill. Encouraged to set up here by the local borough council on an under-used site owned by them, I often wonder if it regrets its precipitous location particularly in the light of the downturn in tourism to the North Wales coastal resorts and the difficulty in getting from the bottom of that hill to the zoo. There are compensations of course and very few zoos can compete with the view on offer here, it is little surprise that this was the first zoo in Britain, possibly the world, to offer falconry displays. Started in 1963 by Robert Jackson the zoo, like so many others, developed in piecemeal fashion through its first two decades and after that period needed many of its developments replacing. Following the death of Robert Jackson in 1969 the zoo was run by his widow Margaret and three sons, Tony, Chris and Nick. The last twenty years have seen redevelopment with exhibits which will stand the test of time.

Largest of these redevelopments is Chimpanzee World and Chimp Encounter from

1990. Basically a piece of hillside surrounded by a brick wall with viewing windows set into the side it isn't wildly attractive but suits the purposes of the large group well. Certainly a huge improvement on their old cage. 'Bear Falls' took the zoo's Brown Bears out of a glum pit into a naturalistic enclosure in 1996 and the Sumatran Tigers received new indoor quarters in 2000. Their spacious outdoor quarters are overlooked by the restaurant. And this must be the only seal rescue centre on top of a mountain having been built in 1997. Other native species with recent enclosures would be European Otters and Red Squirrels. Imaginatively an old cage has been half opened, planted and fronted with a water feature to prevent the escape of the marmosets which live here. There are Snow Leopards, Andean Condors and Red-faced Spider Monkeys (seen occasionally around the UK but not much elsewhere). The zoo's reptile collection is spread across two elderly houses which have seen better days – 'Alligator Beach' contains what surely must be the largest American Alligator in these islands whilst the reptile house has a very dull collection of pet shop reptiles and is the worst thing in the whole zoo.

The accolade of 'National' status is a deserved one for a zoo which plays a full part in the UK zoo community and has to now contend with a difficult location I feel. I would like to think that the new status came with governmental financial support too, it is probably wishful thinking. They would spend it wisely here that is for sure.

NATURELAND SEAL SANCTUARY
North Parade, The Promenade, Skegness, Lincolnshire PE25 1DB

MAP REF: 99/3D
SIZE: 1 ACRE
OPENED: 1965
OWNERS: PRIVATE

GEORGE CANSDALE was a famous zoo face on grainy black and white television screens in the fifties and sixties. As Superintendent of the London Zoo he presented programmes such as 'Looking at Animals' and 'All About Animals'. He also broadcast on radio and wrote a number of books. It wouldn't be unfair to say that he rubbed shoulders with Peter Scott and Desmond Morris as a publicly recognised zoological authority at the time. Cansdale also became involved in a number of zoo projects around the country and his name lent considerable prestige to projects. Marineland at Morecambe is one other that comes to mind. 1965 saw Skegness Natureland open its doors for the first time which Cansdale owned in conjunction with one John Yeadon. The Yeadon family still own this establishment now known as Natureland Seal Sanctuary.

The initial purpose of Natureland was to create a small zoo with the emphasis on marine life. It would appear that the concept of seal rescue came about almost by accident because it was almost 18 months before the first abandoned Common Seal pup came in with the animal living almost 35 years at the zoo. Today two pools contain seals – one for adults with underwater viewing, and a smaller rearing pool for neonates. The Seal Hospital also incorporates a public viewing area and the work in rescuing and rehabilitating seals has become central to Natureland's raison d'être.

The overall feel of Natureland is rather reminiscent of a child's toy zoo with significant houses running around the perimeters of an almost perfectly rectangular site and the seal pool plus a penguin enclosure (African Penguins) in the middle. There is a rather dark Tropical House for reptiles and invertebrates and an Aquarium with thirty tanks representing a cross section of aquatic situations. Local North Sea species are shown in a 25 feet long, 5,000 gallon tank viewed from the outside of the building. The seaward side of Natureland is almost entirely given over to 'The Floral Palace' which is a 175 feet long greenhouse divided into three sections including a desert section with a large cacti collection and two tropical sections – one for birds and another for butterflies. The avian selection is now a rather low-key one of finches, quails, Diamond Doves and a lone Chilean Flamingo.

Natureland Seal Sanctuary ended up performing a valuable function with which there can be little argument, and doubtless in areas apart from pinniped rescue it gives local holidaymakers all they need from an hour's zoological diversion. The connoisseur may find it lacking a little at the sharp end of the collection however, and the zookeeping ethos of the legendary George Cansdale would be a welcome spiritual return to liven things up.

THE NEW FOREST OTTER, OWL & WILDLIFE PARK
Longdown, Marchwood, Nr Southampton, Hampshire SO40 4UH
MAP REF: 100/C4
SIZE: 25 ACRES
OPENED: 1995
OWNERS: PRIVATE

OPENED AS New Forest Nature Quest and surprisingly at one time owned by the Sea Life Centre group this zoo was initiated as a collection of indigenous British species in 1995. By 1998 it had been acquired by Roger Heap who started with the Chestnut Centre up in the Peak District and also now runs Battersea Park Children's Zoo. Mr Heap has extended the scope and area of the collection to include some seventeen species of owl, European Lynx and Wild Boar. There is also a substantial off-show area of pens for the breeding and raising of European Otters as part of a captive breeding and reintroduction programme. As the park exhibits almost entirely northern European species it is perhaps surprising to find that there is a substantial indoor house in the form of a long greenhouse divided into diurnal and nocturnal portions. The diurnal part includes the indoor quarters for the three species of otter kept here (North American River, European and Asiatic Short-clawed) and is surprisingly sweet-smelling despite its inhabitants. Weasels, Harvest Mice, European Hedgehogs are other residents. We don't have too many UK specialities amongst our own higher vertebrates (the Scottish Crossbill comes to mind) but we do have some subspecies and here at the park are Skomer Voles, a subspecies of Bank Vole isolated on the Pembrokeshire island of Skomer. Stoats, Pine Martins, Scottish Wildcats and an imaginative Badger exhibit are also here to be viewed. As might be expected by the name quite a large number of owl aviaries are to be encountered. It is a heavily wooded site but some pleasant glades have been created to welcome in the sunlight. Expect to spend a very pleasant hour or two here.

NEWQUAY BLUE REEF
Towan Blystra Rd, Newquay, Cornwall TR7 1DU
MAP REF: 101/B4
OPENED: 1994
OWNERS: BLUE REEF AQUARIUMS

ONE OF THE small chain of ex-Sea Life Centres which go under the banner of Blue Reef. This particular one overlooks one of Newquay's glorious beaches and has rather a hut-like appearance (the famed Venus Café in another bay looks identical from above). It can be difficult to come up with a radically different critique of this new wave of seaside aquarium which began to appear around twenty years ago, but a wonderfully lively tank for Fly River Turtles, Matamata Turtles and a myriad of small barbs, rainbowfish and others really caught my eye. Anchovies aren't in every aquarium and there are three species of octopus on show including a big Giant Pacific. Despite their sophisticated physiology cephalopods are short-lived so this species can soon change in aquariums. Crabs can be fascinatingly diverse and I was taken by a Sponge Crab with strange pink tips to its claws. The compulsory underwater tunnel goes through a Caribbean theme and can also be viewed from above which is not a common vantage point. It does rather seem that Blue Reef has a slightly different agenda than Sea Life which is to be welcomed by those of us for whom the presence of an aquarium is the first priority on a visit to the seaside.

NEWQUAY ZOO

Trenance Gardens, Newquay, Cornwall TR7 2LZ
MAP REF: 102/B4
SIZE: 13.5 ACRES
OPENED: 1969
OWNERS: WHITLEY WILDLIFE CONSERVATION TRUST
SPECIES: 138

OPENED AS A municipal zoo in 1969 Newquay Zoo is now owned by the Whitley Wildlife Conservation Trust headquartered at Paignton Zoo after the zoo's fortunes were somewhat transformed by the previous owners Mike Thomas and Roger Martin. At the very beginning the local council obviously wanted to merely add to the tourist attractions of this seaside resort and in the late sixties a zoo was a comparatively cost effective way of doing this. But providing a few ephemeral 'oohs' and 'aahs' before sending people back to their ham salads at a local B&B is no longer sufficient justification for keeping animals in captivity and by the 1980's the zoo appeared very dated. Mike Thomas changed this into a situation that the Whitley organisation can build upon and I feel confident that they can take things to a higher level yet given that the economics of this zoo will always be governed by local tourism.

Newquay Zoo is not a large zoo in area however, additional land was available and this has resulted in a new African Savannah exhibit including White-tailed Gnu, Chapman's Zebra and Kafue Flats Lechwe. A Philippines theme has also been adopted in and around the old zebra paddock vacated by the African Savannah. On the down side, there is not much uniformity in enclosure design and architectural statement is often minimal, it is clear that the zoo has grown in a rather ad hoc manner over the years. A new Asiatic area is an indication that this could all change under the new ownership combining a well planted aviary for Red-billed Tree Pies with enclosures for the Asiatic Small-clawed Otters and Owston's Palm Civets in imaginative fashion. Together with The Rare Species Conservation Centre and Paradise Wildlife Park this endangered species was brought into the UK as part of a Vietnamese breeding programme. Sadly these animals are highly nocturnal and unlikely to be seen in any other condition, save for sound asleep!

Newquay's Tropical House is a small one on two levels and rated highly by many. Speaking personally I find it rather too homespun even if it is positively brimming with rainforest flora and fauna. You should see Hoffmann's Two-toed Sloths in here and Newquay claims to be the first British zoo to breed the species. A simple and small Nocturnal House is not far away housing Southern Tamandua, Kinkajou, Potoroo, Seba's Short-tailed Bats and Rodrigues Fruit Bats.

A bear pit was converted for Sulawesi Crested Macaques in 1995 quickly receiving awards from the Federation of Zoos (now BIAZA) and the Universities Federation for Animal Welfare in the process. Carnivores are represented by African Lions, European

Lynx, Red Pandas, Raccoons, Coatis and Fosas apart from those previously mentioned.

The public clearly approves of the 'new' zoo here as visitor figures are almost double those of the old council-owned days. Expect things to improve still further. Clearly the transformation is not complete at Newquay and I feel sure that this small zoo is one to watch in future. Whitley equals quality as far as I am concerned.

NOAH'S ARK ZOO FARM

Clevedon Road, Wraxall, Bristol BS48 1PG
MAP REF: 103/C4
SIZE: 100 ACRES
OPENED: 1997
OWNERS: PRIVATE
SPECIES: 104

THE ANALOGY OF Noah and the fable of his Ark is used quite frequently in the context of wild animal collections, at no point can I ever remember the biblical tale being taken literally... well here they do! Situated 5 miles to the west of Bristol, Noah's Ark Zoo Farm is a religious zoo that eschews evolutionary theory in favour of creationism and the word of the bible. Indeed the zoo is not even open on a Sunday. A large amount of money has been spent on creating a large, model Ark as well as a huge Ark-like climbing frame for children. Enormous effort has gone into detailed explanations of how exactly the Ark worked and how all life on Earth has 'semi-evolved' in a few thousand years from the basic number of species which Noah took with him. This isn't the time or place to discuss religious theory but I can well imagine that most readers of this book would be astounded that such fundamentalism could emerge as a visitor attraction in modern Britain. I might add that some of this zoo is of a low standard rather emphasizing a certain loss of priority. The description of this place as a 'zoo farm' is a very accurate one with a variety of fairly ramshackle cages strewn around a farmyard. To be fair some of these are already being replaced and the once miniscule Reptile House has been greatly enlarged in a somewhat slapdash manner. A tall Siamang cage has also been constructed.

Noah's Ark has over 300 acres at its disposal so one cannot argue with the large agriculturally-styled housing and paddocks for White Rhinoceros and Giraffe. Bactrian Camels, American Bison and Red Deer are also to be found in the paddock area. Rather worryingly the zoo now has Tigers.

We live in a free country and the owners of Noah's Ark Zoo Farm are quite entitled to place their animals within the context of religious dogma, personally I think it is wrong but they are breaking no laws in doing such a thing. What is wrong however, is that much of the collection is housed to an uninspiring level whilst substantial sums of money have clearly been spent on rhetoric. To me that is very unsatisfactory.

THE OTTER TRUST

Earsham, Bungay, Suffolk NR35 2AF
MAP REF: 104/D3
SIZE: 30 ACRES
OPENED: 1975
OWNERS: REGISTERED CHARITY

THE OTTER TRUST was founded by Philip and Jean Wayre in 1971 and has been headquartered at Earsham near Bungay since 1975. Two other centres in Cornwall and County Durham were added later. Philip Wayre was an important figure in the emergent conservation movement in the UK zoo scene of the sixties and seventies, most notably at the Norfolk Wildlife Park. Recent times have seen his interest orientate towards the status of the European Otter in the UK via the Otter Trust, which seeks to both reintroduce the species to its former haunts and to create public awareness of both the animal and wetlands in general. The centre itself revolves around the work undertaken with European Otters although some Asiatic Small-clawed Otters are also kept. Wild Barnacle Geese are also in abundance and a couple of captive species of waterfowl are also to be observed.

When one seeks to examine and dissect the various circumstances and reasons for keeping and displaying animals in captivity the results are surprisingly diverse. Yet here in Suffolk are a few acres of meadow and water which has managed to reverse the decline in population of a species in a given geographical area in a comparatively short period of time (The Otter Trust has been releasing Otters since 1983). That this has been done primarily by captive breeding is a lesson for the zoo community as a whole and a very powerful pro-zoo argument against those who would have it that reintroduction programmes are basically ineffectual.

PAIGNTON ZOO ENVIRONMENTAL PARK

Totnes Road, Paignton, Devon TQ4 7EU
MAP REF: 105/B4
SIZE: 75 ACRES
OPENED: 1923
OWNERS: THE WHITLEY WILDLIFE CONSERVATION TRUST
SPECIES: 280

PAIGNTON ZOO started with a pint of beer. Well, a few pints of beer – millions of gallons of the stuff actually. This is because Paignton Zoo was formed by the reclusive Herbert Whitley, a wealthy heir to a beer brewing fortune who died in 1955. And whilst money was the fuel and lubrication of Whitley's natural history machine, full tribute must be given to a remarkable individual who shone as a breeder of all manner of domestic breeds before turning to exotic animals. He was an exceptional horticulturalist as well, and an early conservationist who bought a unique wetland at Slapton Ley to preserve it as long ago as 1921.

Opened in 1923 as the Torbay Zoological Gardens, away from any significant urban population and with tourism in its infancy, the new zoo grew mainly as a result of its benefactor, although Whitley always kept an astute eye on finances. Nonetheless, a huge collection was accumulated which soon rubbed shoulders with Bristol Zoo as second in size only to London. Upon Whitley's death a trust was hastily formed to take the zoo into the future guided by one Philip Michelmore, a friend and distant relative of Herbert Whitley. The trust's main objective was to be an educational one. However, Whitley did not leave enough money to fund the zoo indefinitely and for the next forty years Paignton Zoo had to stand on its own feet from an attendance base of around 300,000 visitors per annum and with all the attendant vacillations of a zoo in a seaside resort. Progress was slow with only a few major developments for Giraffes (1968), a Baboon Rock (1973) and a Rhino House (1986) in four decades. Yet the animal collection continued to grow with the zoo's first elephants, Orang-utans, rhinos and Giraffes all arriving in the period. My own first visit in 1972 revealed a huge amount of animals often crammed into crumbling old buildings full of atmosphere and skilful husbandry.

By the early nineties it was clear that the zoo needed a major overhaul and the acquisition of a European Regional Development Fund grant of £2.9 million was the catalyst for change. The now commonplace tactic of selling some land for retail development provided further funding and over £7 million was to be well spent, changing the zoo almost beyond recognition. A new name (actually the zoo's fifth!) of Paignton Zoo Environmental Park heralded the new era and with the help of a couple of television series, attendances have increased by over 50%. This has been a remarkable achievement in an age when the British seaside holiday has been in remission due to cheap foreign travel.

I am pleased to report that the winds of change continue to blow strongly at Paignton and this is most certainly one of the UK's top zoos. Upon my first visit to the zoo in many years I was quite disorientated after all the changes, a spanking new entrance area did not particularly help but a new Reptile House had all the 'earthiness' of those old Whitley Tropical and Sub-Tropical Houses, this combined with the current style of naturalistic design soon put me at ease. A recent book about the zoo shows a picture of the inside of the old Tropical House and, as the quip goes, I'm tempted to say that nostalgia isn't what it was! In other words the modern-day Paignton 'jungle' with its free-flying birds truly is tropical in a way that the few hanging baskets and pot plants of yesteryear simply weren't. Next door is the Desert House and I'm not sure that I don't like this even more, enclosures for the like of Gila Monsters and Beaded Lizards melt into the surroundings whilst Hooded Parrots and finches test the length of the building. Even the imitation termite mounds in here have had a UFAW award, one being a food dispenser whilst the other is a nest mound for those Hooded Parrots.

More recent than the above two houses is 2005's Monkey Heights and another excellent development which sees the visitor observe the primates from 'treetop' level inside the house whilst the external quarters consist of hot-wired, grassy meadows (with climbing facilities of course). King Colobus, Black and White Colobus and Sulawesi Crested Macaques are amongst the species here. Apes are also on show at Paignton and once more, it is quite a new exhibit dating from 1997. A bachelor group of Lowland Gorillas live in one half (a very useful studbook facility) and Bornean Orangs in the other half of a very sturdy building. Outside are a couple of islands for the apes which almost vanish into the copious vegetation of the woodland valley which houses the Marie Le Fevre Ape Centre as do some other exhibits, namely Lemur Wood (a walk-through) and an island for Allen's Swamp Monkey.

Not far from the above is the Avian Breeding Centre completed in 1999, a group of aviaries surrounding a kitchen and nursery painted in a sober dark green which seeks to combine an environmental colour with the seriousness of its intentions I feel. There are parrots, hornbills, toucans and more here with a degree of change amongst the inhabitants but on my last visit the raucous display of a Green Oropendola particularly caught my attention. Vital work has been undertaken with the Socorro Dove, probably the world's most endangered pigeon and declared extinct in the wild in the early 1980s. Remarkably, virtually all the specimens of this Mexican island species (Socorro is in the Pacific) are held in European collections. A project exists to return captive-bred individuals to their natural habitat. The Brookside Aviary nearby is a walk-through stocked mainly with wading birds and the endangered White-winged Wood Duck. Double-wattled Cassowaries also have convincing forested enclosures and convince themselves too by breeding here.

The most recent exhibits at Paignton are a Crocodile House (one of only three such buildings in the UK) and a Barbary Sheep enclosure. The former houses Nile, Estuarine and Cuban species in various enclosures as well as a large pond for Matamata Turtles (including Giant Water Lilies – Paignton is a botanic garden too) and an 'open' vivarium for large pythons. I've gone on record before as saying that one or two light-hearted pieces of exhibitory are not to my taste in this house but I should perhaps reserve full judgement until the vegetation has really taken hold in here. As for the Barbary Sheep enclosure, well I've spent a lifetime enclosing bits of quarries, valleys, dells and various holes in my mind's eye as potential animal enclosures and I would definitely have done that with the small dell at the back of the zoo if I had seen it, but the they beat me to it. The result is a bit of fenced-off cliff face and scrub, which I've no doubt the sheep love plus a smart wooden barn to fend off those chilly Devonian nights. It is quite unique and I like it.

Mention was made earlier of elephants and Giraffes arriving at Paignton over the years, the elephants came from Longleat Safari Park in 1977 – they are African and Asiatic female individuals following the old, now out-dated tradition of exhibit – only. They will not be replaced at the zoo and they share a newish agricultural-styled building with the zoo's Rothschild's Giraffes which have bred here. Black Rhinos breed at the zoo too. There are Asiatic Lions, Cheetahs, Sumatran Tigers, Grevy's Zebras, Red River Hogs, as well as a small nocturnal house. The old 1968 Giraffe House now houses Aldabran Giant Tortoises.

In a book of this nature it is impossible to cover every exhibit in every zoo and I've not done so here although every major aspect has been considered. The Whitley Wildlife Conservation Trust has also created Living Coasts in Torquay, bought Newquay Zoo, owns the Clennon Gorge Nature Trail in Paignton, still maintains Slapton Ley and its figurehead in Paignton has been magnificently reinvented. I'm sure Herbert Whitley would have been delighted by his legacy, he is buried in the family grave in the village of Buckland-in-the-Moor up on Dartmoor. Go and thank him sometime.

THE PALMS TROPICAL OASIS
Stapeley Water Gardens, London Rd, Nantwich, Cheshire CW5 7LH
MAP REF: 106/C3
SIZE: 1.5 ACRES
OPENED: 1987
OWNERS: PRIVATE LTD COMPANY

THE PALMS TROPICAL OASIS is an enormous glasshouse situated amongst retail areas for gardening and angling all around a vast central parking lot. In over an acre covered by glass is an interesting indoor zoo comprised of three or four fairly distinct areas. The first of these is actually known as the 'Zoo Room' which concisely explains a mixture of glass-fronted exhibits, Striped Skunks and Golden-handed Tamarins are most notable in this area. 'Jungle Floor' is the next room and is probably the most interesting being full of reptiles, amphibians and invertebrates in well presented vivariums and aquariums. Beaded Lizards give some idea of the quality that can be observed here. The centre of the house is mostly ornamental in the shape of fishponds and flowers but there are birds such as Blue and Gold Macaws and White-fronted Amazons. A final area was given over to aquatic displays but these have recently been largely replaced and the area is under review. Currently, Meerkats, Sugar Gliders and a Screaming Hairy Armadillo are kept here and it is likely that the aquatic exhibits will not return.

There are a surprisingly large amount of animals at The Palms Tropical Oasis and nicely presented too. Easily accessed just off the M6 motorway it is well worth making the detour to see.

PARADISE PARK WILDLIFE SANCTUARY

16 Trelissick Road, Hayle, Cornwall TR27 4HB
MAP REF: 107/B4
SIZE: 13 ACRES
OPENED: 1973
OWNERS: PRIVATE
SPECIES: 175

IT IS REALLY satisfying to see small collections play a significant conservational role and make a contribution to the worldwide plight of endangered species. In some ways we've cornered the market in this type of thing in the UK, instigated by Gerald Durrell, with the result that we have quite a clutch of privately motivated 'doers' and 'shakers'. Paradise Park founder Mike Reynolds was one such person and he started this small bird garden in 1973 in an era when bird gardens were fledging at a rapid rate all over the land. At the very beginning it was known as Bird Paradise.

Parrots had always been Mike Reynolds' motivating passion however, and going back to the late sixties he started a project to remove singular caged birds in private hands into a captive breeding programme. This was to eventually lead to The World Parrot Trust registered as a charity in 1989. One notable achievement of the Trust was the significant financial underpinning of the Echo Parakeet project in Mauritius, a project which pulled this critically endangered species back from certain extinction to a population of almost 200 birds. In Cornwall itself Reynolds was passionate about the disappearance of the Chough from the county and he funded a research programme to investigate the problem. Almost by coincidence three Choughs returned to the Lizard Peninsula in 2001 and breeding occurred in the following year but there is little doubt that the infrastructure is now in place to help the species gain a foothold once more. Sadly Mike Reynolds passed away in 2007.

With regard to Paradise Park itself then recent years have seen the collection move slightly beyond purely birds. Red Pandas, American River Otters, Asiatic Short-clawed Otters and Red Squirrels have been added to the collection. But the park's emphasis is still very much on feathered fauna and over 200 different species have been bred here over the years. As might be expected Parrots dominate the collection with a Parrot Jungle for the larger species including the precious St. Vincent Amazon (which has bred to second generation here). The equally rare St. Lucia Amazon is also here and Paradise was the first place to introduce the public feeding of lorikeets – a fad which is omnipresent in the US but still unusual here in Britain. However, there are lots of other types of bird as well with an Owls of The World area, Humboldt Penguins and a tiny tropical house (where Verditer Flycatchers have bred) all set on a hillside overlooking the fishing village of Hayle. Black-casqued Hornbills can also be seen here and are amongst the more unusual of their type in captivity. Paradise Park will continue with important work in the absence of its founder, of that I am certain.

PARADISE WILDLIFE PARK

White Stubbs Lane, Broxbourne, Herts EN10 7QA
MAP REF: 108/D4
SIZE: 26 ACRES
OPENED: 1964
OWNERS: PRIVATE LTD COMPANY
SPECIES: 85

FORMERLY THE NOTORIOUS Broxbourne Zoo, which was regarded as one of the worst zoos in the country in its day. In 1984 the Sampson family purchased the zoo and to their eternal credit they have created an acceptable and interesting zoo which although not perfect would satisfy any enthusiast making the effort to get there.

In some ways Paradise Wildlife Park reminds me of Drusillas Park in that around half of the total area is given over to children's amusements, but the animal collection itself is considerably more 'adult' with big cats as something of a speciality. This is rather more of a zoo-man's zoo than the Sussex establishment. The enclosures themselves are shoe-horned into the available area and the whole geometry of them is somewhat reminiscent of an archetypal toy zoo at times, that said I do rather appreciate being surrounded by animals in such an intimate fashion. Big cats featured here are Amur Tigers, African Lions (and new in 2007 so-called 'white' Lions which I think are a bit of a damp squib) Snow Leopards, Cheetahs and, best of all, Jaguars, in an excellent spacious cage. Pallas' Cat and Geoffroy's Cat feature amongst the smaller felines. Paradise Wildlife Park was one of three smaller zoos to get involved in the UK captive breeding project for the rare Owston's Palm Civet and a pair can be seen here albeit usually asleep as this species is very nocturnal. There are straight-lined small paddocks for Bactrian Camel, Brazilian Tapir, Common Zebra and Reindeer, a nice wooden Rainforest House specializing in callitrichids and a temple-themed Reptile House which didn't take my fancy despite Madagascan Hog-nosed Snake and a Chinese Alligator being amongst its inhabitants. A Zorilla has now been added to the collection having been absent from the UK zoo scene for quite a while. Another notable singleton is the Black-throated Magpie Jay. There is a bird garden which luxuriates under the name of 'Birds Of Paradise', a clever use of words but one would have to be pretty naïve to expect aviaries full of those remarkable New Guinea avians. The bird garden is in a slightly different area than the zoo proper as is 'Woodland Walk' with European Beavers amongst others. The animal collection can therefore be regarded as being in three distinct areas here.

This is actually one of the country's most interesting smaller zoos, were more of its area given over to animals instead of kiddies rides then I would be even happier. Doubtless the ownership would see that as a slightly naïve comment and I would agree that it takes income to turn a poor zoo into a good one, happily this is now quite a good one.

THE PARROT ZOO

Dickonhill Road, Friskney, Boston, Lincolnshire PE22 8PP
MAP REF: 109/D3
SIZE: 20 ACRES
OPENED: 2003
OWNERS: THE NATIONAL PARROT SANCTUARY TRUST
SPECIES: 90

A NUMBER OF ZOOS around the world specialise in parrots, most notably Loro Parque in Tenerife, yet I can think of no zoo that is entirely psittacine. This relatively new collection in Lincolnshire is the exception. Started by one Steve Nichols in Sheffield the National Parrot Sanctuary Trust was granted charitable status in 1997 after a few years of working with rescued parrots as well as fielding a tidal wave of enquiries, problems and concerns via 'Parrot Line'. Of course, it quickly became apparent that this intelligent, confiding and long-lived family of birds needed serious help on a national basis due to the negative aspects of their popularity as pets and a plan was hatched to establish a permanent parrot sanctuary. Eventually, in 2003, the Parrot Zoo opened on a fairly bland and very flat piece of land in Lincolnshire which is currently undergoing a long-term plan of landscaping.

At the moment the policy here is one of rescue rather than the conservational breeding of the rarer types. The need for this strategy is best exemplified by the fact that already the sanctuary has over 1200 parrots in about 90 species. And quantity is the over-riding impression here with various aviaries containing, in one case, over 80 macaws and in another case, around 250 Grey Parrots. Of course there are cockatoos, amazons, rosellas, lorikeets, lovebirds and not a few Budgerigars and Cockatiels. That such a collection could be assembled largely by the haphazard method of unwanted donations gives a real indication as to the overall size of the problem parrot population in these islands alone. Of course this is all worthy stuff, and to look into the eye of a parrot is to see a sentience unrecognisable in most other birds (except perhaps, hornbills), yet I feel that the parrot family needs more help than sanctuary alone. It would be nice to see the Parrot Zoo taking a serious conservational stance as well, Chester Zoo's Parrot Breeding Centre (an off-show facility by and large) is a good example of the type of thing I am talking about. A zoologist will always take the species over the individual and this needed dimension is currently missing from the Parrot Zoo.

PAULTONS PARK

Ower, Nr Romsey, Hampshire SO51 6AL
MAP REF: 110/C4
SIZE: 140 ACRES
OPENED: 1983
SPECIES: PRIVATE LTD COMPANY
SPECIES: 205

JOHN AND ANNE MANCEY bought an area of land from the Paulton's estate in 1980 with the idea of creating a countryside attraction. For its first few years it was largely a zoological collection based on birds. By 1986 'Kids Kingdom' had been added to what was a fairly genteel place and the descent into the freneticism of today's Paulton's theme park had begun. A high summer visit reveals row after row of parked cars and lengthy queues of paying visitors at the gates waiting to pay a pretty penny to enter it all. Who can blame the owners for adopting this policy? But the unfortunate fact remains that this lovely spot is now basically a funfair with a decent collection of birds in some quiet corners of still-impressive gardens. For instance, a trip from the macaw aviary to the penguins involves negotiating 'The Stinger', 'Kontiki Ride', Jumping Jack', Pirate Ship' and 'Magic Forest'. In all fairness a look at their map reveals the animal collection to be divided into two fairly distinct areas that are not infiltrated too much by the razzmatazz but it does not feel that way when you are walking around.

My two recent visits to Paulton's were separated by only a couple of years but even within that short period I gained the impression that the collection was in remission. Some aviaries near the entrance had just been torn down and I'll bet that it won't be new bird accommodation that replaces them. There is a delightful Tropical Bird Garden based on a Japanese theme and with an interesting collection of barbets in 2005; by 2007 these had all gone to be replaced by more usual fare. Without a doubt the bird collection here is still worth a visit however, there is a good collection of hornbills in at least half a dozen species and the Trumpeter Hornbill has bred here. Other notable species would be Rhinoceros and Crowned Hornbills. Talking of breeding results Paultons was the first in the UK with Yellow-faced Mynah. There are some nice laughing thrushes such as the Chestnut-crowned and Red-winged plus a large collection of waterfowl. All in all around 200 species of bird are kept here.

It would be surprising if myself or the IZES took less than a dim view of the commercial development of Paulton's Park because a British Walsrode could easily have grown here. Sadly the majority of people want rollercoasters not rollers and big dippers not dippers – here is the proof, I just hope they can hold on to what they have as this is still a major bird collection – one of the country's biggest in fact.

PENSTHORPE WATERFOWL PARK & NATURE RESERVE

Fakenham, Norfolk NR21 0LN
MAP REF: 111/D3
SIZE: 500 ACRES
OPENED: 1988
OWNERS: CHARITABLE TRUST

THIS PLACE really is a gem, combining a captive collection with beautiful formal gardens and a nature reserve in a manner which outshines all other similar establishments, even a much more famous one in south west England. More of an accent is put on wetland species rather than just waterfowl and the result is a couple of fantastic aviaries for shorebirds and waders – the Dulverton Aviary is beautifully laid out for the likes of Black-tailed Godwit, Arctic Tern, Bearded Tits (which breed here) even Pine Grosbeak. Another aviary contains Little Grebe, Ruff, Avocets, Common Lapwing, Curlew and Redshank – truly a sight for sore avian eyes. Tropical ducks such as African Pygmy Geese, Pink-eared Ducks and Freckled Duck have an aviary and diving ducks in the form of the stunning Harlequin Duck and rarely seen Scaly-sided Merganser have their own aviary termed the Waterfall Aviary. Ibis too have their enclosure even if, dare I say it, theirs is a little less inspiring than the others. Recently Pensthorpe has added a substantial area for the breeding of cranes and has attracted Common Cranes to the reserve. Now under the stewardship of Bill and Deb Jordan, famed as manufacturers of upmarket breakfast cereals, this wonderful place should go from strength to strength.

PORFELL ANIMAL LAND WILDLIFE PARK

Trecangate, Nr Lanreath, Liskeard, Cornwall PL14 4RE
MAP REF: 112/B4
SIZE: 20 ACRES
OPENED: 1989
OWNERS: PRIVATE
SPECIES: 51

ROLLING CORNISH COUNTRYSIDE provides the home for Porfell Animal Land Wildlife Park – a long name but not a large collection, situated on one side of a verdant valley. Despite an attractive setting it has to be said that the zoo itself needs a good deal of tidying up with various enclosures seemingly unfinished and all haunted by untold amounts of domestic chickens clucking around! As for the animal collection – Capybaras that breed here, Ocelots, a Kinkajou, Caracal Lynx and Common Zebra represent the more unusual mammals with a rather predictable selection of other species including a handful of birds.

A few years ago Porfell beefed up at least a part of its imagery via some rather neat graphic design on publications and the entrance; to be perfectly honest this professional approach now needs to extend to the actual collection. Curiously this establishment shares its car park with another wildlife attraction in the shape of a small building devoted to the Tropic Days Butterfly House, although you may be fortunate to find the latter open.

PORT LYMPNE WILD ANIMAL PARK
Lympne, Nr Ashford, Kent CT21 4PD
MAP REF: 113/D4
SIZE: 395 ACRES
OPENED: 1976
OWNERS: HOWLETTS AND PORT LYMPNE ESTATES LTD
SPECIES: 104

THE BACKGROUND to Port Lympne Wild Animal Park purchased by John Aspinall in 1973 is best explained in the review of the elder sibling Howletts. Port Lympne is some twenty miles away to the south and occupies the grounds of a mansion built between the wars with a quite breathtaking aspect overlooking the Romney Marshes and the English Channel. Opened as a zoo in 1976 it has a quite unique and wonderful setting with spectacular gardens and panoramic views, although it could also be said that the hillside location makes for a rather challenging visitor experience. Some 25 years ago the park acquired an adjoining farm, which was used for maintaining surplus stock. Much of this area was converted for visitor access in 2004 via a truck ride known as 'The African Experience'.

As at Howletts, mammals predominate at Port Lympne and the areas of strength are more or less the same as well. There are important differences however, and the two collections certainly do not duplicate each other. Of course Gorillas have found a home at Lympne as might be expected with such a burgeoning 'Aspinall' population. Indeed, there are two locations for these apes at the zoo and these combine the 'Gorillarium' aspects of Howletts with open meadow areas and are more pleasing to the eye than the cages at the parent collection. At one time Asian Elephants were kept at Lympne but all is now African to assist in breeding protocol. And whereas it might be observed that the above species have 'overflowed' in effect from Howletts, the cut and thrust of Black Rhinoceros breeding has happened here with over 20 births thus far as well as some reintroductions to wild environments.

Carnivores are well represented at Port Lympne and not only cats (including the UK's only Rusty-spotted Cats) but canids as well with Maned Wolves, Bush Dogs, Dholes and African Hunting Dogs as well as a pack of very dark-coloured Timber Wolves. Brown Hyenas have recently returned to the UK zoo scene here at Port Lympne and have already reproduced.

The Aspinall policy of viable zoo enclosures rather than architectural zoo enclosures is in evidence at Port Lympne too with various towering monkey cages seeming at the same time to be both ramshackle and ideal. Notable amongst the inhabitants of these are Guinea Baboons and Drills, both taxa are rare in zoos. Some rare lemurs too – Crowned Sifaka live with Grey Gentle Lemurs, and Greater Bamboo Lemurs are of course one of the world's rarest mammals. One enclosure bucks the Aspinall trend and I've never seen the style adopted to quite the same extent anywhere else. Quite simply a patch of woodland has been fenced off for a combination of De Brazza's Monkey and Black and White Colobus to good effect, but it was the minimalist nature of the fencing which really intrigued this observer and made me wonder if it could be employed elsewhere.

Wild cattle too find a home at this collection with Lowland Anoa, Banteng, and both species of bison. The Water Buffalo here resemble the wild form but are not truly the wild type. Much of the hoofstock is kept on the previously mentioned 'African Experience' which has improved greatly in 4 years but, as an additional charge, makes this the most expensive zoological collection to enter in the UK. Halfway around the trip is a pit stop which includes the Discovery Centre – a small reptile collection housed in two thematic areas, one tropical and one arid. I must admit to finding most drive-around animal experiences essentially unsatisfying and Lympne's is no different even if a useful driver commentary compensates for the discomfort of the ride. It might also be worth mentioning that almost half of the African Experience comprises Asiatic species such as Barasingha, Blackbuck and Axis Deer. The more adventurous visitor can even stay overnight in a mock-safari camp known as the Livingstone Safari Camp.

Partly due to its location I think I actually prefer Port Lympne to Howletts, the Aspinall zoos have always under-performed as visitor attractions and, in the case of Lympne in particular, even the non-animal orientated visitor is missing a great deal. Yet there has always been a sense at both that the public is tolerated rather than welcomed, that is their prerogative of course, but until that changes then these two fine places will not see the kind of attendances that they so dearly deserve.

PORTSMOUTH BLUE REEF AQUARIUM

Clarence Esplanade, Southsea, Portsmouth, Hants PO5 3PB
MAP REF: 114/C4
OPENED: 1986
OWNERS: BLUE REEF LEISURE CO. LTD

PORTSMOUTH, or more accurately Southsea, was the place for only the third of the Sea Life chain when this aquarium was opened in 1986, the official opening being performed by Princess Diana. At the time of course these places were a new concept, in fact Portsmouth Sea Life was the first totally enclosed aquarium in the group – the previous two (Oban and Weymouth) both having an open-air element to them. Ultimately Sea Life was to sell several of the smaller aquariums off and three of these, Portsmouth,

Tynemouth and Newquay, became part of a new group known as Blue Reef. Recently Underwater World at Hastings was added to the group with a new facility soon to open in Bristol.

I would like to state that Blue Reef added a new dimension to the Sea Life brand but, at times the difference between the presentations of the two companies is hardly discernible. So it is then at Portsmouth that there is a tropical ocean tank with an underwater viewing tunnel, a 'Seahorse Ranch', rockpool encounters, local marine species, amphibian displays and Asiatic Short-clawed Otters in a rather dull indoor enclosure. As I write it is less than a year since I made my one and only visit to Blue Reef, Portsmouth and actually I can remember very little about it, which speaks volumes in truth.

RAPTOR FOUNDATION
St. Ives Road, Woodhurst, Cambridgeshire PE28 3BT
MAP REF: 115/D3
SIZE: 4 ACRES
OPENED: 1996
OWNERS: REGISTERED CHARITY
SPECIES: 46

FOUNDED AS Ramsey Raptor Centre in 1990 the Raptor Foundation moved to its current location 12 years ago. Adjoining a farm the centre is perhaps rather more substantial and stoutly built than many of its type. Rescue and rehabilitation of indigenous species of birds of prey and owls are a major element of the facility but the seasoned observer will find some very interesting aspects to the exotic collection as well. The collection is compactly housed in an area comprising less than an acre and in uniquely-shaped geodesic rounded aviaries as well for the most part. It was explained to me that this somewhat unusual shape is to allow some species to 'wheel' around and achieve a flight pattern. It must be said that I have seen various species of kite, for instance, flying fairly frequently and successfully in aviaries so this is probably worth taking into account. There are quite a number of these aviaries and the overall effect of the layout is pleasing – very zoo-ish and reminiscent of a more general bird garden. The Raptor Foundation has a number of uncommon species too, in particular a pair (and a spare) of Crested Serpent Eagles (*Spilornis cheela*) which looked like the lighter form *burmanicus* as would be expected from birds confiscated from an illegal shipment from Thailand. Other unusual taxa included Changeable Hawk Eagle and a juvenile Black-chested Eagle-buzzard which will in time adopt a slate-grey and cream appearance greatly different from its current tawny colours. Brahminy Kites also struck me as an attractive species now not seen as much as they were. A pair of Bald Eagles occupy the largest aviary built in a more conformist style. The owl collection is perhaps rather less idiosyncratic with the usual plethora of eagle owls and some UK species. This is possibly due to the general lack of heated housing which would limit the collection to palearctic species.

In an age and a time when falconry centres have proliferated throughout the land and vary greatly in quality and intention it is always a pleasure to come across a more serious approach to birds of prey as a whole and the Raptor Foundation rather lives up to the serious intent inherent in its name.

RARE SPECIES CONSERVATION CENTRE & ZOOLOGICAL GARDEN

Sandwich, Kent CT13 0DG
MAP REF: 116/D4
SIZE: 1.5 ACRES
OPENED: 2006
OWNERS: RARE SPECIES CONSERVATION TRUST
SPECIES: 40

A NEWCOMER to the British zoo scene is the Rare Species Conservation Centre, just outside of Sandwich in Kent which opened in 2006 on the former site of a primate centre. Although a very compact zoo due to the small area it covers, there is a fascinating mixture of species already on display and an eye for detail which is most encouraging. The centre has already fostered relationships with a number of in situ projects such as the Small Carnivore Project in Vietnam or the Rare Lemur Consortium in Madagascar and the result has often been the direct importation of species rarely seen today in zoos, or vital new bloodlines for existing zoo populations.

The entrance to the zoo also combines a coffee shop and a tasteful gift shop. This aspect is unsurprising given that owner Todd Dalton owns a company specializing in unusual food stuffs – curried crickets anyone? Upon leaving this area the visitor is straight into the Tropical House which features Rhinoceros Hornbills, some callitrichids, Jaguarundis (which have bred here), Bali Starlings and Smooth-coated Otters *(Lutrogale perspicillata)*. The otters are the first to be seen in Europe for some years and again the zoo supports an *in situ* project for this declining species in Cambodia. Also unique to European zoos and found in the Tropical House is a group of Little Red Fruit Bats *(Pteropus scapulatus)*, an Australian member of this large, tropical genus.

Small felines could be described as something of a speciality, there are Ocelots, Pallas' Cats, Black-footed Cats, Pumas and Indochinese Clouded Leopards. The latter two species are hardly small but, technically at least, are not big cats either. Clouded Leopards are amongst the most frustrating of zoo animals – arguably the most beautiful of all the felids, they can be shy and temperamental captives with a curious and fragile dynamic between the sexes which makes breeding fraught to say the least and murderous at worst.

Some of the centre's inhabitants are quite a bit larger than small cats, such as a Malayan Tapir and a Giant Anteater, with the UK mainland's only Sun Bears as something of a highlight. Again, these bears have come to the Rare Species Conservation Centre as part of an Australian organisation that rescues Asian bears from adverse circumstances. The Trust that owns the centre has supplied medical equipment and building materials to this organisation.

The reader may wonder how all of the above, plus lemurs, gibbons, Binturongs, flamingos, Owston's Palm Civet and more, have been squeezed into one and a half acres. Most specimens are in cages, but not small ones and by use of convincing artificial rockwork, water, glass viewing windows, raised wooden walkways and hot wire, it all just about works. You know, I've travelled the globe quite a bit looking at zoos and most of the time I find myself at the more famous names. Maybe there just isn't the time to do lots of smaller zoos but when I do come across them they are often poor. It strikes me that the 'little gem' has become something of a UK speciality ever since Len Hill gave us Birdland. And we still have one or two, here is such a place.

RHYL SEAQUARIUM

East Parade, Rhyl, Denbighshire LL18 3AF, Wales

MAP REF: 117/C3
OPENED: 1993
OWNERS: PRIVATE LTD COMPANY

YET ANOTHER in the chain of Sea Life Centres which has been sold off, in this case to the same company who also own the Weston-Super-Mare counterpart and West Midland Safari Park. Unlike the heavily engineered Seaquarium at Weston, Rhyl's equivalent is housed in a rather everyday shed built largely from corrugated section. Rather too much of the entrance area is given over to cheap food and even cheaper gifts. It is always a pleasure to observe animals in close proximity, it enhances any day and is a wonderful way to while away an hour or two. There are magical little corners at the aquarium at Rhyl such as a tall tank for Lionfishes lit almost nocturnally and I enjoyed a Dog-faced Pufferfish canoodling with Coral Catfish but overall I felt that this was an unloved and uncared for establishment. Too many exhibits with wildly incorrect labelling, tanks containing little or no life, shortage of pizzazz or flair. If the aquariums of Britain are often formularized (which they are) then at Rhyl Seaquarium the formula looks tired indeed. The small walk-through tank seemed to sum it all up – a few Lesser Dogfish, an odd Conger Eel, lots of Sea Bass and masses of tiny anemones covering the glass. Very uninspiring.

ST ANDREWS AQUARIUM

The Scores, St Andrews, Fife KY16 9AS, Scotland
MAP REF: 118/C1
OPENED: 1998
OWNERS: PRIVATE
SPECIES: 45

THE PROLIFERATION of the Sea Life chain over the last three decades has spawned a number of aquariums which are no longer a part of their masterplan and were sold off as part of recapitalization in the nineties. One such place is the St Andrews Aquarium located at the famous golf resort in Scotland but situated on the very seafront with the beach running up to the entrance. Interestingly this aquarium is owned by the Mace family who actually set off the whole Sea Life chain of events back in 1979 when they started the Oban Sea Life Centre over on the west coast of Scotland. Consolidation and interpretation have been the main themes of the second ownership. Individual aquaria have been redesigned and much more emphasis placed on explaining a reduced collection. It might also be said that there is an increasing move away from local species of marine life towards tropical ones. In addition to the aquarium itself there is a seal pool outside for Common Seals. Considering that the Fife coast is not over-populated St Andrews Aquarium can consider itself unlucky that Deep Sea World is not too far away at Queensferry and it will be interesting to see how the aquarium squares up to the ongoing challenge of that establishment.

SCARBOROUGH SEA LIFE

Scalby Mills, Scarborough, North Yorkshire YO12 6RP
MAP REF: 119/D3
OPENED: 1991
OWNERS: MERLIN ENTERTAINMENTS

MANY OF THE usual Sea Life attractions are to be seen at the Scarborough Sea Life including Jellyfish, 'Kingdom of The Seahorse' and various 'sanctuaries' for the likes of Humboldt Penguins and Asiatic Short-clawed Otters. Scarborough is one of four Sea Life Centres doing good and valuable work with the rescue of our two seal species. The latest £200,000 addition to this particular Sea Life is in the form of yet another 'sanctuary' this time for turtles and it is to be hoped that something significant can be achieved with freshwater species here. Not in the 'Turtle Sanctuary' itself but in the walk-through tank is a rescued Loggerhead Turtle from Greek waters and now quite unusual in UK aquariums given that the few remaining sea turtles are virtually all the Green species. Local marine species are presented here as 'Jurassic Seas' and there is also a small 'Great Barrier Reef'.

SCOTTISH SEA LIFE SANCTUARY

Barcaldine, Oban, Argyll PA37 1SE, Scotland
MAP REF: 120/2B
SIZE: 600 SQUARE YARDS
STARTED: 1978
OWNERS: MERLIN ENTERTAINMENTS

HIDDEN AMONGST the woods of Loch Creran a revolution was started by John Mace back in 1978, when a seal rescue facility was started backed by a local food company and inadvertently set off the whole chain of Sea Life Centres. It wasn't the seal rescue particularly as this was a worthy task already undertaken by others across the country; it was the aquatic displays which made the straight rows of aquaria in other establishments look rather dated. At Oban open-topped tanks could be approached from different directions and exhibits were set in random ways rather than in straight lines. In the UK this was a radical approach and through the 1980s the Sea Life brand proliferated around the country's coast before being purchased by Vardon Attractions who were to expand the concept much further before growing into Merlin Entertainments.

Known today as the Scottish Sea Life Sanctuary, the centre is perhaps most notable for its beautiful, secretive location and its history. The work with both our native species of pinniped is notable, the displays of local species of fish quite worthy, but with only 600 square yards of exhibition space this isn't a large facility. Perhaps it is to be regretted that here, on the west coast of Scotland, the species of otter displayed is not our own, but North American River Otters. A rarely-seen exhibit of Herrings also failed to establish itself and has been replaced by trout. This was unfortunate as Sea Life centres need all the idiosyncrasies they can acquire in order to have any individuality. Even here there is a place for Nemo it would seem!

SCREECH OWL SANCTUARY

Nr. Indian Queens, Goss Moor, Cornwall TR9 6HP
MAP REF: 121/B4
SIZE: 10 ACRES
OPENED: 1990
OWNERS: PRIVATE
SPECIES: 37

DESPITE THE FACT that there are such things as screech owls and despite the fact that some owls do screech, the Screech Owl Sanctuary is actually named after neither circumstance and is named after owner Tom Screech! The centre is situated right next to the busy A30 and apparently road improvements have led to some changes in the positioning of the collection itself. For certain, as I write, there is a real sense of 'newness' about much of the collection with brand new pathways, sapling trees and timber-framed aviaries only recently constructed. The collection itself is surprisingly large with around 50 taxa and it is clear that the owners take owl collecting pretty seriously. When people get into various subspecies you can be assured that a certain mindset is in place and one which I rather approve of in truth. For instance, not that many places bother with the exact provenance of *Bubo bubo*, the Eurasian Eagle Owl, but at Screech Owl Sanctuary one can compare both Eastern and Western Siberian varieties of that species. Barn Owls here have been identified to the mid-European race (and it would be a good bet to nominate the Barn Owl as amongst the species of bird with most named subspecies). Many of the owls here are the usual suspects but can a Milky Eagle Owl or a White-faced Scops ever be any the less beautiful for that? Definitely on the rarer side of things is the Ashy-faced Owl from the island of Hispaniola in the Caribbean, a kind of Barn Owl with a dirty face!

One cannot fail to be impressed with the depth of the collection at Screech Owl Sanctuary, hopefully when the site has matured a little more the place will acquire more of a homely feel.

SEAL SANCTUARY
Quebec Road, North End, Mablethorpe, Lincolnshire LN12 1QG
MAP REF: 122/D3
SIZE: 2 ACRES
OPENED: 1974
OWNERS: REGISTERED CHARITY

ONLY 16 MILES up the Lincolnshire coast from Natureland Seal Sanctuary in Skegness is another establishment with a similar function and an even more abbreviated name. Both the name and function of the Seal Sanctuary at Mablethorpe have changed over the years starting rather tautologically as North Dunes Animal and Bird Gardens with not too much thought as to seal rescue back in 1974, but it wasn't long before the waifs and strays of our native pinnipedia, which are rather commonplace in this neck of the woods, arrived at the door. Interestingly not only are Common and Grey Seals 'patients' here but over the years an odd, disorientated, Bearded, Ringed or Hooded Seal from Arctic waters has contrived to need the Seal Sanctuary's assistance as well. Well over 600 seals have been rehabilitated and returned to the wild – a remarkable contribution. And an expensive one too helped by charitable status acquired in 1990. Seabirds are also on the rescue agenda as are any other animals that are brought in to the sanctuary.

For all the above there is a small zoo here as well rather unusually built into the dunes of the coastal location. Not surprisingly this site doesn't really lend itself to zoo architecture on the grand scale and the layout could perhaps be best described as rather informal.

Please do not confuse this description with 'poor' however, whilst some cages for Vervet Monkeys and Scottish Wild Cats are unremarkable then the European Lynx enclosure is rather good with sweeping views of the surrounding countryside (although we will probably never know if felines really appreciate such vistas). The collection here orientates around local species but there is an odd exotic such as Crested Porcupines or Emus. The seabird aviary is a temporary home for most of its inhabitants but does afford a nice, close, view of species now seen infrequently in zoos such as the North Atlantic Gannet, Razorbill, Guillemot and Atlantic Puffin. More idiosyncratic exhibits exist in the form of 'Time Walking' (which traces prehistory) and 'Ice-Age Caves' which delves into the natural history of the local area over the last 20,000 years.

One further unusual aspect of the Seal Sanctuary is the influence of the noted, now-deceased, zoo eccentric Clinton Keeling on the place via CEO Paul King. The etymology of scientific names is fully explained (no bad thing), there is a decent guide book and even a Clinton Keeling Education Room. To be honest Paul King is the only person I have ever known to be enchanted by Keeling's own zoo in Ashover (which by all accounts was of a rather low standard), yet if such a worthy establishment can emerge from such unlikely inspiration then that is justification alone. The Seal Sanctuary is a classic case of valuable work being undertaken, driven along and perpetuated by one inspired individual. Paul King is an animal man through and through; he even sees little need to provide children's entertainment in the form of playgrounds arguing that zoology, geology and history are entertainment enough. And whilst that view may be a little unrealistic today I do find myself nodding feverishly in agreement – inside at least!

SEAVIEW WILDLIFE ENCOUNTER

Seaview, Isle Of Wight PO34 5AP

MAP REF: 123/C4
SIZE: 10 ACRES
OPENED: 1971
OWNERS: PRIVATE

FORMERLY KNOWN as Flamingo Park which had it confused, by some at least, with the North Yorkshire collection of the same name. Today neither place has the name, with the Yorkshire establishment becoming Flamingo Land. Seaview still has flamingos however, in fact three species – Chilean, Caribbean and slightly-less-seen Lessers. There is still an emphasis on birds, particularly waterfowl with several different enclosures running down the side of the site. Humboldt Penguins are also on show in a rather curious brick terraced enclosure which they obviously like as they breed here. It almost hurts to report on a mammal collection of Meerkats, Bennett's Wallabies and Asiatic Short-clawed Otters so predictable is it. The most interesting aspect of Seaview is probably the Tropical House which has rather more the feel of a garden centre greenhouse than a rainforest but which does contain some interesting birds such as Greater Necklaced Laughing Thrush, Great Kiskadee and Bruce's Green Pigeon. A peculiar narrow corridor for a few vivaria and aquaria serves only to emphasize the idiosyncrasy of the Tropical House here. In the most predictable manner Seaview Wildlife Encounter is everything it says on the box with a quite splendiferous outlook over the Solent, and we do indeed encounter wildlife although it would be nice if there were rather more of it.

SHALDON WILDLIFE TRUST

Ness Drive, Shaldon, Nr Teignmouth, Devon TQ14 0HP

MAP REF: 124/B4
SIZE: 2 ACRES
OPENED: 1964
OWNERS: SHALDON WILDLIFE TRUST
SPECIES: 44

THIS TINY ZOO started life as one of Ken Smith's chain of three small zoos on the south coast (the others at Exmouth and Poole have long since vanished). Smith is perhaps best remembered as the one-time right hand man to Gerald Durrell. At times this small collection which clings perilously to a wooded hillside has clung perilously to survival itself and its fortunes were changed by two ex-London zoo keepers Mike Moore and Stuart Muir who took over in 1979. The emphasis was sensibly placed on small mammals and modern zoo protocols, the result being that the local community started to fall in love with its local little zoo. To this day a great deal of work at Shaldon is undertaken by unpaid volunteers. In 1985 the zoo was granted charitable status and the years have seen consolidation of the collection in the direction of a contemporary, conservation-led approach to the species kept.

Given the restrictions on space it is not surprising that Shaldon's speciality is small mammals but instead of the rabbits, guinea pigs and miscellaneous macaques of the early years, such rare species as Buffy-headed Capuchins, Alaotran Gentle Lemurs and Pied Tamarins can be seen today. Obviously virtually all the species maintained at Shaldon are kept in cages but a good deal of ingenuity has been employed in providing adequate facilities. In the case of the Prevost's Squirrels the system of arboreal runways has greatly increased the usable space for these rodents. Another rare rodent on show is the Giant Jumping Rat from Madagascar, critically endangered with a small natural range on that island, it is something of a British zoo speciality being almost unknown in captivity outside of these islands.

Very recently Shaldon has acquired an acre of adjacent land, thus doubling the area of the zoo. As yet future plans for this land are a little unclear but if it can be put to such good usage as the old one acre then I will look forward to seeing what they can do with it.

SHEPRETH WILDLIFE PARK

Station Road, Shepreth, Hertfordshire SG8 6PZ

MAP REF: 125/D4
SIZE: 17 ACRES
OPENED: 1984
OWNERS: CHARITABLE TRUST
SPECIES: 98

BRITISH ZOOS ARE poorly served by the nation's rail network. Unlike Germany where many a train or tram drops the prospective visitor off virtually at the zoo entrance, railways in Britain seem designed to be as far away from the zoo as possible. Even London's underground service leaves the London Zoo visitor with a healthy walk from any one of three stations (and don't even think about the one marked 'Regent's Park'). Yet Shepreth Wildlife Park, despite a semi-rural location, happens to be almost next to a railway station as the address would indicate. Started by a builder (strange how often this occupation has created zoos, or perhaps it isn't) named Terry Willers, the zoo began as a rescue centre and general hotchpotch of domestics and unwanted zoo animals. For many years it was known as Willersmill Wildlife Park. A legacy of the building trade is that many of the zoo's houses are fashioned from stone or brick giving the zoo a professional air rather than the 'Soweto' wooden cages often encountered in sanctuaries.

Shepreth is now managed by Terry Willers's son Jake and the last dozen years have seen a transformation into a genuine zoological garden (although there are still far too many domestic animals mixed in). The acquisition of Wolves in 1999 and Tigers in 2001 (zoo hybrids) marked the zoo as moving up a division or two, to use a football analogy. The Tigers have a solid fenced enclosure with a particularly good display of information on the various subspecific forms, next door are cages for Pumas (now rare in the UK) and European Lynx. More unusual is a recent Nocturnal House which in effect builds itself into an earth bank and uses that slope inside, all this hemmed between the perimeter fence which in itself backs on to the railway track. Sounds bizarre? It is! Inside are two portions, one glass fronted for Pygmy Slow Loris the other almost a walk-through for Potoroos and Egyptian Fruit Bats.

Elsewhere the Tropical House is basically a large greenhouse but with the added 'excitement' of a small area for reptiles dedicated to the memory of Princess Diana (hopefully not for her services to herpetology). There are sturdy, walled outside enclosures for the likes of coatis, Raccoons and Red Foxes. The monkeys are quite interesting including species such as Vervets and Crab-eating Macaques now out of fashion in the conservationally motivated zoo mainstream. Yet still we have not finished with the idiosyncrasies of Shepreth – there is an animal graveyard and for an extra admission charge, Bug City, which offers a few invertebrates, reptiles, amphibians and fish in rather a pet shop style which I'm not sure is worth the extra fee.

Shepreth Wildlife Park is not a top zoo although it is improving all the time, you may gather from the above report that it is most certainly 'different'. In the course of compiling this book I have been motivated by quality in both large and small collections, yet there has been joy at the oddities of our zoo scene – aquariums in chapels, tropical houses in shopping centres etc, for that reason if nothing else Shepreth should be seen and cherished.

SILENT WORLD AQUARIUM
Mayfield Drive, Tenby SA70 8HR, Wales
MAP REF: 126/B4
OPENED: 1989
OWNERS: PRIVATE

THE OWNERS of this unique little aquarium were once involved in another animal collection in Tenby. They are part of the family that once ran Tenby Zoo located in a Victorian fort on St Catherine's Island. The location of Silent World Aquarium is just as bizarre, situated as it is in a 19th century chapel restored from a derelict condition by the owners. Occupying two floors it is very small but delightfully idiosyncratic. On the ground floor is a marine aquarium with various tanks specializing in local species and upstairs comprises of a tiny reptile collection and a café. There isn't a car park but there is a substantial graveyard surrounding the chapel. Places like this make you want to write a book about them and maybe this short paragraph more or less sums everything up but virtue of its location it deserves at least a few words.

SLIMBRIDGE WETLAND CENTRE (WWT)
Bowditch, Slimbridge, Gloucestershire GL2 7BT
MAP REF: 127/C4
SIZE: 110 ACRES
OPENED: 1946
OWNERS: WILDFOWL AND WETLANDS TRUST
SPECIES: 157

IF EVER THE conservation movement had a founding father it was Sir Peter Scott, in a lifetime of outstanding achievements the concept of the World Wildlife Fund (now the Worldwide Fund for Nature) and the Severn Wildfowl Trust (now the Wildfowl and Wetlands Trust) stand out as his greatest, and most enduring, feats. Truly Scott was a man amongst men with sporting endeavour and wartime heroics on his CV. He was a talented artist too. Scott's intention after the war was to study and preserve wildfowl both through the natural assets of the site he chose and by assembling as comprehensive a collection of the world's species and subspecies as possible. He selected Slimbridge on the basis of its appeal for wild geese brought there by the marshy, estuarine, conditions on the banks of the River Severn. The combination of a captive collection sitting alongside natural populations of wildlife was a world first and indeed, although not usually thought of as such, was Britain's first bird garden. In time the Wildfowl Trust, headquartered at Slimbridge was to become one of the tiny band of zoos that can point directly to the saving of a species in the shape of the Hawaiian Goose.

Today's Slimbridge greets the public with a quite enormous timber visitor centre. In its exhibitions, observation tower, bookshops and restaurants there is the tangible essence of serious intent. There is even an animal exhibit entitled 'Toad Hall' which takes the visitor through huge mock bullrushes into a small display of various amphibians including Great Crested Newts, Alpine Newts, Marsh and Pool Frogs, plus a bizarre albino American Bullfrog. Of course the ponds, pools and paddocks outside are the real Slimbridge; others would argue that those wild geese (and others) are the real Slimbridge. I suspect, in reality, that it is the captive collection that provides most of Slimbridge's visitors.

The collection is zoogeographically arranged for the most part even if the Hawaiian Geese never seem to know where they belong and vast numbers of Mallards irritatingly dilute the impact of the collection. It is still the only zoo in Europe, possibly the world, where all six types of flamingo can be observed. And the wildfowl collection is, of course, a mighty one running in at around 120 taxa. This figure is around a third less than the heyday of Sir Peter's vision of a truly comprehensive collection and it is clear that this approach has been overtaken at Slimbridge. Particularly disappointing is the dissolution of the sea duck collection which, on my last visit (2009) was almost non-existent. On a more positive note the small Tropical House seemed much more vibrant than for some time containing Orange-headed Ground Thrush, Grey-winged Trumpeter, Speckled Mousebird, Madagascar Teal and others. Adjoining aviaries for White-winged Wood, Freckled and Pink-eared species of duck ensure that at least some of the rarer species can be seen and identified (quite a problem on the grounds as a whole I found).

In recent years the Wildfowl and Wetlands Trust has paid more attention to the latter part of its name and the collections are expanding a little beyond waterfowl alone. 2010 should see the 'Back From The Brink' a new exhibit for European Otters, Water Voles and European Beavers. Of course the WWT has become a highly respected and valued member of the conservational community, yet again here in the UK key individuals made a huge contribution. Yet Slimbridge itself is not beyond criticism and in terms of presentation of the captive collection is neither the most disciplined nor aesthetically pleasing, even of the WWT centres, let alone one or two wildfowl collections in the UK that are now more comprehensive. It is almost certain that Slimbridge will go for a broader wetlands perspective; perhaps it does need to reinvent itself a little.

SOUTH LAKES WILD ANIMAL PARK

Crossgates, Dalton-In-Furness, Cumbria LA15 8JR
MAP REF: 128/C3
SIZE: 34 ACRES
OPENED: 1994
OWNERS: PRIVATE
SPECIES: 135

CERTAIN AREAS OF our country almost cry out for animal attractions. One of these areas always was the Lake District and it is no great surprise that a zoo situated there has rapidly proliferated and grown. Now fifteen years old the South Lakes Wild Animal Park can count on over 250,000 visitors per year and is involved in numerous overseas *in situ* conservation projects.

In truth South Lakes is not really in the Lake District proper being situated on the southern coast amongst a run of small towns and on a major arterial which takes the traveller to the industrial town of Barrow. In some ways it can extract the benefit of a reasonably sized local populace and tourism all at the same time. The park sits on a once barren hillside which runs straight down to a busy dual carriageway and must have caused many a double-take in its time with Giraffes and rhinos almost at the very roadside. Things are not quite as dramatic these days, in summer at least the growth of trees obscures the views somewhat. Indeed the growth of vegetation and the maturing of the site has greatly served to lessen the unattractive impact of a utilitarian approach. Unfortunately the zoo is situated on brick-red soil giving an unfortunate pink tinge to many white or cream-coloured inhabitants, this circumstance is hard to avoid and anything other than a summer visit will also find the zoo visitor contending with this factor. Possibly in an attempt to avoid this a number of tree level walkways have been created from timber recalling a similar plan which London Zoo had fifty years ago and did not put into practice.

The collection here is rather mammal orientated and also seeks to mix species wherever possible, so we can observe Spectacled Bears mixed with Asiatic Short-clawed Otters and Brazilian Tapirs, or Pygmy Hippos mixed with Mandrills. White Rhinos breed well here and there is also a bachelor group of Giraffes comprising of Rothschilds and the country's only Kordofan subspecies (due to arrive at the time of writing). Nowadays Australian walkabouts and lemur walk-throughs are commonplace but South Lakes was one of the first places I saw doing this. And the zoo has sizeable collections of both lemurs and macropods with some half dozen species of the latter including Swamp, Tammar and Agile Wallabies – all now rarely seen in Western zoos.

As the zoo quickly grew there was some opposition to the acquisition of big cats, initially in the form of Sumatran Tigers. Some farmers even suggested that the cats would affect the dairy yield! Of course these fears were totally unfounded and today South Lakes sees both Amur and Sumatran Tigers plus African Lions. I dare say you can still buy a pint of milk in the town. Feeding of the Tigers is rather a show here with the meat being placed at the top of wooden climbing poles providing quite a spectacle. Nor is the opportunity lost, just after the jaw-dropping sight, of collecting donations for Tiger conservation projects.

There is little at South Lakes for the herpetologist and aviculturists don't fare too much better save for one enormous flight cage given over to Andean Condors, King Vultures and a variety of macaws although there are also quite a lot of waterfowl. The owner and founder of South Lakes, David Gill, would currently like to expand the zoo much further but has, not for the first time, found himself at loggerheads with the local council. He has threatened to either move the park or indeed give up all together. I do not know the truth of the matter at all but certainly his success so far in creating a conservationally-orientated zoo deserves as much co-operation as the rules will allow.

SOUTHEND SEA LIFE ADVENTURE

Eastern Esplanade, Southend, Essex SS1 2ER

MAP REF: 129/D4
OPENED: 1992
OWNERS: PRIVATE LTD COMPANY

YET ANOTHER in the chain of small purpose-built seaside aquariums started and disposed of by the Sea Life group (Merlin Entertainments). Amongst British seaside resorts Southend has to be one of the least appealing so a little zoological diversion is probably welcome although there is nothing special at all about Sea Life Adventure. Initially one is enticed into a cave like area in the age-old aquarium tradition yet those Victorian innovators can scarcely have imagined such poor artificial rockwork as this. Jules Verne and his bolted submarine forms the inspiration for another room in the aquarium which is rather less than authentic. There is a 'sunken ship', a small walk-through, an estuary exhibit but little to eschew the formulaic approach save possibly a deep sea area in which Pogge *(Agonus cataphractus)* relieved the monotony of the inventory. After all this brash commercialism the aquarium then had the effrontery (on my visit) to give over a significant area to anti-cetaceans-in-captivity propaganda much of which was arguable in the extreme. Rather a high handed attitude I thought from an establishment whose sole purpose seems to be one of removing money from sticky-handed daytrippers.

THRIGBY WILDLIFE GARDENS
Filby, Nr Great Yarmouth, Norfolk NR29 3DR
MAP REF: 130/D3
SIZE: 10 ACRES
OPENED: 1979
OWNERS: PRIVATE
SPECIES: 85

OCCUPYING THE GARDENS of a Victorian country house this neat and pristine zoo specializes in the fauna of Asia reflecting part of the life and times of owner Ken Sims (he was a rubber planter from 1961 to 1974). An aerial view of this small zoo would reveal something of the shape of a wellington boot – the 'foot' contains woodland, ornamental gardens and a lake whilst the 'leg' heads up a slight slope towards agricultural land. In this latter part cages are connected and surrounded by wooden walkways offering a variety of levels to view the likes of gibbons (Lar and Siamang), Sulawesi Crested Macaques and Snow Leopards. At the bottom of the slope is the Swamp House dedicated primarily to crocodilians such as Muggers (becoming unusual in zoos) and American Alligators which of course tweak the zoogeography a little. The various species are separated and even offered summertime external accommodation in some cases, whilst the house inside works at two levels with a few reptile vivaria down below. Next door is the Forest House – a small tropical house that also includes Estuarine Crocodiles.

Thrigby could be defined as being strong on felines: apart from the previously mentioned Snow Leopards there is England's only Asiatic Golden Cat as well as Clouded Leopards and Leopard Cats. There are Sumatran Tigers too and special mention should be made of Thrigby's narrow wooden walkways which take the more agile visitors around at treetop level and indeed, over the Tiger enclosure itself. I've never come across anything else quite like them and I'm sure there is no risk, nonetheless there is a certain thrill in that one quick vault could take you into the lair of a known man-eater. Nearby is a walk-through aviary with Blyth's Hornbill being noteworthy amongst the inhabitants. Look out for Painted Storks as well, found at very few zoos in Europe, indeed Thrigby's are the only ones in the UK.

There is a wonderful simplicity to the concept behind Thrigby Wildlife Gardens. You find yourself a nice rural house, they often have a decent size of garden or even adjoining land and you fill it full of nice animals in nice enclosures. You then hope people will pay to come along and look at it all. Usually they do because the public love zoos – and they love this one as well.

TILGATE NATURE CENTRE

Tilgate Drive, Crawley, Sussex RH10 5PQ
MAP REF: 131/D4
SIZE: 12 ACRES
OPENED: 1973
OWNERS: LOCAL AUTHORITY
SPECIES: 96

FREE-OF-CHARGE zoological collections are not commonplace in the UK, or even continental Europe for that matter, so the local government in Crawley is to be commended on providing quite a substantial local amenity. Part of a much larger park in general, the Tilgate Nature Centre mixes wild animals with domestic breeds in a manner which I don't really approve of but then the overall protocol should be remembered and a little bit of something is better than a whole lot of nothing! The centre occupies a wooded hillside which eventually dissipates into a swampy meadow at the bottom. This area is quite perfect for cranes – Sarus, White-naped and the Stanley species can be seen here in various enclosures. Some substantial aviaries house the likes of Common Chough, Raven, Gough Island Moorhen, Waldrapp and Purple Gallinules. Red Squirrels have an interconnecting set of cages and there is a small indoor vivarium which puts the accent on endangered species of all kinds.

TRENTHAM MONKEY FOREST

Trentham Estate, Stone Road, Stoke-On-Trent, Staffordshire ST4 8AY
MAP REF: 132/C3
SIZE: 60 ACRES
OPENED: 2004
OWNERS: LIMITED COMPANY
SPECIES: 1

I OFTEN USED TO drive past Trentham Gardens and contemplate that it would make an ideal location for a zoological attraction. And so it came to pass with the Trentham Monkey Forest which opened in 2004. A walk-through single-species exhibit was not exactly what I had been imagining but that was the result. Although a first for the UK this concept is not new on the continent, indeed the owners of Trentham Monkey Forest actually own two similar establishments in France and one in Germany. The principle is based around the Barbary Macaque of which around 150 animals are kept here free-ranging in 60 acres of woodland and clearings on an undulating site. It is an attractive spot. The species is now an endangered one and best known to British people as the so-called 'apes' of Gibraltar. More typical habitat for the monkeys is the Atlas Mountains of Morocco, the altitude of which determines that this is one of only 3 or 4 species of monkey which could tolerate English winters without heated indoor accommodation (Japanese Macaques, Tibetan Macaques and probably a couple of species of snub-nosed monkeys being the others). Work has been done on successfully reintroducing these monkeys to the wild but for the moment this has been halted. Outside of Europe the Barbary Macaque is an uncommon zoo species.

As might be expected in over-regulated Britain the macaques are constantly overseen by attendants but in that respect the walk-through is no different than the proliferation of lemur walk-throughs now to be found around the nation. One very interesting aspect of the exhibit is that it is large enough for the monkeys to form social structures largely uninhibited by boundaries and therefore they select their own captive areas as-it-were. In the event two groups largely equal in size have formed with comparatively little interaction between the two and they make use of fairly small areas on a regular basis. The zoo theory that provision of an animal's basic requirements would in itself restrict the movements of an animal has therefore largely proved to be correct.

I might have expected that the provision of only the one attraction might have ultimately proved problematical for visitor numbers, but an entrance fee of only £6 for an adult (£4.50 for a child) and some truly excellent catering facilities have overcome this. Trentham Monkey Forest has entered the UK with a new concept which isn't entirely in keeping with the philosophy of the IZES (we believe in captive biodiversity). Nonetheless this is a very worthwhile addition to the scene here with one or two aspects that zoos might take note of.

TROPICAL WINGS WORLD OF WILDLIFE ZOO
Wickford Rd, South Woodham Ferrers, Essex CM3 5QZ
MAP REF: 133/D4
SIZE: 10 ACRES
OPENED: 2000
OWNERS: PRIVATE
SPECIES: 94

A GROWING COLLECTION which initially was a tropical greenhouse and a few aviaries but which is now spreading out in a rather too commonplace non-architectural style. The Tropical House is suitably verdant and surrounding cages contain Hawk-headed Parrots, Red-flanked Lorikeets and Lesueur's Water Dragons amongst others including butterflies. Outside a traditional bird garden is rather functional but perfectly acceptable with Yellow-collared Macaws and Severe Macaws amongst the highlights. A huge bowl of a Meerkat enclosure was recently added (but with only two Meerkats at the time of writing) and you won't be surprised to find that Asiatic Short-clawed Otters, Ring-tailed Lemurs and

Bennett's Wallabies have followed them. If you are fortunate enough to see them (they are usually sound asleep). Tropical Wings also has Marbled Polecats. Rather too much of this collection is given over to non-animal attractions and the labelling contained one or two enormous howlers upon the occasion of my visit but there are one or two interesting not-often-seen species here.

TROPICAL WORLD
Roundhay Park, Leeds, West Yorkshire LS8 1DF
MAP REF: 134/C3
OPENED: 1988
OWNERS: LOCAL AUTHORITY

REMARKABLY the local authority in Leeds seems to have little problem with not only maintaining a few wildlife collections, but actually subsidizing their public usage as well. The bird garden at Lotherton Hall is free to enter and for a number of years Tropical World at Roundhay Park was free as well. These days the latter costs a few pounds to enter but nothing that would embarrass most families. Tropical World was started in 1988 to celebrate seven years in office of one Councillor Elizabeth Nash, a quite underwhelming origin upon reflection and hardly a lifetime of servitude either. Anyway this peculiar tribute is our gain as Tropical World rambles through various greenhouses to give us an insight into the flora and smaller fauna of the tropics. All of this has been achieved within the councils' parks department and the result is higher on practical presentation than aesthetic statement. Tropical World was always rather amateurish in appearance but in recent years this has largely been overcome as greenery proliferated and some of the more blunt pieces of 'architecture' were covered-over.

It would not surprise me if the butterfly jungle, or 'Swamp Zone' as they call it here, wasn't amongst the country's largest, for certain it is one of only a few to appear convincingly as a rainforest. In between this area and the 'Rainforest Zone' is a fairly uninspiring aquarium which does at least look better since the breeze blocks were covered over with half-logs. The pathway winds around another verdant area which actually consists of two galleries and this is the 'Rainforest Zone'. There are a few largish birds such as Puna Ibis, whistling ducks and Grey-headed Chachalaca but the vivarium annex is now home to a few small mammals as well as reptiles. Common Tree Shrews and Turkish Spiny Mice would be two examples. I always rather like desert houses in zoos for some reason and although Meerkats can ecologically justify their recent inclusion (and certainly do as a public attraction) their glass sided enclosure has rather spoilt this room I thought. The 'Nocturnal Zone' is small but good. Five reasonably-sized floor-to-roof glass-fronted enclosures house the likes of Douroucouli, Pygmy Slow Loris, Malagasy Jumping Rat and Egyptian Fruit Bats. Yet another twist in this surprise-around-every-corner indoor zoo. Expect to spend a very worthwhile hour and a half or so in Tropical World.

TROPIQUARIA

Washford Cross, Watchet, Somerset TA23 0QB
MAP REF: 135/C4
SIZE: 4 ACRES
OPENED: 1989
OWNERS: PRIVATE LTD COMPANY
SPECIES: 114

IF YOU DRIVE along the A39 on the North Devon coastal route you will see signs of Tropiquaria long before you get to it in the shape of towering radio masts. This is because Tropiquaria inhabits an old radio transmission building and the grounds immediately around it. the building itself is a huge concrete bunker, hardly attractive it now houses an indoor jungle and a basement aquarium which has recently been refurbished. I don't feel the building particularly lends itself to a rainforest quite honestly and, all in all, it is rather gloomy.

A small variety of enclosures and cages represent the outdoor zoo with a fair mix of callitrichids and lemurs as the prime inhabitants and Northern Helmeted Curassows as the rarest of the bird collection, there are Brazilian Tapirs too. New in 2009 is a Serval enclosure. Pirate Ships, Indoor Play Castle, Play Fort and Puppet Theatre also inhabit the outside section, indeed dominate the outdoor section, to the detriment of the zoological side of things. Tropiquaria advertises itself as 'animals and adventure', therein lies the problem. New owner Chris Moiser is a long time zoo enthusiast fulfilling a personal dream purchasing Tropiquaria, it is hoped that he can place more zoological emphasis on things. There are after all over one hundred species to work with, no mean number! Incidentally the first ever UK zoo breeding of a Pancake Tortoise occurred here.

TROTTERS WORLD OF ANIMALS

Coalbeck Farm, Bassenthwaite, Keswick, Cumbria CA12 4RD
MAP REF: 136/C2
SIZE: 24 ACRES
OPENED: 2004
OWNERS: PRIVATE LTD COMPANY
SPECIES: 102

AN UNPROMISING NAME for a wildlife collection but actually a place that promises much! Trotter's World of Animals is owned by the Graves family who own the adjacent Armouthwaite Hall Hotel- a decidedly upmarket establishment – and it was originally opened as a rare breeds centre in 2004, even now it is fairly obvious that it was once a farm. As for the name, well, that makes reference to the domestic pigs which once dominated things here. Surprisingly, it was the Foot and Mouth epidemic of 2000 which ultimately changed the nature of this particular place due to the fact that all hoofed stock here had to be culled in the dreadful outbreak of the disease. A decision was made afterwards to broaden the scope of the collection and to move into so-called exotics, one cannot help but think that the success of the South Lakes Wildlife Park some fifty miles to the south was very influential. Whatever the reason, it has proved to be a wise choice with a significant increase in visitor numbers to some 75,000 in 2008.

Already a sizeable collection has been assembled on a site near to Bassenthwaite Lake and although some impressive Lakeland scenery can be seen from the park, it is not at the very top of the scenic list for zoological parks (without trying too hard I can think of three which are even nicer). Nonetheless it is in a very pretty position and ideally placed to take advantage of tourism in the northern Lake District with Keswick some seven miles away. A significant stream runs through the park and the enclosure for a pair of Brazilian Tapirs. At the beginning of 2004 severe flooding hit the area badly with the effects on the town of Carlisle being widely reported and Trotters becoming submerged under a couple of feet of water rather less famously, although it is impossible to identify any after-effects now.

These are not times when wild animals have to be purchased from dealers and as a result Trotter's has many of the likely suspects in a line-up of successful U.K. breeding species Black and White Ruffed Lemurs, Ring-tailed too, Asiatic Small-clawed Otters, Red Pandas, Mara, Capybara, Bennett's and Parma Wallabies. Courtesy of hot-wiring techniques many are kept in grassy paddocks, personally speaking this takes some getting used to, lots of room for sure but occasionally not enough climbing facilities. Occasionally at Trotter's, a whole mature oak tree is offered for this purpose and the primates here seemed to be loving every branch. Most notable is one of the two groups of Mandrills from Southport Zoo (now closed) and two youngsters have been born here. A group of Lar Gibbons are also noteworthy and Fishing Cats have recently bred here.

Birds are mostly represented by birds of prey although plans are afoot to create some aviaries and diversify. Much of the collection is kept tethered in the falconry manner and whilst birds of prey are noted energy conservers, I can't help but think that this method of display differs little from the parrot stands of a hundred years or more ago. Exceptions to this rule are a pair of Striated Caracaras and a large aviary containing Griffon Vultures. There is a small and rather dark Reptile House which is scheduled for replacement and a much better Monkey House with Squirrel Monkeys, Geoffroy's and Common Marmosets, also Cotton-top Tamarins.

Simple, clean lines and spotless enclosures caught my attention. A move towards a zoo-geographic layout has been undertaken and this will also contain a certain anthropological approach represented at the moment by a small Native American camp at the edge of the bison enclosure. Zoowatchers will note nearby a couple of Canadian Lynx, a species now rare in Europe and these are thought to be the only ones in a U.K. zoo. Events have moved very quickly at Trotter's possibly accelerated by the unexpected availability of species from closed collections and the future looks bright for this zoo in such a lovely location.

TWYCROSS ZOO

Twycross, Nr Atherstone, Warwickshire CV9 3PX
MAP REF: 137/C3
SIZE: 52 ACRES
OPENED: 1963
OWNERS: EAST MIDLANDS ZOOLOGICAL SOCIETY
SPECIES: 184

NOW TAGGED 'The World Primate Centre' Twycross is at the beginning of a new era after being created, developed and run by Molly Badham and Natalie Evans. No zoo had a more devoted directorship which saw Twycross become a major attraction in the East Midlands yet it would also be correct to state that change and development did not occur with the frequency that it might have. Twycross is rightly famous for its primate collection and always has been. At public level a series of television advertisements for a tea brand used their Chimpanzees for a number of years whilst at enthusiasts' level the rarities came thick and fast (Proboscis Monkeys, Kloss's Gibbon, Douc Langurs, etc etc). These days anthropomorphic Chimpanzees are no longer amusing and the primate species housed are more in keeping with the policies of the European zoo community as a whole. Of more concern is the fact that the long sheds for gibbons and monkeys, of which there are several housing much of the collection, appear very dated with poor breeding records to boot. There are major challenges ahead facing the new management.

I am a great believer that an impressive entrance to a zoo sets the right tone and for a number of years now Twycross has virtually had a non-entrance comprised of two functional toll booths. As I write all that is about to change with a huge new entrance complex under construction which will include a Snow Leopard exhibit. Other new developments include the 'Mary Brancker Waterways' which has totally revamped the rather dark and dingy waterfowl ponds running along the roadside perimeter of the zoo. Although the general theme in this exhibit is an Asiatic one there are also Saddle-billed Storks, Chilean Flamingos, Striated Caracaras, Allen's Swamp Monkeys and Scottish Wildcats. In keeping with the main theme in this area Malayan Tapirs are also to be found and Tufted Deer have bred for the first time in this country. Recent times have also seen the outdated Reptile House converted into a walk-through South American rainforest experience which inconveniently is undertaken by guided tour and deserves a definite thumbs down by virtue of that factor.

However, this is 'The World Primate Centre' don't forget and I have already made reference to the straight, long, sheds housing much of the collection. Obviously this does not include the Great Apes which require much sturdier accommodation. Twycross is the only UK zoo to hold Bonobos, there are also Lowland Gorillas, Bornean Orang Utans and a bewildering array of Common Chimpanzees. All of these species have their own houses, in the case of the Chimpanzees a wide variety of assorted dwellings. Again, whilst there is nothing poor (God forbid that Badham and Evans would have ever permitted that), the housing is uninspired consisting mainly of ersatz bungalows and suburban-styled lawns. One of the problems with any older generation (Molly Badham died, aged 93, in 2007) is that their conception of 'modern' is often outdated. Decade in, decade out, Twycross built in the same way and whilst the ape premises are perfectly adequate they are unimaginative. The various monkey houses are defined by overall type ie. colobus, langur, callitrichid etc consisting simply of a fairly narrow public passage, glass viewing windows and caged outdoor runs. You will probably never get a better view of a Javan Brown Langur or a Siamang but the design deficiencies are too numerous to even mention and the replacement of the houses a major task. It is no real surprise that excellent breeding results for Black Howlers and Humboldt's Woolly Monkeys are achieved in individual houses of a different design. There are around 50 species of primate at Twycross which is indeed a world class number. Highlights would include both Diana and Roloway Monkeys, six species of gibbon, Lowe's Guenon and an odd Crowned Guenon. The last remaining Phayre's Langur in the Western world is also to be seen but astounds this writer by remaining alive to an age of 33 as I write.

Quite apart from the monkeys and apes Twycross is rather mammal-orientated in any case. The Elephant House is another fairly straightforward building with a group of four female Asian Elephants worked under full keeper contact. Twycross has no bull accommodation but is quite willing to access the latest artificial insemination techniques resulting in the birth of a male baby elephant as I write. For many collections this could be the way forward – apart from the fact that as many males as females will probably be produced thus presenting further husbandry problems. Amur Leopards, Asiatic Lions, Dholes, Bat-eared Foxes and a lone Aardwolf represent the carnivores with Patagonian Sea Lions as the lone pinniped species. At 76 species perhaps the bird collection should not be underestimated too much, after all there are Blue-throated Macaws, Boat-billed Herons, Little Pied Cormorants and Montserrat Orioles (only two zoos outside of Britain have the species).

Twycross seems to have developed in a fairly haphazard manner with little thought as to the relationships between various buildings or landscaping. The development of the 'Mary Brancker Waterways' gives encouragement that this fact is acknowledged somewhat and that the zoo can perhaps embrace a little design. This may well be 'The World Primate Centre' but it rather needs to live up to that title in appearance. The initial signs under new management are uplifting however and promise that much-needed change is underway.

TYNEMOUTH BLUE REEF AQUARIUM

Grand Parade, Tynemouth, Tyne & Wear NE30 4JF

MAP REF: 138/C2
OPENED: 1994
OWNERS: BLUE REEF LEISURE CO. LTD

TYNEMOUTH isn't a well known seaside resort. Rather like its near neighbour Whitley Bay they are local resorts for Newcastle and Sunderland scarcely frequented by those from outside the area. It's rather a plain looking place by my judgement not particularly gaudy but not very classy either. Anyway on the very front, looking out to sea amidst an ocean of grass lawns is the Blue Reef Aquarium, one of a group of three ex-Sea Life Centres acquired by a private company. Actually, it is a rather impressive building in the manner of a small airport arrivals construction.

If the Blue Reef aquariums have any theme at all then it would appear to be 'a little bit of everything' to be honest. And that's the way it is at Tynemouth. There's a bit of tropical (Sea of Cortez), the usual seahorse thing, piranhas of course but one or two things did stand out such as a silvery, slippery shoal of Anchovies in a tall round exhibit and I always enjoy Alaskan King Crabs although I end up contemplating that the enormous crustaceans do not seem to get a fair deal in terms of space. Interestingly, this aquarium has a Frog Room and although the combination of Cane Toad, White's Tree Frog, Tomato Frog, Red-eyed Tree Frog and various poison arrow frogs was somewhat predictable, it is still nice to see these amphibians given centerstage. In the centre of the aquarium is an Asiatic Small-clawed Otter exhibit clearly converted from one of those ray tanks that Sea Life introduced to the UK.

On a fair Saturday in May the Blue Reef Aquarium in Tynemouth was packed to discomfort, the North East has never been well served with animal attractions and possibly this very paucity accounted for the crowds on the day of my visit. Newcastle Zoo anyone?

WADDESDON MANOR AVIARY

Waddesdon, Oxfordshire HP18 0JH

MAP REF: 139/C4
OPENED: 1889
OWNERS: THE NATIONAL TRUST

WADDESDON MANOR was created by Ferdinand De Rothschild, of the famous banking dynasty, in the 1870s and 1880s. Ferdinand was uncle to the legendary Walter Rothschild who gave so much to British zoology including the Natural History Museum at Tring. Not that all the zoological genes lay with Walter for Ferdinand commissioned an aviary in the ornate fashion of the English chateau that is the manor. Not only that but he kept Barbary Sheep and Llamas in the grounds as well! By 1889 Ferdinand's cast iron aviary was complete. During the Second World War the aviary fell into disrepair but 1977 saw the appointment of an Aviary Keeper and a return to former glories. A further restoration project occurred in 2003.

For most of its history the aviary at Waddesdon was little more than an ornamental fancy and the birds kept in keeping with that aspect. Recent times have seen a serious avicultural profile specializing in softbills, rarer pigeons and partridges. Species such as the White-bellied Go-Away Bird and Spot-flanked Barbet have been bred for the first time in the country here. Rarities such as the Blue-crowned Laughing Thrush and Black and White Laughing Thrush can be seen in a total of ten aviaries. And of course Rothschild's Mynah which took its name from that famous nephew is here as it should be. An afternoon spent at Waddesdon will be an interesting and enchanting one well worth undertaking at any time – some fantastic birds and well maintained aviaries are almost a bonus.

WALES APE & MONKEY SANCTUARY
Caehopkin, Abercrave, Swansea Valley SA9 1UD, South Wales
MAP REF: 140/B4
SIZE: 8 ACRES
OPENED: 1998
OWNERS: REGISTERED CHARITY

THE OWNERS of this sanctuary high upon the Welsh hills inform me that it is not a zoo. Maybe this is as well because if it was it would be amongst the worst in the country. The sanctuary was created to house the unwanted Chimpanzees of Penscynor Wildlife Park some dozen miles away when that zoo closed its doors in 1998. Other Chimpanzees have since been acquired as unwanted zoo animals to be followed by Hamadryas Baboons, Lar Gibbons, a variety of other primates, Crested Porcupines and a few other odds and sods. Apart from one stout and reasonable Chimpanzee cage the rest is shoddy and untidy with small concrete bunkers as the favoured form of indoor housing. The magic word is of course 'sanctuary', this has enabled one or two organisations to commend the work here with blissful blindness towards the circumstances created. It is a fact that zoos create, on occasion, unwanted surplus animals and if someone wants to take these animals in at an adequate level then I've no real argument with the process. I would however argue that the word 'adequate' is debatable for much of this establishment.

WASHINGTON WETLAND CENTRE (WWT)

District 15, Washington, Tyne & Wear NE38 8LE

MAP REF: 141/C2
SIZE: 101 ACRES
OPENED: 1975
OWNERS: WILDFOWL & WETLANDS TRUST
SPECIES: 65

WASHINGTON WILDFOWL & WETLANDS CENTRE is situated at the very southern edge of the Tyne and Wear conurbation that is largely comprised of the two cities of Sunderland and Newcastle. It is at the very point where the old industries have transformed themselves into newer technology parks and lives amongst them at the very frontier of countryside proper. Unusually amongst the various WWT centres it is not a flat site (although not hilly really either, more undulating I would say) and as a result seeks to create riverine habitats.

The captive collection takes a roughly circular route and, as is often the case, we are greeted by flamingos first, in this case the Chilean species which breeds here. Geese seem to dominate the collection as a whole with one large meadow given over to a familiar variety of species including Swan Geese, seemingly familiar as a domestic breed but actually highly endangered as a wild species. Individual pens house a variety of wildfowl without any particular direction – White-winged Wood Duck, Trumpeter Swans, one for Hooded Mergansers and Smew – all highly interesting of course.

In 1996 Washington WWT opened the James Steel Waterfowl nursery with a huge variety of rearing pens both inside and outdoors, I was surprised to see it so under-used but was informed at a later time that all rearing is now centralized at Slimbridge.

All in all the collection houses some 65 species and is another example of the WWT's policy as a whole of moving away from truly representative collections. That said, all WWT centres have proved themselves to be both a reliable public resource and important habitat for a variety of wild populations of animal, perhaps this is even more pertinent to the fauna-starved folks of the North East.

WEST MIDLAND SAFARI & LEISURE PARK

Spring Grove, Bewdley, Worcestershire DY12 1LF
MAP REF: 142/C3
SIZE: 200 ACRES
OPENED: 1973
OWNERS: PRIVATE LIMITED COMPANY
SPECIES: 136

THE WILDLIFE DIRECTOR of West Midlands Safari Park, Bob Lawrence, reflects in his autobiography 'My Wildlife' that, on national television, he challenged the inventor of safari parks, Jimmy Chipperfield, with the notion that the safari park concept had stagnated. It was a perceptive viewpoint and one I would still agree with over thirty years on. In a recent guidebook West Midland claims to be 'passionate about conservation' yet in the same guidebook I have to reach page ten to find a seriously endangered species in the shape of the African Wild Dog, turning swiftly past white Lions, Bennett's Wallabies and Emus we eventually find Banteng on page 21! Whilst I know that virtually every safari park operates to create a removable monetary surplus and is therefore somewhat hampered in making a meaningful contribution it is still unacceptable that these places have yet to start any captive breeding initiative. (Woburn Deer Park was a quite different circumstance). At the moment they exist merely as spacious repositories for zoo breeding programmes.

Of all the safari parks West Midland is probably the least deserving of criticism having at least sought to broaden the biodiversity of their green acres with the likes of Cape Buffalo and Brindled Gnu. And, unlike Longleat, at least it chooses to keep elephants (1.2 African) which are of course tailor-made for these places. Britain's safari parks keep only sixteen out of the nation's 72 elephants as I write. Did someone mention the word 'stagnate'?

The reader is entitled to question the whereabouts of 136 species if the usual safari park circumstances prevail. Of course West Midland has its White Rhinos, Rothschild's Giraffes, white Tigers, Wolves, Ostriches and other species suited to a drive-through (although no monkeys after numerous escapes) but also a rather decent zoological garden. This zoo is separated from the park by a large pool for a sizeable herd of Common Hippopotamus viewed from a wooden walkway. West Midland touts the herd as the largest in Europe. Actually in truth it is a small theme park which is separated from the safari park by the Hippos, fortunately the zoo is separated from this nightmare of cheap thrills and cheaper smells by a road. In the zoo 'Leopard Valley' displays African Leopards and also enables the safari park to advertise the so-called 'big five' of game legend. There is a decent Reptile House which has had a long-term association with television herpetologist Mark O'Shea so I expected rather more from the species shown. Nonetheless there are some venomous snakes and three separate crocodile enclosures. South African Fur Seals nearby have a couple of rather un-naturalistic pools leaving 'Discovery Zone' as probably the best thing in the whole park. This house is a combination of insectarium, aquarium and a small nocturnal section complete with an Aye-aye. The invertebrate part is very nicely designed and, on my visit, contained some unusual insects such as Goliath Beetles and Giant Katydids (of course most invertebrates do not live very long so these may not be there now). West Midland is a part of a group which also owns the seaquariums at Rhyl and Weston-Super-Mare so not surprisingly the eight different aquarium tanks are nicely presented and also take the name of 'Seaquarium'.

In this volume safari parks have been given rather a critical overview yet I refer once more to Bob Lawrence and his stagnation comments. Many zoos are greatly different than they were thirty years ago, safari parks are not. And if West Midland really is passionate about conservation then it will knock down its helter-skelters and give us a Maned Wolf enclosure (poor drive-through exhibits, they hide by and large, but the EEP is desperate for new holders). I don't think it will happen somehow.

WESTON-SUPER-MARE SEAQUARIUM
Marine Parade, Weston-Super-Mare, Somerset BS23 1BE
MAP REF: 143/C4
OPENED: 1995
OWNERS: PRIVATE LTD COMPANY

THE SEAQUARIUM at Weston-Super-Mare doesn't really have an address as such for the simple reason that it is located on stilts on a beach! Purpose built by the Sea Life Group the aquarium was opened in June 1995 at a cost of £1.6 million. Built with a wooden bridge connecting it to the main promenade it therefore qualifies as a pier and as such was the first pier to be built in Britain for 25 years. It stands 12 feet off the surface of the beach. Since 2001 it has been owned by the same company who also own the Seaquarium at Rhyl and West Midlands Safari Park. Although not a large aquarium it nonetheless has an interesting selection of aquatic animals – an enormous Stonefish *(Synanceia verrucosa)* caught my eye as well as Bearded Grouper, Virgate Rabbitfish and Double-saddled Butterflyfish. As with most smallish aquariums now there are a selection of themed tanks or areas (25) here at Seaquarium they include 'Amazone', 'Ocean Zone' (a small walk through tunnel under a tank of native species), 'Ray Zone' (speaks for itself) and 'Evozone' (a catch-all area for lungfish and Dwarf Caiman). Apart from the magnificence of its beaches I find Weston-Super-Mare to be neither fish nor fowl, it has neither brash kiss-me-quick commercialism or any discernible style, so I would have thought that the Seaquarium was rather an important item on Weston's list of attractions.

WETLANDS WATERFOWL RESERVE & EXOTIC BIRD PARK

Off Lound Low Rd, Sutton-Cum-Lound, Long Sutton, Notts DN22 8SB

MAP REF: 144/C3
SIZE: 32 ACRES
OPENED: 1985
OWNERS: PRIVATE

THE WETLANDS WATERFOWL RESERVE & Exotic Bird Park certainly lives up to its name with the majority of its 32 acres covered by a number of lakes formed from old gravel pits. Evidence of its industrial roots still exist on one side of the centre in the shape of a noisy quarrying operation although thankfully the noise soon dies away as the visitor leaves that particular area of the grounds. The visitor's route is simple enough and very basically comprises of a circular trek around the lakes which are full of a conservative selection of waterfowl and, judging by the number of anglers, well stocked with fish as well. Mammals as large as Yak occupy a series of larch-pole style paddocks and other residents include Collared Pecarry, Guanaco, Fallow Deer (in a rather nice wooded glade) and Bennett's Wallaby. A less predictable selection of smaller species occupy some long narrow cages backing onto open agricultural land along one side of the lake. The range of cages remind me somewhat of the old birds of prey aviaries at Chester (now long gone). White-fronted Capuchins can be seen here and there are Brown Capuchins as well as Black and White Ruffed Lemurs. Various marmosets, coatis and Meerkats won't surprise the regular zoo enthusiast with their presence. I'm not too sure that the park has quite decided what it wants to be yet. The sizable lakes are doubtless perfect for waterfowl yet in some ways are too large affording little more than a vague impression of the collection. On the other hand the 'zoo' side of things is not really professional enough in appearance to take this establishment into the realms of the serious collection that the area cries out for.

WEYMOUTH SEA LIFE PARK & MARINE SANCTUARY

Lodmoor Country Park, Weymouth, Dorset DT4 7SX

MAP REF: 145/C4
SIZE: 4 ACRES
OPENED: 1983
OWNERS: PRIVATE LTD COMPANY

WEYMOUTH SEA LIFE PARK is the nearest thing the UK has to a Sea World or a Marineland. Of course this being Britain we are not allowed Killer Whales or Bottle-nosed Dolphins... and who says not? Well the Sea Life Centres of course! Y'know if I were a cynical man I might just say that a commercial-for-profits-organisation being against species that require multi-million dollar investment smacks of a certain degree of self preservation. Then again we must ignore the 'Splash Lagoon', 'Dino Dig', 'Panning For Gold' and 'Golden Galleon' because this is (voice rising to a bellow) a SANCTUARY! Yes, the Humboldt Penguins and Asiatic Small-clawed Otters are safe after being born in captivity, safe from being installed in any other almost identical exhibit that might be found in numerous zoos around the nation. And of course this refuge for marine life has a real mission – to transform crazy golf into a true pirate adventure!

Amongst all the fairground razzmatazz is actually quite an interesting marine zoo. Some of the Common Seals in the Seal Sanctuary actually are rescued so there is justification for the sanctuary tag here (and Common Seals are quite rare on a world scale). 'Mysteries of the Deep' includes Giant Frogfish and an absolutely enormous Giant Spider Crab in the equivalent of a huge jar to be quite frank. And you don't see Mackerel in captivity very frequently either. Other exhibits are 'Amazone' (their spelling), 'Bay Of Rays', 'Seahorses and Sharks'. A brand new ride whizzes past a few Spectacled Caiman whilst branding itself as some kind of reptilian risk.

I might also point out that in high summer Weymouth Sea Life Park is around the same price to enter as London Zoo and I will leave you to draw your own conclusions from that amazing fact.

ZSL WHIPSNADE ZOO

Whipsnade, Nr Dunstable, Beds LU6 2LF
MAP REF: 146/D4
SIZE: 548 ACRES
OPENED: 1934
OWNERS: ZOOLOGICAL SOCIETY OF LONDON
SPECIES: 215

As is well known, Whipsnade was the idea of Sir Peter Chalmers Mitchell, Secretary of the Zoological Society of London from 1903 – 1935. In truth the concept of the ZSL acquiring additional areas other than the Regent's Park site was not a new one. Indeed as early as 1829 the Society took the lease on a 33 acre farm in Richmond Park, one of the intentions of which was to provide a more secluded area for breeding purposes. The venture rapidly lost a great deal of money for the embryonic organisation and was abandoned after only five years. The prospect of the ZSL acquiring extra room never quite went away and by the early part of the 20th century was most firmly back on the agenda, with proposals either to move the zoo entirely (Crystal Palace and Wembley were considered) or to set up an additional facility. 'Cometh the hour, cometh the man' proved to be an adage born of truism with Chalmers Mitchell a strong advocate of fresh air for exotic animals. Even the offer of extra land in Regent's Park was not considered to be the ideal solution due to the adverse atmosphere of Central London at the time (a regrettable decision it must be said). Eventually Hall Farm, Whipsnade, was purchased and again, as has been oft-documented, an Act of Parliament was needed to close certain public access to the edges of the property and the right to dig flints as well as the right to charge an admission fee on a Sunday. The idea was to provide a back-up collection for the diversity of Regent's Park in essence and even increase the diversity by removing surplus specimens of species to Bedfordshire. Happy days indeed! Chalmers Mitchell was well aware of the plight of wild populations, beating WAZA by some eighty years in advocating a seamless interaction of zoos with the wild.

By May 1931 the Whipsnade Zoological Park was open causing such arousal in interest on its first weekend that trains from London to Dunstable had to be cancelled. Buses, cars, vans and pedestrians clogged the small country lanes around the zoo. It has been said that Whipsnade was the first 'country' zoo – and this is largely true. Hagenbeck's moated zoo at Stellingen near Hamburg was certainly an inspiration and in the late eighteenth century there started a fashion amongst the higher echelons of the landed gentry for exotic animal collection reaching its pinnacle with the 13th Earl of Derby's menagerie at Knowsley near Liverpool, but I can think of no other open, rural, public zoo before Whipsnade.

Gradually the idea of a 'rest home' for animals from the London collection evaporated and in truth the collection became a zoo with fields rather than animal houses. Schomberg wrote in his 1970 Penguin Guide to British Zoos that the future for Whipsnade was as 'a breeding station for rare species'. It is probably only in recent years that this outlook could be claimed with real conviction. Certainly a dolphinarium built in 1972 (now for Californian Sea Lions) and a children's zoo, were more about drawing visitors to a collection that could offer surprisingly little to see in its vast paddocks if you were unlucky on a particular day. Of course the Pere David's Deer, Przewalski's Horse and White Rhinos were trotted out as the stars of conservation, overlooking the fact that the park was also knee-deep in Fallow Deer, Blackbuck and Ankole Cattle. Despite notable early breeding successes with the likes of Cheetahs and Moose, these were often unsustained. In retrospect it is obvious that much more could have been done in terms of collection planning.

For all the criticisms of the ZSL at its Regent's Park headquarters, I do think that a great deal has been achieved over the last twenty years at Whipsnade. It took the park some years to breed an elephant, hardly surprising in that Lubetkin's Tecton Elephant House was not designed for a bull elephant. Today the building is rightfully preserved and forms a backdrop to a lemur walk-through exhibit, but the Asian Elephants have moved out to a purpose-built breeding facility where fecundity can prosper. Indian Rhinos have long been a speciality at Whipsnade and now a whole complex is given over to the species with a quite superb semi-aquatic house for the animals as its centre. Cheetahs are back with a bang and a new breeding facility for the species, with an emphasis on the Ethiopian Cheetah *(Acinonyx jubatus soemmeringii)*. Sloth Bears moved from Regent's Park have a huge paddock, even their own mini-forest! I'm a bit less convinced about the new African Lion exhibit which fails to overcome the age-old Whipsnade problem of visibility of the inhabitants as far as I am concerned. The old children's zoo has for some years now been a bird garden and is starting to lose the 'nakedness' of its early years.

Some parts of vintage Whipsnade have stood the test of time remarkably well – the Brown Bear enclosure still looks like a perfect place for these animals, in fact some of the ancient rusty fencing at the rear almost seems natural. The Hippopotamus complex (for both species) has lost nothing with age and an old Rhino House serves the country's only Gaur rather well. I still think that more could be done with rare ungulates at Whipsnade. This isn't a place that should compare poorly with Tierpark, Berlin's collection of hoofstock, but it does. And I almost forgot dear old Home Farm as well. Over the years the original farm building has served as offices and a restaurant, these days it's the Discovery Centre – a charming zoo within a zoo, with an astounding variety of creatures on show for a small building. The building has an almost Tardis-like quality of appearing much bigger on the inside than it appears externally. Fish, reptiles, invertebrates, amphibians, an odd bird and some small mammals such as Dwarf Mongoose and White-faced Saki are all squeezed in here. There is a breeding centre for rare chelonians such as Chinese Three-striped Turtles also the McCord's and Zhou's species of box turtle. Roti Island Snake-necked Turtles are also to be found but in the tiny aquatic section. I like it a great deal; it's the kind of thing you think you could own yourself.

As a confirmed urban zoo lover, many will suspect that the open spaces of Whipsnade are not enormously to my taste. They would be wrong. Chalmers Mitchell had a great vision and even if I believe that the zoo has occasionally failed itself in the past, I do also believe that today it is meeting its destiny. Whipsnade is a unique place and on a warm summer's day there are few finer places to be.

WILDWOOD TRUST
Herne Common, Herne Bay, Kent CT6 7LQ
MAP REF: 147/D4
SIZE: 42 ACRES
OPENED: 1999
OWNERS: CHARITABLE TRUST
SPECIES: 41

A COMMON ATTRACTION in Germany is a type of zoo known as a 'wild park'. These are zoos specializing in European animals which, by their nature, usually require little in the way of heated accommodation. Highland Wildlife Park is our best example of this type of thing but there are a couple of others specializing in UK fauna and Wildwood is the largest of these. Initial portents are not encouraging as the zoo hides itself behind a small industrial estate, but once inside there is little to disabuse the visitor that he is not in a Kentish woodland. Industry seems many miles away.

Wildwood not only involves itself in today's British wild species but also fauna of the historical past. These include Wolves and Lynx, only Brown Bears are missing at the moment. Of course the European Beaver has caused much consternation amongst landowners as a reintroduction species. Other taxa receiving similar help include Water Voles, Hazel Dormice and Red Squirrels. Wildwood has also worked with reintroduction of the Pool Frog, after the long-held opinion that it was an introduced species was disproved.

As I mentioned earlier most of this collection is situated amongst forest and nowhere has a better feel to it than the area where Wild Boar, Roe Deer and Red Deer roam amongst towering conifers creating the mystique of a Central European scene. Another nice exhibit represents a cutaway earthen view into a Badger set – so often in the past this species got a bit of a raw deal in captivity, but can be kept easily and well as a few places are now proving. I like the fact that smaller species don't get ignored at Wildwood – Stoats, Weasels, various reptiles in open-air vivaria and Coypu, once the bane of East Anglia as an introduced pest; amazingly Wildwood's are now the only ones in the land. Birds are perhaps the weakest area at Wildwood, true there are Common Cranes, Ravens (in a clever enclosure which seems to vanish into the woods), owls and a wetland aviary but so many more species could be here. Yet this is a good zoo, only ten years old and playing an important conservational role under charitable status. We lost the Norfolk Wildlife Park recently which was, in its day, a noted European collection so perhaps we are fortunate that something even better in the form of Wildwood took its place.

WILLIAMSON PARK BUTTERFLY HOUSE

Williamson Park, Lancaster, Lancashire LA1 1UX
MAP REF: 148/C3
OPENED: 1990
OWNERS: LOCAL AUTHORITY

IF YOU'VE EVER taken the journey north to the lakes or Scotland, for instance, via the western route of the M6 or even by train you will almost certainly have seen Lancaster's Williamson Park. A St Paul's cathedral-like dome is the Ashton Memorial named after local philanthropist Lord Ashton (his family, the Williamsons, were responsible for the park itself). In 1907 Lord Ashton built a palm house behind the huge memorial in order to display 'the plants of the Empire'. 19 years ago it was decided to open the palm house as a free-flying butterfly exhibit in rather more substantial surroundings than is usually the case for these invertebrates and it is a little surprising to see these fragile animals fluttering around up to 25 feet from the ground. It could be said that things are not as pristine as they are in many hot houses and one reason for this is that the house really is dominated by the Blue Morphos, Glasswings and Owl Butterflies that live here (amongst 30 or so species), with a legion of caterpillars dutifully munching through much of the floral collection.

As is often the way of things with animal collections in local parks a gentle expansion of the collection has taken place in the area behind the palm house. A Mini-beast House takes the form of a simple wooden building decorated inside in the age-old form of a cave with various vivaria inserted in the walls. Personally speaking I rarely feel satisfied with these troglodytic experiences – exhibits of genuine cave-dwelling animals are rare in themselves and taking Williamson Park as an example, a small but diverse collection from African Giant Land Snails, through Senegal Chameleons and Ocellated Skinks to Harvest Mice is actually shown in totally the wrong context and I cannot understand what dwellers of tropical forest, desert and temperate meadows have to do with caves. A tiny walk-through aviary and a small mammal section that is really a pets corner complete the collection. I spent an absorbing hour or so here but I'm not really sure that it is in itself entirely worth the fairly hefty £4.50 entrance fee, add the attractions of the surrounding park (which are free) and I would probably have to change that viewpoint.

WINGHAM WILDLIFE PARK
Wingham, Canterbury, Kent CT3 1JL
MAP REF: 149/D4
SIZE: 21 ACRES
OPENED: 1987
OWNERS: PRIVATE
SPECIES: 130

FORMERLY A BIRD GARDEN now expanded to include a few mammal species as well. Situated in open, rolling, Kent countryside, Wingham isn't nearly as good as it should be. On the other hand as the park's raison d'etre would appear to be purely commercial I find it difficult to wish them well with the more worthy ideals of Howletts, Wildwood and the Rare Species Conservation Centre just up the road. I would hate to think that money was being spent here that could help the vital zoo work of its neighbours. Seemingly, Wingham Wildlife Park justifies its existence by 'rescuing' animals – I have an issue with this. Wildlife and wild places face extreme pressure from mankind, I passionately believe that zoos can make a positive contribution to alleviate at least some of that pressure – for the life of me I cannot see the point in keeping a few abandoned Fallow Deer alive when the space could be allocated to captive stocks of an endangered species. This whole 'rescue' business is, at best, woolly minded anthropomorphism and at its worst little more than a confidence trick. I'm not suggesting that Wingham is of the latter school but with at least half of the area committed to either playgrounds or domestic animals I'm entitled to be cynical.

A not so positive introduction to Wingham Wildlife Park then! So what of the collection itself? There are two substantial buildings. Firstly a Tropical House with, surprise surprise, Green Iguanas and Burmese Pythons, it is all fairly basic. Secondly the Parrot House which can best be described as a depressing and dark psittacine vault. For me to use the term 'vault' in the context of a zoo takes some doing as I have a strong aversion to the sheer meaning of the word but to see these beautiful birds incarcerated in gloomy, red brick cells was disappointing and what's more it is quite a large collection too. Some bird of prey aviaries looked fairly new and aren't too bad despite the bizarre style of netting used to enclose and cover them. Asiatic Small-clawed Otters, Meerkats and prairie dogs live in uninspiring but adequate surroundings, a wildfowl pond at the top of the meadow in which the park is situated was unattractively devoid of vegetation. Recently Patas Monkeys and Barbary Macaques have been added to the wildlife park. Those seriously interested in zoology will struggle to spend much more than an hour at Wingham Wildlife Park and may well find themselves on the way to the better collections of the area soon enough.

WOBURN DEER PARK

Woburn, Bedfordshire MK17 9QN
MAP REF: 150/D4
SIZE: 3000 ACRES
OPENED: 1955
OWNERS: PRIVATE

THERE IS A LONG tradition of animal keeping at Woburn going back as far as the 6th Duke of Bedford, but it is the 11th Duke who is the stuff of zoological legend as it was he who imported Pere David's Deer from China and laid the foundation for the preservation of a species which became extinct in its native land. Together with his wife, they brought many species to Woburn with a particular interest in the deer family. The 12th Duke preserved the prominence of the collection and it was his son who opened the house (Woburn Abbey) and its grounds to the public in 1955. Surprisingly, the first guide book to the animal collection at that time refers to Woburn Zoo Park. It was indeed possible to see both species of bison at the park of the time but most other animals wandered at will in the vast acreage.

Ten species of deer still inhabit the park to this day and although the safari park is adjacent the deer park is a quite separate entity. The species are Barasingha, Red, Axis, Hog, Rusa, Manchurian Sika, Reeves' Muntjac, Chinese Water Deer and the aforementioned Pere David's. Actually the nearby safari park holds an eleventh type in the shape of Vietnamese Sika *(Cervus nippon pseudaxis)* kept there to avoid hybridizing this rare subspecies which may well be extinct in the wild. I'm bound to say that the spotting of the various deer species is not easy in such a large area and binoculars are a 'must'. Nonetheless, to see a large group of Pere David's Deer moving as one through the long grass in these hallowed acres is a tremendous, if not a little moving, sight.

WOBURN SAFARI PARK

Woburn, Bedfordshire MK17 9QN
MAP REF: 151/D4
SIZE: 350 ACRES
OPENED: 1970
OWNERS: PRIVATE TRUST
SPECIES: 80

AS AT KNOWSLEY SAFARI PARK there is a long tradition of animal keeping at Woburn (see Woburn Deer Park) although many were surprised when a safari park opened on the Woburn estate. After all an enormous open-plan zoo existed just up the road at Whipsnade, what's more the various Dukes of Bedford had always maintained a close relationship with the Zoological Society of London. In the event things have worked out amicably, which they often do, and I doubt that there is too much rivalry today.

If some people think that all zoos are the same then even I would concede to something similar about safari parks. So is there anything different about Woburn? Well a mixed exhibit of Wolves and some ageing American Black Bears is unusual, as the latter are now pretty rare in European collections. The primate forest is rather more than a single type of baboon as well with Patas Monkeys, Black and White Colobus, Drills, Barbary Macaques and Grivet Monkeys. It is the only drive-through monkey area where I personally risk my windscreen wipers by bothering to enter. What might be termed the 'zoo' portion of Woburn Safari Park does perhaps manage to tone theme park overtones down a little in an area termed Wild World by the park itself. There is an enclosure for European Lynx, Land of Lemurs (what, a walk-through, you surprise me!) decent Sea Lion (Californian) and Penguin (Humboldt) enclosures, even a large vivarium for Bornean River Turtles as part of the EAZA rescue package from a few years ago.

There is no doubt that every safari park is about commercial opportunity, it is the reason why each and every one of them exists. And one need only look around the pedestrian area of any safari park to see a much higher level of non-zoological entertainment than would occur in any serious zoo. However, in the early 1990s Woburn divested itself of one significant business aspect by buying out the Chipperfield family who ran the safari park 'franchise' as-it-were, leaving the way open for a more conservational approach manifested by commencement on The Woburn Centre for Conservation and Education (WCCE). Despite its name this centre is actually all about a 60 acre facility for Asian Elephants, obviously this will involve a breeding herd of up to a dozen animals but will also involve public relations, research and a training school for personnel from around the world who may be involved in *ex situ* or *in situ* Asian Elephant programmes. It is easily the most important project ever undertaken by a safari park and one which I hope will set the tone for a more responsible future rather than the animals existing as a financial contributor to the preservation of inherited bricks and mortar.

WOODSIDE ANIMAL FARM & LEISURE PARK

Woodside Road, Slip End, Luton, Bedfordshire LU1 4DG

MAP REF: 152/D4
SIZE: 10 ACRES
OPENED: 1988
OWNERS: PRIVATE LIMITED COMPANY

JUST A SHORT DISTANCE from the very same A5 arterial which heads off towards Whipsnade are a couple of meadows converted to rural free enterprise. You can have your car washed here (or your dog!), buy some poultry feed or a loaf of bread, eat a decent fry-up or purchase some logs. And you can see some wild animals too, mixed up in a jumble of barnyards, paddocks, cages and fairground amusements. To be honest, it is not of the highest standard. There are Asiatic Short-clawed Otters in a dark but otherwise adequate converted aviary, Squirrel Monkeys, lots of waterfowl mixed in with domestics, a few reptiles. A small walk-through aviary is clearly converted from fruit-growing cages but included are some superbly coloured Scarlet Ibis. Great White Pelicans occupy a grubby little corner near a Prairie Marmot exhibit. And there are lemurs – Black and White Ruffed and Ring-tailed, the former species in particular is endangered of course and in my childhood was a very rare zoo animal indeed. Did we really succeed with this species in captivity to see them end up in catchpenny establishments such as this? Other than that, one could regard Woodside as a harmless entertainment aimed primarily at children apart from the fact that it exists so near to such a serious and worthy establishment as Whipsnade. I can forgive Woodside much by virtue of its sheer irrelevance, but I cannot forgive it removing even one pound from the serious zoology up the road and on an odd occasion that must surely happen.

WORLD OWL CENTRE

Muncaster Castle, Ravenglass, Cumbria CA18 1RQ

MAP REF: 153/C3
SIZE: 10 ACRES
OPENED: 1988
OWNERS: REGISTERED CHARITY
SPECIES: 48

WE LIVE IN an 'owl nation', or so it often seems these days, yet this is a recent syndrome and one that can be traced back to the World Owl Centre when it opened in 1988 for it was in fact the first such specialist centre in the world. Occupying the spectacular grounds of Muncaster Castle on the coastal fringe of the Lake District, there had in fact been a bird garden at the castle since 1970 which even included a pair of Asiatic Black Bears. The remnants of the bird garden – including those bears – were taken over by Tony Warburton and the British Owl Breeding and Release Scheme in 1987. A brave new era was born and it would be incorrect to regard the World Owl Centre as a continuum of the old Muncaster Castle Bird Garden. After all, a serious and well-defined role had begun which was essentially at odds with the old haphazard animal attraction.

Over twenty years on and the World Owl Centre can be justifiably proud of its contribution towards conservation. A notable collection of around 50 taxa of owl has been built up, amongst these are Mottled Owl, Magellan Horned Owl, Pallid Scops Owl, Pharaoh Eagle Owl, Ashy-faced Owl and Buffy Fish Owl; expect to see over 160 owls at any one time. The collection is housed in two major sections. First of these are the original ranges of aviaries which contain the larger species and subspecies including the 90 foot long Layburn Aviary which houses all the UK species of owl communally (without taking the position of the Eagle Owl and Snowy Owl in British ornithology too seriously!). A set of steps then takes the visitor to the Owl Garden where the smaller species are maintained. Red Kites are also kept here. As might be expected the World Owl Trust has an impressive breeding record and particularly with some of the smaller, trickier species such as the European Pygmy Owl or Ferruginous Pygmy Owl.

Clearly Tony Warburton always wanted to make a difference to the natural world, to attempt to redress imbalances caused by mankind. His Barn Owl release scheme released well over one thousand captive-bred Barn Owls into the wild, enforcing the notion (often in the face of vociferous opposition) that this policy can work and work well. In places such as Nepal, India and particularly the Philippines, the World Owl Trust has made significant contributions to *in situ* conservation projects as well. The Trust has done whatever it can for owls and their habitats. As far as I am concerned it is a model for the smaller animal collection in terms of commitment, application and dedication.

YORKSHIRE WILDLIFE PARK

Brockholes Lane, Branton, Doncaster, South Yorkshire DN3 3NH
MAP REF: 154/C3
SIZE: 25 ACRES
OPENED: 2009
OWNERS: PRIVATE LIMITED COMPANY
SPECIES: 20

IF THERE WAS ONE area in the whole of the United Kingdom that has long cried out for a wildlife attraction then it is the highly urbanized county of South Yorkshire. In the fifties there was a brief attempt to start a zoo in Doncaster but basically the Sheffields, Rotherhams and Barnsleys have never been accorded such a worthy institution. Now South Yorkshire has such a place, and although fairly modest at the moment the signs are encouraging, the location just right.

The zoo is on the site of a former riding school and the courtyard here has been converted into an entrance area of some professionalism including excellent catering facilities. Poor zoos always have poor cafes so I suppose the signs are encouraging. Major exhibits in this, the very first summer, would be Lemur Woods and an African Savannah with a large group of Kafue Flats Red Lechwe. There is a bachelor group of African Wild Dogs in a pleasant enclosure and Raccoon Dogs which are a rare exhibit in the UK. A high profile scheme is currently underway to rescue a group of African Lions from a Romanian 'slum' zoo and bring them to the Yorkshire Wildlife Park. The more idiosyncratic side of this collection is represented by Guayaquil Squirrels.

As yet it is early days obviously but intentions are right and the first exhibits well made. If my zoo radar is in any way tuned in the Yorkshire Wildlife Park could be in for quite a successful ride.

SMALLER WILDLIFE ATTRACTIONS

ENGLAND

• ALFORD
CLAYTHORPE WATERMILL & WATERFOWL GARDENS
Claythorpe, Alford, Lincolnshire

Some 300 birds up to the size of Grey-necked Crowned Crane, Chilean Flamingo and White Stork but mostly waterfowl.

• ALTON
ALTON TOWERS RESORT
Alton, Staffordshire

The addition of a Sea Life Centre via the theme park's mutual owners is hardly likely to overcome a rather steep admission price as far as zoo enthusiasts are concerned, especially as the aquatic element replicates the more predictable elements of the Sea Life brand here touted as 'Sharkbait Reef'.

• BARROW-IN-FURNESS
FURNESS OWLS
Sandscale Park, Barrow-In-Furness, Cumbria

Opened in 2006 and now home to over 100 owls. Furness Reptiles is planned on the same site in the near future. No permanent buildings are allowed on the site so all structures are of a temporary nature.

• BEDALE
FALCONS OF THORP PERROW
The Walled Garden, Thorp Perrow Arboretum, Bedale, North Yorkshire

A fairly extensive collection of birds of prey in beautiful surroundings has now moved into mammals such as Raccoons, Meerkats and wallabies.

• BERKELEY
BERKELEY CASTLE BUTTERFLY CENTRE
Berkeley Castle, Berkeley, Gloucestershire

• BIGGLESWADE
ENGLISH SCHOOL OF FALCONRY BIRD OF PREY CENTRE
Old Warden Park, Biggleswade, Bedfordshire

• BIRDHAM
SUSSEX FALCONRY CENTRE
Locksacre Farm, Wophams Lane, Birdham, W. Sussex

• BLACKBURN
VISITOR CENTRE WITTON COUNTRY PARK
Preston Old Rd, Blackburn, Lancashire

An indoor collection of British small mammals such as Harvest Mice and Bank Voles.

• BLENHEIM PALACE
BLENHEIM PALACE BUTTERFLY HOUSE
Blenheim Palace, Oxfordshire

• BIDEFORD
MILKY WAY ADVENTURE PARK BIRD OF PREY CENTRE
Milky Way Adventure Park, Nr Clovelly, Bideford, Devon

• BOLTON
ANIMAL WORLD
Moss Bank Park, Bolton, Greater Manchester

A small free-of-charge children's zoo populated mostly by domestics and with a small Butterfly House.

BOLTON MUNICIPAL AQUARIUM
Le Mans Crescent, Bolton, Greater Manchester

Situated in the basement of Bolton Town Hall is a small aquarium of some ten tanks originally opened in 1939. Rare Madagascan cichlids such as the Pinstripe Damba now extinct in the wild are kept and bred here. Other fish include Ripsaw Catfish and Giant Green Knifefish.

SMALLER WILDLIFE ATTRACTIONS

- BRIDLINGTON
SEWERBY HALL ZOO
Sewerby Park, Bridlington, East Yorkshire

There has been a small zoo in the grounds of stately Sewerby Hall since 1946. A group of around a dozen Humboldt Penguins are probably the highlight. In addition there are some aviaries, Rheas and capuchin monkeys.

- BRISTOL
BRISTOL CITY MUSEUM & ART GALLERY AQUARIUM
Queens Road, Bristol

A small freshwater aquarium for local species.

- BUCKFASTLEIGH
BUCKFAST BUTTERFLIES & DARTMOOR OTTER SANCTUARY
The Station, Buckfastleigh, Devon

Three species of otter – Eurasian, North America River and Asiatic Short-clawed plus a butterfly house.

- CLACTON ON SEA
CLACTON PIER SEAQUARIUM
Clacton Pier, Clacton On Sea, Essex

A small aquarium with some 18 tanks split quite evenly between marine and freshwater species. The old end-of-pier animal entertainment is not quite dead!

- CLEETHORPES
THE JUNGLE ZOO
Lakeside, Kings Road, Cleethorpes, Lincolnshire

Originally opened as a butterfly house in 1998 this small zoo centres around an indoor tropical house with reptiles, a few parrots and Sulphur-breasted Toucans. Outdoors there is uninspiring accommodation for capuchins, Ring-tailed Lemurs and Meerkats.

- CHIPPING
BOWLAND WILD BOAR PARK
Chipping, Nr Preston, Lancs

- CRANHAM
PRINKNASH BIRD & DEER PARK
Cranham, Gloucestershire

A rather pleasant 9 acres of wooded valley with an idiosyncratic combination of waterfowl, pheasants and Fallow Deer mixed in with small architectural Follies. The park was started by the artist Philip Meigh in the early 1970s.

- EAST AYTON
BETTON BIRDS OF PREY & CONSERVATION CENTRE
Betton Farm Visitor Centre, Race Course Road East Ayton, Nr Scarborough, North Yorkshire

- ECCLESHALL
GENTLESHAW BIRDS OF PREY & WILDLIFE CENTRE
Fletcher's Country Garden Centre, Stone Road, Eccleshall, Staffordshire

Founded in 1993 as a centre for rescuing unwanted exotic mammals, reptiles and birds of prey. Surprisingly animals as large as a Puma can be found here as can Rhesus Monkeys, Raccoons, Coatis and others. Until recently the centre looked quite run-down but an effort has been made to provide better enclosures and a more pleasant environment.

- FILEY
FILEY BIRD GARDEN & ANIMAL PARK
East Lea Farmhouse, Scarborough Road, Filey, North Yorks

A recently opened (May 2008) collection of the commoner aviary birds and some domestic breeds of other animals.

- HIGHBRIDGE
ALSTONE WILDLIFE PARK
Alstone Hall, Alstone Road, Highbridge, Somerset

A small childrens zoo with Bactrian Camels, Emus, deer and owls amongst the domestic animals.

SMALLER WILDLIFE ATTRACTIONS

- **GIGGLESWICK**
YORKSHIRE DALES FALCONRY CENTRE
Crows Nest Road, Nr Giggleswick, Settle, North Yorks

- **GODALMING**
BUSBRIDGE LAKES EXOTIC WATERBIRDS & GARDENS
Hambledon Road, Godalming, Surrey

A large and impressive collection of wildfowl (130 taxa) held and often bred in the idyllic grounds of Busbridge Hall. Were it not for the fact that this collection is only open for a few days per year, around Bank Holidays, then it would have easily warranted a main review.

- **GREAT ELLINGHAM**
GREAT ELLINGHAM TROPICAL BUTTERFLY WORLD
Long St Nursery & Garden Centre, Great Ellingham, Norfolk

- **GREAT YARMOUTH**
AMAZONIA WORLD OF REPTILES
Marine Parade, Great Yarmouth, Suffolk

On the seafront around 100 yards from the Sea Life Centre. An indoor display of around 50 species of reptile, amphibian and invertebrates. A fairly predictable selection but quite good on geckos plus there is a large American Alligator and Cuvier's Dwarf Caiman.

- **GUERNSEY**
THE GUERNSEY AQUARIUM
La Vallette, St Peter Port, Guernsey, Channel Islands

- **HAGLEY**
FALCONRY CENTRE (HAGLEY)
Kidderminster Road South, Hagley, West Midlands

Quite a large collection of birds of prey and owls including vultures, African Fish Owl, Golden Eagle, Bateleur Eagle.

- **HARLESTON**
OASIS CAMEL CENTRE
Orchard Farm, Cratfield Road, Linstead, Halesworth, Suffolk

All the camelid species apart from Vicunas.

- **HECKMONDWIKE**
PONDEROSA RURAL THERAPEUTIC CENTRE & RARE BREEDS FARM
Off Smithies Lane, Heckmondwike, W. Yorks

Founded in 1992 to help bridge the gap between able-bodied and disabled people there are a surprising variety of animals at the farm including Military Macaw, Boobook Owl, Brown Lemurs, Reindeer, even a Brazilian Tapir! Also a number of reptiles.

- **HEMPSTED**
THE BARN OWL CENTRE OF GLOUCESTERSHIRE
Netheridge Farm, Netheridge Close, Hempsted, Gloucestershire

A new home (2008) for this Barn Owl conservation body established in 1997. Plans are to build an extensive centre with some 34 aviaries and incorporating a Bird of Prey Centre, at the moment a modest temporary centre is available for visitors.

- **HOLDENBY**
HOLDENBY HOUSE FALCONRY CENTRE
Holdenby House, Holdenby, Northamptonshire

- **HORSHAM**
HUXLEYS BIRDS OF PREY
Hillier's Garden Centre, Brighton Road, Horsham, West Sussex

- **IPPLEDEN**
DEVON BIRD OF PREY CENTRE
Fermoys Garden Centre, Totnes Road, Ippleden, Devon

SMALLER WILDLIFE ATTRACTIONS

- **ISLE OF WIGHT**
BUTTERFLY & FOUNTAIN WORLD
Staplers Road, Wootton, Isle Of Wight

FORT VICTORIA MARINE AQUARIUM
Fort Victoria, Isle Of Wight

A tiny marine aquarium housed in a couple of arches within the 19th century Fort Victoria. Mostly local species. Opened in 1984.

ISLE OF WIGHT OWL & FALCONRY CENTRE
Appuldurcombe House, Isle Of Wight

OWL & MONKEY HAVEN
Five Acres, Staplers Road, Newport, Isle of Wight

As I write, this collection aimed at housing surplus primates from other zoos is still to open but work is well underway. Expect it to be visitable in 2010.

- **KIELDER WATER**
KIELDER WATER BIRD OF PREY CENTRE
Leaplish Waterside Park, Kielder, Hexham, Northumberland

- **KINGTON**
SMALL BREEDS FARM PARK & OWL CENTRE
Kington, Herefordshire

A fairly sizeable collection of owls, with a few less commonly observed, smaller species. Also to be found here are some waterfowl, pheasants and Red Squirrels (the latter being housed in a cage from the defunct Windsor Safari Park).

- **KNUTSFORD**
GAUNTLET BIRD OF PREY, EAGLE & VULTURE PARK
Next To Fryer's Rose Nursery, Manchester Road, Knutsford, Cheshire

Over 40 species of bird of prey and owl. This centre works with a South African research programme for the African White-backed vulture as well as the Gyps Vulture Restoration Project in Pakistan which is working with the critically endangered Oriental White-backed Vulture.

- **LANGWATHBY**
EDEN OSTRICH WORLD
Langwathby, Nr Penrith, Cumbria

A farm given over to a few exotic species such as three different ratites, Collared Peccary, Crested Porcupines and Raccoon Dogs.

- **LANREATH**
TROPIC DAYS BUTTERFLY HOUSE
Porfell Animal Land, Trecangate, Nr Lanreath, Liskeard, Cornwall

A tiny butterfly house situated on the edge of the car park at Porfell Animal Land but a quite separate entity.

- **LAUNCESTON**
TAMAR OTTER & WILDLIFE CENTRE
North Petherwin, Nr Launceston, Cornwall

Eurasian and Asiatic Short-clawed Otters plus deer, owls and waterfowl.

- **LINCOLN**
WOODSIDE WILDLIFE & FALCONRY PARK
Newball Wood, Nr Langworth, Lincolnshire

- **LIVERPOOL**
WORLD MUSEUM
William Brown St, Liverpool, Merseyside

This substantial museum housed technically the third aquarium in the world. Records show fish tanks displayed as early as 1857. The current aquarium dates back to the 1930s and was recently refurbished. There are six larger thematic tanks plus around a dozen smaller ones. Elsewhere in the museum is a rather nicely presented invertebrate room, small but with living species.

SMALLER WILDLIFE ATTRACTIONS

• LONDON
BRENT LODGE ANIMAL CENTRE
Brent Lodge Park, London

A small free-of-charge park zoo run by Ealing Council. Nonetheless it is of sufficient stature to belong to BIAZA and has undertaken a Hazel Dormouse breeding programme. The largest animals would be Common Rhea but there is also an indoor area with callitrichids, Turkish Spiny Mice, reptiles and invertebrates.

GOLDERS HILL PARK ZOO
Golders Hill Park, West Heath Ave, London

A small parks zoo that until recently housed a fair collection of tropical birds in two main blocks of aviaries. Unfortunately the collection was almost entirely owned by a private individual who removed the birds in 2007. Decent enclosures remain but have remained empty for some time now so clearly the solution is not a simple one. Paddocks remain for Mara, Rhea and Fallow Deer.

KEW GARDENS (ROYAL BOTANIC GARDENS)
Kew Road, Richmond, London

Surprisingly this world famous botanic gardens actually has a couple of small but rather decent aquariums. In the basement of the 1848 Palm House is a marine display of a dozen tanks and tropical freshwater aquaria can be found in The Princess of Wales Conservatory. Also in the latter building Mountain Horned Dragons *(Acanthosaura armata)* run at liberty as a biological pest control.

NATURAL HISTORY MUSEUM
Cromwell Road, London

A butterfly exhibit was opened in the summer of 2009 at the famous museum. At the time of writing this exhibition runs from May to September. It is not known if it is likely to become a permanent feature.

• LONG SUTTON
THE BUTTERFLY & WILDLIFE PARK
Long Sutton, Spalding, Lincs

A tropical house of some size is the main feature here. Butterflies predominate but there are some reptiles as well. There are half a dozen aviaries and a birds of prey centre. Brush-tailed Possums can also be seen here and are not a species found frequently outside of Australia and New Zealand (where they are an introduced species).

• LYME REGIS
LYME REGIS MARINE AQUARIUM
The Cobb, Lyme Regis, Dorset

A small collection of local marine species housed in an 18th century harbour building known as the Cobb. The aquarium first opened in 1958.

• MANSFIELD
SHERWOOD FOREST FARM PARK
Lambs Pen Farm, Edwinstone, Nr Mansfield, Nottinghamshire

Basically specializing in rare domestic breeds but also has Mara, wallabies, Water Buffalo and wildfowl.

• MATLOCK BATH
MATLOCK BATH AQUARIUM
110 North Parade, Matlock Bath, Derbyshire

• MEVAGISSEY
MEVAGISSEY HARBOUR AQUARIUM
Old Boat House, Mevagissey, Cornwall

Opened in 1955 the aquarium is housed in the former Lifeboat House. Following structural problems the aquarium closed in 2004 to open two years later with £50,000 spent on refurbishments raised locally and with some help from the Heritage Lottery Fund. Admission is free and the aquarium specializes in local species.

SMALLER WILDLIFE ATTRACTIONS

- **MELTON MOWBRAY**
GAUNTLET BIRDS OF PREY
Twin Lakes Theme Park, Melton Spinney Road, Melton Mowbray, Leicestershire

- **NORTHWICH**
CHESHIRE WATERLIFE, AQUATIC & FALCONRY CENTRE
Blakemere Craft Centre, Chester Road, Sandiway, Northwich, Cheshire

- **NORTH ANSTON**
TROPICAL BUTTERFLY HOUSE & FALCONRY CENTRE
Woodsetts Road, North Anston, Sheffield, South Yorkshire

A tropical house with a small garden attached with a few aviaries and a bewildering assortment of other attractions and facilities even including a private daytime nursery.

- **OAKHAM**
RUTLAND FALCONRY & OWL CENTRE
Burley Bushes, Exton Lane, Oakham, Rutland

- **PENRITH**
LAKELAND BIRD OF PREY CENTRE
Lowther Castle, Lowther, Penrith, Cumbria

- **PORLOCK**
EXMOOR FALCONRY & ANIMAL FARM
West Lynch Farm, Allerford, Nr Porlock, Somerset

Includes the 'World of Owls Barn'.

- **PORT ISAAC**
PORT ISAAC HARBOUR AQUARIUM
Port Isaac, Cornwall

- **PRESTON**
TURBARY WOODS OWL & BIRDS OF PREY SANCTUARY
92 Chain House Lane, Whitestake, Preston, Lancs

- **REEDHAM**
PETTITTS ANIMAL ADVENTURE PARK
Church Road, Reedham, Norfolk

Mara, Raccoons, callitrichids, Ring-tailed Lemur, owls etc but much more in the way of amusements and rides.

- **REDCAR**
KIRKLEATHAM OWL & ENDANGERED SPECIES CENTRE
Kirkleatham Village, Redcar, North Yorkshire

Located in the grounds of the Old Hall and opened in 1990. There is perhaps a rather wider perspective to the bird of prey and owl collection here with species such as the Abyssinian Ground Hornbill, King Vulture and Tawny Frogmouth to be seen. The owl collection is notable and a number of species such as Spectacled and Ural have bred here.

- **RIPON**
LIGHTWATER VALLEY BIRDS OF PREY CENTRE
Lightwater Valley, North Stanley, Ripon, North Yorkshire

Located within this theme park is a dedicated bird of prey centre and 'Creepy Crawly Cave' for invertebrates and a few predictable reptile species.

- **RODBASTON**
ANIMAL ZONE VISITOR CENTRE
Rodbaston Campus, South Staffordshire College, Rodbaston, Staffordshire

A mixture of a few exotic mammals (Common Marmosets, Bennett's Wallabies) birds, reptiles and fish rather nicely presented. Open weekends only.

SMALLER WILDLIFE ATTRACTIONS

- ST ALBANS
BIRDS OF A FEATHER FLYING DISPLAYS
The Lodge, Bowmansgreen Farm, Lowbell Lane, London Colney, St Albans, Herts

Despite the name there is a small row of newly constructed and attractive aviaries.

- ST COLUMB
CORNISH BIRDS OF PREY CENTRE
Winnards Perch, St Columb, Cornwall

- SILLOTH ON SOLWAY
BANK MILL BUTTERFLY HOUSE & REPTILIA
Bank Mill Nursery And Visitor Centre, Beckfoot, Silloth On Solway, Cumbria

- SKIPTON
CONISTON FALCONRY CENTRE
Coniston Cold, Skipton, North Yorkshire

- SPALDING
BAYTREE OWL CENTRE
High Road, Weston, Spalding, Lincs

Over 100 birds up to the size of a Secretary Bird, also including Snowy Owls, Spectacled Owls and Northern Hawk Owl.

- STANLEY
BEAMISH WILD BIRD OF PREY CONSERVATION CENTRE
Beamish Hall Country House Hotel, Beamish, Stanley, Co. Durham

African White-backed Vultures, Bald Eagles, Golden Eagles and around 50 other birds of prey and owls.

- STOCKTON-ON-TEES
BUTTERFLY WORLD
Preston Park, Yarm Road, Stockton-On-Tees, Teeside

- STONHAM ASPAL
SUFFOLK OWL SANCTUARY
Stonham Barns, Pettaugh Road, Stonham Aspal, Stowmarket, Suffolk

Specializing in British species of owl and birds of prey with particular emphasis on rescue projects.

- STRATFORD UPON AVON
STRATFORD UPON AVON BUTTERFLY FARM
Swans Nest Lane, Stratford Upon Avon, Warks

- SWINDON
BUTTERFLY WORLD
Studley Grange Garden & Leisure Park, Hay Lane, Wroughton, Swindon

- SWINGFIELD
BUTTERFLY CENTRE
Macfarlanes Nursery, Swingfield, Dover

- SYMONDS YAT
WYE VALLEY BUTTERFLY ZOO
Jubilee Park, Symonds Yat West, Ross-On-Wye, Herefordshire

- TARPORLEY
PECKFORTON FALCONRY
Peckforton Castle, Stone House Lane, Peckforton, Tarporley, Cheshire

- TARVIN
TARVIN SANDS REINDEER CENTRE
Kelsall Road, Tarvin, Chester, Cheshire

A guided walk-through experience of Reindeer, Sika, Fallow Deer and Red Deer.

- THIRSK
FALCONRY UK BIRD OF PREY & CONSERVATION CENTRE
Sion Hill Hall, Kirby Wiske, Thirsk

- TORPOINT
CORNISH OWL CENTRE
Sconner Nurseries, Polbathic, Torpoint, Cornwall

SMALLER WILDLIFE ATTRACTIONS

• TUNBRIDGE WELLS
GROOMBRIDGE PLACE GARDENS RAPTOR CENTRE
Groombridge Place, Groombridge Hill, Tunbridge Wells, Kent

• WEST KNOYLE
BUSH FARM BISON CENTRE
West Knoyle, Nr Mere, Wiltshire

American Bison, Wapiti, Raccoons, Guanacos and Prairie Dogs with meat products from the first two species for sale.

• WILDEN
WILD BRITAIN
Renhold Road, Wilden, Bedfordshire

Formerly Bedford Butterfly Park this still amounts to a few miscellaneous invertebrates plus a butterfly encounter.

NORTHERN IRELAND

• RANDALSTOWN
WORLD OF OWLS CENTRE
Randalstown Forest, Co. Antrim

• SEAFORDE
SEAFORDE TROPICAL BUTTERFLY HOUSE
Seaforde Nursery, Seaforde, Co. Down

SCOTLAND

• ABERDEEN
NORTH EAST FALCONRY CENTRE
Broadland, Cairnie, Huntly, Aberdeen

• AUCHINGARRICH
FALCONRY CENTRE AUCHINGARRICH WILDLIFE CENTRE
Comrie, Perthshire

Confusingly the falconry centre within Auchingarrich Wildlife Centre is independent of the park it is within and a separate charge is made.

• CAMPBELTOWN
SCOTTISH OWL CENTRE
Witchburn Road, Campbeltown, Argyll

• CUMBERNAULD
PALACERIGG COUNTRY PARK
Cumbernauld, Glasgow

Sadly, a collection that once contained Chamois, Pine Martens and Snowy Owls amongst others has been largely disbanded. There are still a few vivaria containing native species in the visitor centre.

• CUPAR
SCOTTISH DEER CENTRE
Bow of Fife, Cupar, Fife

Nine species of deer plus Wolves, Red Foxes and birds of prey.

• DALKEITH
EDINBURGH BUTTERFLY & INSECT WORLD
Dobbies Garden World, Melville Nursery, Lasswade, Midlothian

• ISLE OF CUMBRAE
ROBERTSON MUSEUM & AQUARIUM
Millport, Isle of Cumbrae

A display of local marine species maintained by the University Marine Biological Station.

• ISLE OF SKYE
SKYE SERPENTARIUM
The Old Mill, Broadford, Isle of Skye

Opened in 1991, specializes in abandoned and rescued reptiles. In 2006 a fire killed 149 reptiles and destroyed the breeding unit but the serpentarium continues with its work.

• LADYBANK
FIFE ANIMAL PARK
Birniefield, Collesie, Ladybank, Fife

A small general collection opened in 2007 and aimed primarily at children including

Capybaras, Meerkats, Crested Porcupines, birds of prey, a small reptile house/aquarium even Common Zebra.

• LOCH LOMOND
LOCH LOMOND BIRD OF PREY CENTRE
Stirling Road, Ballagan, Nr Balloch, Alexandria, Dunbartonshire

• MOTHERWELL
AMAZONIA
Strathclyde Country Park, Motherwell

Touting itself as 'Scotland's Only Indoor Tropical Rainforest' this small attraction features Kinkajous, some callitrichids, frogs, reptiles and Leafcutter Ants amongst others.

• ORKNEY
ORKNEY MARINE LIFE AQUARIUM
Pool Farmhouse, St Margarets Hope, Orkney

An imaginative display of local marine life which bases its main display on a walkaround fish transportation lorry!

• PORT LOGAN
LOGAN FISH POND – MARINE LIFE CENTRE
Port Logan, Stranraer, Wigtownshire

A unique wildlife attraction that sees local marine species of fish held for a couple of years and then released. The fish pond is based on a 200 year old live fish larder and has been adapted to maintain living fish in its 48,000 gallons.

• WEST CALDER
FIVE SISTERS ZOO PARK
Gavieside, West Calder, West Lothian

WALES

• ABERYSTWYTH
THE MAGIC OF LIFE BUTTERFLY HOUSE
Cwmrheidol, Aberystwyth, Cardigan

• ANGLESEY
PILI PALAS
Menai Bridge, Anglesey

A converted farmhouse is home to a surprising variety of small animals from birds to reptiles but principally butterflies, in a small 'jungle'.

• BARRY
WELSH HAWKING CENTRE
Weycock Road, Barry, South Glamorgan

Occupies the site of the old Barry Zoo.

• FELINWYNT
FELINWYNT RAINFOREST CENTRE
Felinwynt, Cardigan

Butterflies, stick insects and Leafcutter Ants.

• LLANDUDNO
BODAFON FARM PARK
Bodafon Road, Llandudno, Gwynedd

Situated just above the seafront heading west out of Llandudno is the home of the North Wales Bird Trust a collection, mainly of owls, with a few other species of birds totalling about 50 animals.

• SWANSEA
PLANTASIA
Parc Tawe, Oasis Park, Swansea

A local council owned glasshouse of some size situated in a shopping mall with the entrance in amongst the shops! Although the botanical collection predominates there is a small walk-through aviary, Cottontop Tamarins, invertebrates, a few reptiles and some aquaria. In its own way, quite impressive.

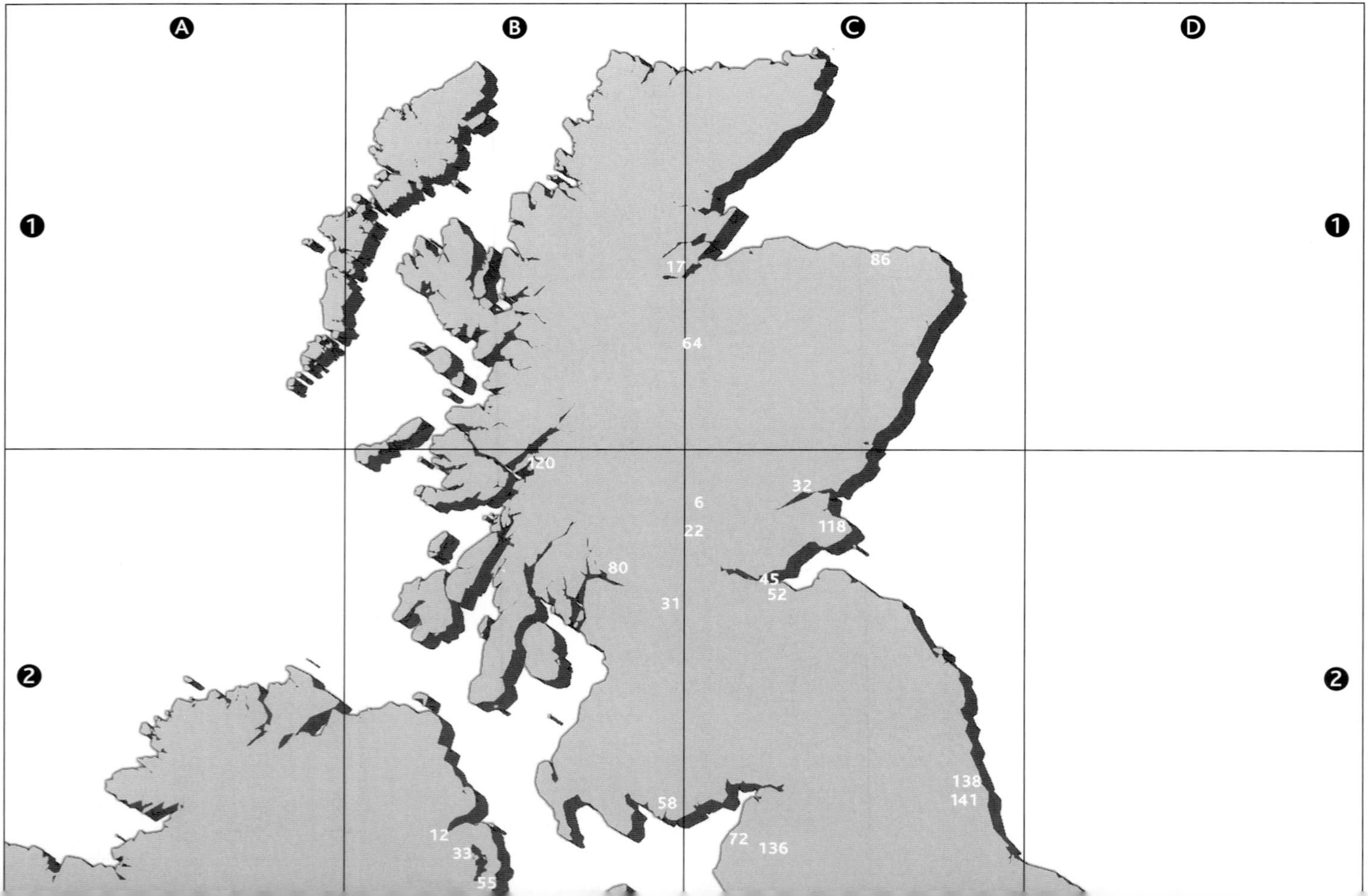
A
B
C
D
1
2
17
86
64
120
32
6
118
22
80
45
52
31
138
141
58
72
136
12
33
55
1
2

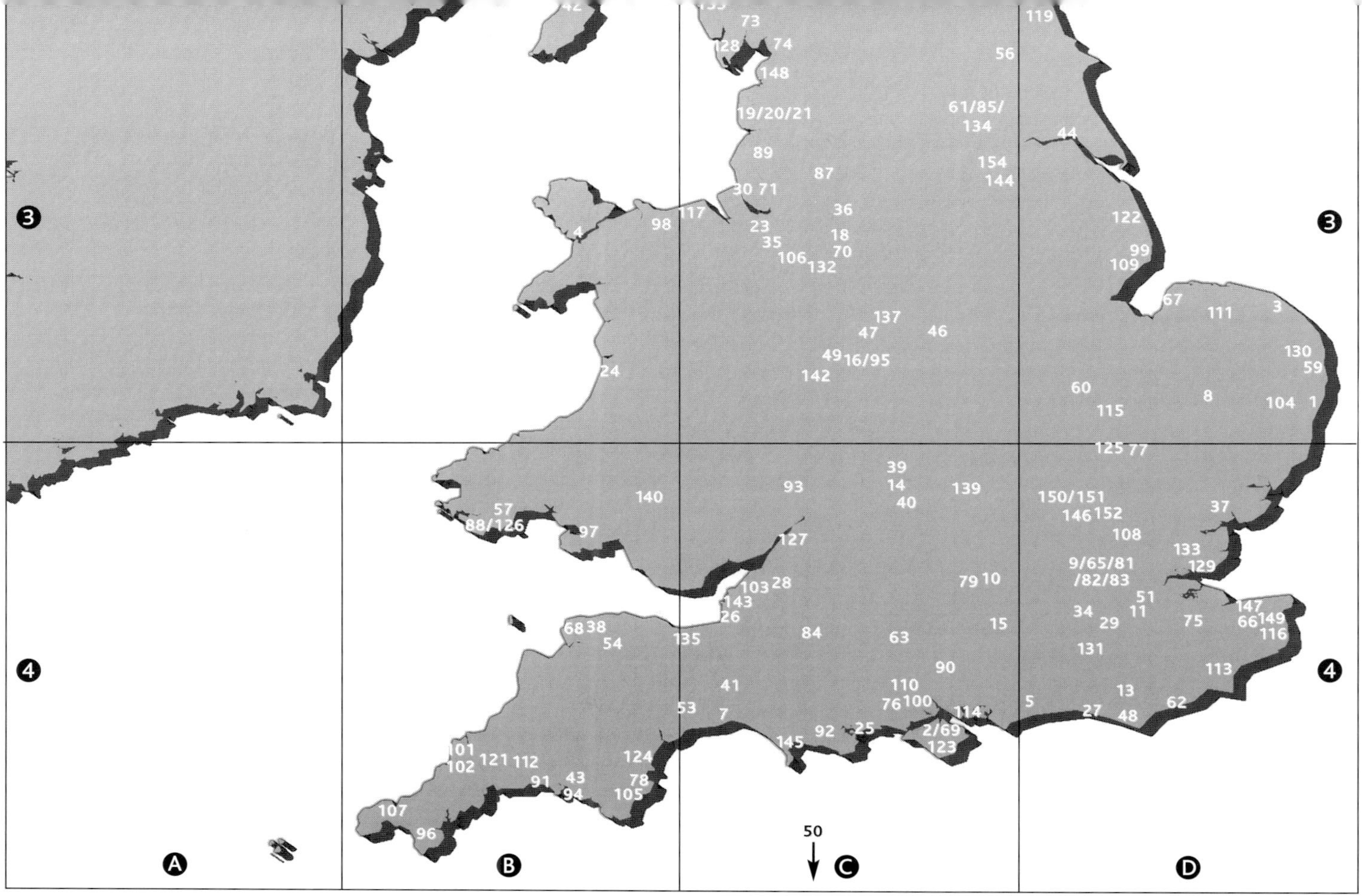

3
3
4
4
A
B
C
D
50
73
74
128
119
56
148
19/20/21
61/85/
134
44
89
87
154
144
30
71
117
98
36
122
4
23
35
18
70
106
132
99
109
67
111
3
137
47
46
49
16/95
130
24
142
59
60
8
104
1
115
125
77
39
14
93
139
40
140
150/151
146
152
37
57
88/126
97
127
108
133
9/65/81
/82/83
129
103
28
79
10
143
26
51
147
34
11
29
75
66
149
116
68
38
54
135
84
63
15
131
90
113
41
110
13
53
7
76
100
114
5
27
48
62
92
25
2/69
123
145
101
102
121
112
124
91
43
94
78
105
107
96

MAP REF		POSTCODE (SAT NAV)	PAGE NUMBER
1	AFRICA ALIVE!	NR33 7TF	10
2	AMAZON WORLD ZOO PARK	PO36 0LX	11
3	AMAZONA ZOO	NR27 9JG	12
4	ANGLESEY SEA ZOO	LL61 6TQ	13
5	ARUNDEL WETLAND CENTRE (WWT)	BN18 9PB	14
6	AUCHINGARRICH WILDLIFE CENTRE	PH6 2JS	14
7	AXE VALLEY BIRD & ANIMAL PARK	EX13 7RA	15
8	BANHAM ZOO	NR16 2HE	16
9	BATTERSEA PARK CHILDREN'S ZOO	SW11 4NJ	17
10	BEALE PARK WILDLIFE PARK & GARDENS	RG8 9NH	17
11	BEAVER WATERWORLD ZOOLOGICAL GARDENS	TN16 2JT	19
12	BELFAST ZOO	BT36 7PN	20
13	BENTLEY WILDFOWL COLLECTION	BN8 5AF	21
14	BIRDLAND	GL54 2BN	22
15	BIRDWORLD	GU10 4LD	23
16	BIRMINGHAM NATURE CENTRE	B5 7RL	24
17	BLACK ISLE WILDLIFE & COUNTRY PARK	IV1 3XF	25
18	BLACKBROOK ZOOLOGICAL PARK	ST13 7QR	25
19	BLACKPOOL SEA LIFE	FY1 5AA	26
20	BLACKPOOL TOWER AQUARIUM	FY1 4RZ	27
21	BLACKPOOL ZOO	FY3 9RS	28
22	BLAIR DRUMMOND SAFARI & ADVENTURE PARK	FK9 4UR	30
23	BLUE PLANET AQUARIUM	CH65 9LF	32
24	BORTH ANIMALARIUM	SY24 5NA	33
25	BOURNEMOUTH OCEANARIUM	BH2 5AA	33
26	BREAN DOWN TROPICAL BIRD GARDEN	TA8 2RS	34
27	BRIGHTON SEA LIFE	BN2 1TB	35
28	BRISTOL ZOO	BS8 3HA	36
29	BRITISH WILDLIFE CENTRE	RH7 6LF	38
30	THE BUG WORLD EXPERIENCE	L3 4AA	39
31	CALDERGLEN CHILDREN'S ZOO	G75 0QZ	40
32	CAMPERDOWN WILDLIFE CENTRE	DD2 4TF	41
33	CASTLE ESPIE WILDFOWL & WETLANDS TRUST	BT23 6EA	42
34	CHESSINGTON WORLD OF ADVENTURES	KT9 2NE	42
35	CHESTER ZOO	CH2 IEU	44
36	CHESTNUT CENTRE, OTTER, OWL & WILDLIFE PARK	SK23 0QS	46
37	COLCHESTER ZOO	CO3 0SL	47

MAP REF		POSTCODE (SAT NAV)	PAGE NUMBER
78	LIVING COASTS	TQ1 2BG	91
79	THE LIVING RAINFOREST	RG18 0TN	92
80	LOCH LOMOND AQUARIUM SEA LIFE	G83 8QL	93
81	LONDON SEA LIFE AQUARIUM	SE1 7PB	93
82	LONDON WETLAND CENTRE (WWT)	SW13 9WT	94
83	ZSL LONDON ZOO	NW1 4RY	95
84	LONGLEAT SAFARI PARK	BA12 7NW	98
85	LOTHERTON HALL BIRD GARDEN	LS25 3EB	99
86	MACDUFF MARINE AQUARIUM	AB44 1SL	100
87	MANCHESTER MUSEUM VIVARIUM	M13 9PL	101
88	MANOR HOUSE WILDLIFE PARK	SA70 8RJ	102
89	MARTIN MERE WETLAND CENTRE (WWT)	L40 0TA	103
90	MARWELL ZOOLOGICAL PARK	SO21 1JH	104
91	THE MONKEY SANCTUARY	PL13 1NZ	105
92	MONKEY WORLD APE RESCUE CENTRE	BH20 6HH	106
93	THE NATIONAL BIRDS OF PREY CENTRE	GL18 1JJ	107
94	NATIONAL MARINE AQUARIUM	PL4 0LF	108
95	NATIONAL SEA LIFE CENTRE BIRMINGHAM	B1 2JB	109
96	NATIONAL SEAL SANCTUARY	TR12 6UG	110
97	NATIONAL WETLAND CENTRE WALES (WWT)	SA14 9SH	110
98	THE NATIONAL ZOO OF WALES	LL28 5UY	111
99	NATURELAND SEAL SANCTUARY	PE25 1DB	112
100	THE NEW FOREST OTTER, OWL & WILDLIFE PARK	SO40 4UH	113
101	NEWQUAY BLUE REEF	TR7 1DU	114
102	NEWQUAY ZOO	TR7 2LZ	115
103	NOAH'S ARK ZOO FARM	BS48 1PG	116
104	THE OTTER TRUST	NR35 2AF	117
105	PAIGNTON ZOO ENVIRONMENTAL PARK	TQ4 7EU	117
106	THE PALMS TROPICAL OASIS	CW5 7LH	120
107	PARADISE PARK WILDLIFE SANCTUARY	TR27 4HB	121
108	PARADISE WILDLIFE PARK	EN10 7QA	122
109	THE PARROT ZOO	PE22 8PP	123
110	PAULTONS PARK	SO51 6AL	124
111	PENSTHORPE WATERFOWL PARK & NATURE RESERVE	NR21 0LN	125
112	PORFELL ANIMAL LAND WILDLIFE PARK	PL14 4RE	125
113	PORT LYMPNE WILD ANIMAL PARK	CT21 4PD	126
114	PORTSMOUTH BLUE REEF AQUARIUM	PO5 3PB	127

#	Name	Postcode	Page
38	COMBE MARTIN WILDLIFE & DINOSAUR PARK	EX34 0NG	49
39	COTSWOLD FALCONRY CENTRE	GL56 9AB	50
40	COTSWOLD WILDLIFE PARK	OX18 4JW	50
41	CRICKET ST. THOMAS WILDLIFE PARK	TA20 4DD	52
42	CURRAGHS WILDLIFE PARK	IM7 5EA	53
43	DARTMOOR WILDLIFE PARK	PL7 5DG	54
44	THE DEEP	HU1 3UF	55
45	DEEP SEA WORLD	KY11 1JR	56
46	DESFORD TROPICAL BIRD GARDEN	LE9 9GN	57
47	DRAYTON MANOR ZOO	B78 3TW	58
48	DRUSILLAS PARK	BN26 5QS	59
49	DUDLEY ZOO	DY1 4QB	60
50	DURRELL WILDLIFE CONSERVATION TRUST	JE3 5BP	62
51	EAGLE HEIGHTS WILDLIFE PARK	DA4 0JB	64
52	EDINBURGH ZOO	EH12 6LR	65
53	ESCOT	EX11 1LU	67
54	EXMOOR ZOOLOGICAL PARK	EX31 4SG	68
55	EXPLORIS	BT22 1NZ	69
56	FLAMINGO LAND THEME PARK & ZOO	YO17 6UX	69
57	FOLLY FARM ADVENTURE PARK & ZOO	SA68 0XA	71
58	GALLOWAY WILDLIFE CONSERVATION PARK	DG6 4XX	72
59	GREAT YARMOUTH SEA LIFE	NR30 3AH	72
60	HAMERTON ZOO PARK	PE28 5RE	73
61	HAREWOOD BIRD GARDEN	LS17 9LQ	75
62	HASTINGS BLUE REEF	TN34 3DW	76
63	HAWK CONSERVANCY TRUST	SP11 8DY	76
64	HIGHLAND WILDLIFE PARK	PH21 1NL	77
65	HORNIMAN MUSEUM AQUARIUM	SE23 3PQ	79
66	HOWLETT'S WILD ANIMAL PARK	CT4 5EL	80
67	HUNSTANTON SEA LIFE SANCTUARY	PE36 5BH	81
68	ILFRACOMBE AQUARIUM	EX34 9EQ	82
69	ISLE OF WIGHT ZOO	PO36 9AA	83
70	KINGSLEY BIRD & FALCONRY CENTRE	ST10 2BX	83
71	KNOWSLEY SAFARI PARK	L34 4AN	84
72	THE LAKE DISTRICT COAST AQUARIUM	CA15 8AB	86
73	LAKELAND AQUARIUM	LA12 8AS	87
74	LAKELAND WILDLIFE OASIS	LA7 7BW	88
75	LEEDS CASTLE AVIARY	ME17 1PL	89
76	LIBERTY'S OWL, RAPTOR & REPTILE CENTRE	BH24 3EA	90
77	LINTON ZOO	CB21 4NT	90

#	Name	Postcode	Page
115	RAPTOR FOUNDATION	PE28 3BT	128
116	RARE SPECIES CONSERVATION CENTRE & ZOO	CT13 0DG	129
117	RHYL SEAQUARIUM	LL18 3AF	130
118	ST ANDREWS AQUARIUM	KY16 9AS	131
119	SCARBOROUGH SEA LIFE	YO12 6RP	131
120	SCOTTISH SEA LIFE SANCTUARY	PA37 1SE	132
121	SCREECH OWL SANCTUARY	TR9 6HP	132
122	SEAL SANCTUARY	LN12 1QG	133
123	SEAVIEW WILDLIFE ENCOUNTER	PO34 5AP	134
124	SHALDON WILDLIFE TRUST	TQ14 0HP	135
125	SHEPRETH WILDLIFE PARK	SG8 6PZ	136
126	SILENT WORLD AQUARIUM	SA70 8HR	137
127	SLIMBRIDGE WETLAND CENTRE (WWT)	GL2 7BT	137
128	SOUTH LAKES WILD ANIMAL PARK	LA15 8JR	139
129	SOUTHEND SEA LIFE ADVENTURE	SS1 2ER	140
130	THRIGBY WILDLIFE GARDENS	NR29 3DR	141
131	TILGATE NATURE CENTRE	RH10 5PQ	142
132	TRENTHAM MONKEY FOREST	ST4 8AY	142
133	TROPICAL WINGS WORLD OF WILDLIFE ZOO	CM3 5QZ	143
134	TROPICAL WORLD	LS8 1DF	144
135	TROPIQUARIA	TA23 0QB	145
136	TROTTERS WORLD OF ANIMALS	CA12 4RD	145
137	TWYCROSS ZOO	CV9 3PX	147
138	TYNEMOUTH BLUE REEF AQUARIUM	NE30 4JF	149
139	WADDESDON MANOR AVIARY	HP18 0JH	149
140	WALES APE & MONKEY SANCTUARY	SA9 1UD	150
141	WASHINGTON WETLAND CENTRE (WWT)	NE38 8LE	151
142	WEST MIDLAND SAFARI & LEISURE PARK	DY12 1LF	152
143	WESTON-SUPER-MARE SEAQUARIUM	BS23 1BE	153
144	WETLANDS WATERFOWL RESERVE & EXOTIC BIRD PARK	DN22 8SB	154
145	WEYMOUTH SEA LIFE PARK & MARINE SANCTUARY	DT4 7SX	154
146	ZSL WHIPSNADE ZOO	LU6 2LF	155
147	WILDWOOD TRUST	CT6 7LQ	157
148	WILLIAMSON PARK BUTTERFLY HOUSE	LA1 1UX	158
149	WINGHAM WILDLIFE PARK	CT3 1JL	159
150	WOBURN DEER PARK	MK17 9QN	160
151	WOBURN SAFARI PARK	MK17 9QN	161
152	WOODSIDE ANIMAL FARM & LEISURE PARK	LU1 4DG	162
153	WORLD OWL CENTRE	CA18 1RQ	162
154	YORKSHIRE WILDLIFE PARK	DN3 3NH	163

The Independent Zoo Enthusiasts Society

IZES